INSIGHTS

A Contemporary Reader

Edited by
AUSTIN FLINT

American Language Program
Columbia University

Newbury House Publishers, Inc. / Rowley / Massachusetts / 01969
ROWLEY • LONDON • TOKYO
1981

Library of Congress Cataloging in Publication Data
Main entry under title:

Insights: a contemporary reader.

Bibliography: p.
1. English language—Text-books for foreigners.
2. College readers.   I. Flint, Austin.
PE1128.I48   428.6'4   80-26023
ISBN 0-88377-185-3

Cover design by Diana Esterly.

NEWBURY HOUSE PUBLISHERS, INC.

Language Science
Language Teaching
Language Learning

ROWLEY, MASSACHUSETTS 01969

First printing: February 1981
5   4   3   2   1

Printed in the U.S.A.

Acknowledgments

Many teachers at the American Language Program have been involved in the preparation of this book. It is impossible to mention all of them, for so many offered valuable suggestions and criticisms along the way. In particular, though, I would like to thank Isabella Halsted and Harvey Zuckerman, who did a vast amount of reading as we were searching for appropriate articles and short stories, and who also contributed much of the supporting material for these selections. Bernard Alter, Richard Faust, Louis Levi, and George Whiteside took part in various phases of the preparation: commenting on the readings, contributing materials, and trying them in the classroom.

In addition to being a contributor, Louis Levi, chairman of the American Language Program since 1977, encouraged and supported this project in its final stages. The late Francis Juhasz, chairman from 1974 to 1977, contributed a great deal to the basic approach and design of this work.

We are grateful to Dean Ward Dennis of the School of General Studies at Columbia University for aiding the work on this book through generous grants of released time from teaching duties.

I also wish to thank Linda Ferreira of the School of General Studies for her invaluable assistance.

Editor's Biography

Austin Flint has been on the faculty of the American Language Program since 1960. He was chairman from 1966 to 1974 and is currently in charge of the courses in college-level English composition and literature for foreign students at Columbia University. In 1971–1972 he was chairman of the Consortium of Intensive English Programs and from 1971 to 1975 served on the Committee of Examiners for the Test of English as a Foreign Language (TOEFL). He also teaches courses in creative writing at Columbia and is the author of several published short stories and poetry translations.

Contents

Introduction

This book of essays and short stories, with introductory material, follow-up questions, and suggested theme topics, is designed for people with a foreign-language background who are at or near college- or professional-level English. It is the result of several years' planning by the faculty of the American Language Program of Columbia University's School of General Studies and derives from our awareness of the special needs of people who have reached advanced levels of English proficiency. For a long time, we have been aware that students of English as a second language are frequently brought by carefully guided steps to an intermediate or high-intermediate level, only to be abandoned to "sink or swim" with students and colleagues in a school or profession requiring a sophisticated grasp of English.

Our own classroom experience has shown that advanced students still need a great deal of practice in three areas: reading, discussion, and writing. For readings, we have chosen fourteen selections by American and English authors, predominantly American. We have tried out all the reading selections several times in the American Language Program classes, and only those readings which teachers and students repeatedly found it stimulating to work with were placed on our final list. In making these selections, we looked for pieces that were well written and were neither archaic nor ultra-modern in style. To ensure the greatest student interest and the most natural language, we selected articles and stories written after the Second World War, but at the same time we avoided selections that were so immediately topical they would soon be outdated.

The articles deal with a wide range of subjects: social and philosophical questions (for example, Julian Huxley, "Is War Inevitable?" Eric Hoffer, "The Role of the Undesirables," Bertrand Russell, "Education for a Difficult World"), personal viewpoints (for example, George Orwell, "Why I Write," Willie Morris, "A Provincial in New York"), language and style (Donald Hall, "A Clear and Simple Style"), music for the lay person (Leonard Bernstein, "The Happy Medium"), and other subjects of general interest.

The short stories were selected because they reveal the feelings, conflicts, and problems of people very concretely in the context of their society, and because they shed light on some of the questions raised more abstractly in the essays. For example, Joyce Carol Oates's story, "First Views of the Enemy," whose protagonist is a middle-class woman afraid of Mexican-American migrant farm workers, may be compared and contrasted with Michael Harrington's "The Invisible Land," about poverty in America, or with Eric Hoffer's "The Role of the Undesirables," which sees the valuable contributions such so-called "misfits" have made to American society. Other short stories lend themselves to discussions and compositions on related topics; for example, George Elliott's "Love among the Old Folk" has stimulated discussions on the problems of old age, and Willie Morris's "A Provincial in New York" has given students a chance to discuss their own feelings on coming to a strange city or on moving from one culture to another.

Because this book is designed to prepare advanced or advanced-intermediate students to understand original texts in English, we have not altered or simplified the selections in any way, but we have added extensive footnotes to explain obscure references, colloquial phrases, and other words or expressions that would probably not be found in an average dictionary.

To help comprehension and to stimulate discussion, introductory and follow-up material accompanies each reading selection. The introductory material, shorter than the follow-up, is designed to "set the scene" for the reader, who may not be familiar with the cultural background and context of a story or article. This material provides some information, but it also asks a few general questions so that the reader may become oriented to the concerns expressed in the selection.

The follow-up questions are much more extensive, generally proceeding from concrete questions that test an understanding of the various points in an article or of the events in a story, to more abstract, interpretive questions, giving the reader a freer range. The questions, proceeding from one point to the next, are arranged much the way a well-organized discussion or a programmed set of materials might proceed, from the specific to the more abstract. Like the reading selections themselves, the introductory and follow-up materials have been tested several times in our American Language Program classes and have been revised as a result of our experience.

These supporting materials can be used in several ways: by a classroom teacher in the United States or abroad, as a guide to discussion, or independently by students on their own. We have worked on making the questions develop so naturally that students who continue through the question sequence should have little trouble knowing whether or not they are on the right track.

To cover the last important point, writing, we provide a choice of composition topics at the end of each selection. Some of the suggested theme topics are very closely related to the article or story; others encourage writing or discussion on topics suggested by the reading. Once again, American Language Program teachers have tested these topics, and we have revised them as a result of our experience.

In any case, people using this book should not be bound by its structure but should feel free to use the supporting materials as flexibly as they wish. Teachers at the American Language Program have done exactly that. Some have more or less followed the questions in sequence as written; others have modified the sequence or departed from it as the discussion has developed; still others have had students go over the questions in advance at home, and with those points clarified, the teachers have concentrated all their class time on discussion of broader, interpretive questions or on related topics. Students using this book on their own would probably benefit from following the sequence of questions more closely, since they will not be taking part in discussions guided by a teacher.

INSIGHTS

Education for a Difficult World*
Bertrand Russell

INTRODUCTION

In this essay, Bertrand Russell discusses his theory of modern education.
A. When you refer to a person as "well-educated," what do you usually mean?
B. What do you consider essential for a good education?
C. How might a good education today differ from a good education of a hundred years ago?
D. Do you feel that the educational system of your country provides students with the necessary background to deal with the modern world? Why?
E. How would you evaluate your own education up to this time? What are some benefits you have gained from attending school? What are some deficiencies in your education, if any?
F. Looking back over your own educational experiences, what changes would you have made? How might these changes have aided your development as a student? Would they have changed your life in any way? How?

Young people who are not completely frivolous are apt to find in the world of the present day that their impulses of goodwill are baffled by failure to find any clear course of action which might diminish the perils of the time. I will not pretend that there is any easy or simple answer to their bewilderment, but I do think that a suitable education could make young people feel more capable of understanding the problems and of critically estimating this or that suggested solution.

There are several reasons which make our problems difficult to solve, if not to understand. The first of these is that modern society and modern politics are governed by difficult skills which very few people understand. The man of science is the modern medicine man.[1] He can perform all kinds of magic. He can say, "Let there be light,"[2] and there is light. He can keep you warm in winter, and keep your food cool in summer. He can transport you through the air as

---

*Reprinted by permission of George Allen & Unwin, Ltd., from *Education and the Modern World* by Bertrand Russell.

[1] Medicine man — a person believed to heal sickness by using drugs or charms having magic or supernatural powers.

[2] "Let there be light." From "The Book of Genesis" in the Bible, referring to the creation of the world.

quickly as a magic carpet in the *Arabian Nights*.[3] He promises to exterminate your enemies in a few seconds, and fails you only when you ask him to promise that your enemies will not exterminate you. All this he achieves by means which, if you are not one in a million, are completely mysterious to you. And when mystery-mongers[4] tell you tall stories[5] of future marvels you cannot tell whether to believe them or not.

Another thing that makes the modern world baffling is that technical developments have made a new social psychology necessary. From the dawn of history until the present century the road to success was victory in competition. We descend from many centuries of progenitors who exterminated their enemies, occupied their lands, and grew rich. In England this process took place in the time of Hengist and Horsa.[6] In the United States it took place during the eighteenth and nineteenth centuries. We therefore admire a certain sort of character, namely the sort of character that enables you to kill skillfully and without compunction. The milder believers in this creed content themselves with inflicting economic rather than physical death, but the psychology is much the same. In the modern world owing to increase of skill this process is no longer so satisfactory. In a modern war even the victors suffer more than if there had been no war. To the British, who are enduring the results of complete victory in two great wars, this is fairly obvious. What applies in war, applies also in the economic sphere. The victors in a competition do not grow so rich as both parties could by combination. The half-unconscious appreciation of these facts produces in intelligent young people an impulse towards general goodwill, but this impulse is baffled by the mutual hostility of powerful groups. Goodwill in general—yes; goodwill in particular—no. A Hindu may love mankind, but must not love a Pakistani; a Jew may believe that men are all one family, but dare not extend this feeling to the Arabs; a Christian may think it his duty to love his neighbour, but only if his neighbour is not a Communist. These conflicts between the general and the particular seem to make it impossible to have any one clear principle in action. This trouble is due to a very general failure to adapt human nature to technique. Our *feelings* are those appropriate to warlike nomads in rather empty regions, but our technique is such as must bring disaster unless our feelings can become more co-operative.

Education if it is to be adapted to our modern needs must fit young people to understand the problems raised by the situation. The imparting of knowledge in education has always had two objects: on the one hand, to give skill; and on

---

[3]Magic carpet in the *Arabian Nights* — according to the old Arabian legends, a carpet that could fly through the air, carrying people from one place to another.

[4]Mystery mongers — people who spread stories about mysterious events. This use of the word *monger* implies that the person is spreading something undesirable, as in *warmonger, scandalmonger,* etc.

[5]Tall stories — stories that are untrue, or where the truth is "stretched."

[6]Hengist and Horsa — brothers from Jutland (now part of Denmark) who led an invasion of the British Isles in the fifth century A.D.

the other, to give a vaguer thing which we may call wisdom. The part of skill has become very much larger than it used to be and is increasingly threatening to oust the part devoted to wisdom. At the same time it must be admitted that wisdom in our world is impossible except for those who realize the great part played by skill, for it is increase of skill that is the distinctive feature of our world. During the late war, when I dined among the Fellows of my College,[7] I found that those who were scientific were usually absent, but on their rare appearances one got glimpses of mysterious work such as only very few living people could understand. It was the work of men of this sort that was the most decisive in the war. Such men inevitably form a kind of aristocracy, since their skill is rare and must remain rare until by some new method men's congenital aptitudes have been increased. There is for example a great deal of important work which can only be done by those who are good at higher mathematics, and the immense majority of mankind would never become good at higher mathematics, even if all their education were directed to that end. Men are not all equal in congenital capacity, and any system of education which assumes that they are involves a possibly disastrous waste of good material.

But although scientific skill is necessary, it is by no means sufficient. A dictatorship of men of science would very soon become horrible. Skill without wisdom may be purely destructive, and would be very likely to prove so. For this reason, if for no other, it is of great importance that those who receive a scientific education should not be *merely* scientific, but should have some understanding of that kind of wisdom which, if it can be imparted at all, can only be imparted by the cultural side of education. Science enables us to know the means to any chosen end, but it does not help us to decide what ends we shall pursue. If you wish to exterminate the human race, it will show you how to do it. If you wish to make the human race so numerous that all are on the very verge of starvation, it will show you how to do that. If you wish to secure adequate prosperity for the whole human race, science will tell you what you must do. But it will not tell you whether one of these ends is more desirable than another. Nor will it give you that instinctive understanding of human beings that is necessary if your measures are not to arouse fierce opposition which only ferocious tyranny can quell. It cannot teach you patience, it cannot teach you sympathy, it cannot teach you a sense of human destiny. These things, in so far as they can be taught in formal education, are most likely to emerge from the learning of history and great literature.

Familiarity with great literature has been one of the nominal aims of education ever since the time of Peisistratus.[8] The Athenians pursued this aim wisely: they learnt Homer[9] by heart, and were therefore able to appreciate their great dramatists in spite of their being contemporary. But modern methods have

---

[7]Fellows of my College — his faculty and research colleagues at the university.

[8]Peisistratus — Greek statesman (605?–527 B.C.).

[9]Homer — epic poet of ancient Greece (around 850 B.C.). Author of the *Iliad* and the *Odyssey*.

improved on all this. I was given when I was very young a little book called *A Child's Guide to Literature*. In this book, the child, guided by some preternatural intelligence, asked about the great English writers in correct chronological sequence beginning, "Who was Chaucer?"[10] I regret to say that I never got any further on this little book. If I had, I should have been able to say just the sort of thing that Examiners[11] wish you to say without having read a single word of any of the authors concerned. I am afraid that the needs of examinations and of an unduly extended syllabus have made this way of studying literature all too common. You may be the better for reading Chaucer, but if you do not read him, knowing his dates and what eminent critics have said about him does you no more good than knowing the dates of some obscure nobody. The good that is to be derived from great literature is not derived with any fullness except by those who become so familiar with it that it enters into the texture of their everyday thoughts. I think it is an admirable thing when children at school act a play of Shakespeare.[12] There is then an obvious reason for getting to know it well, and the enterprise is co-operative rather than competitive. I am quite sure that to take part in acting one of Shakespeare's good plays is a better way of acquiring what is valuable in a literary education than the hasty reading of the whole lot. In former generations English speaking people acquired the same sort of training in prose through familiarity with the Authorized Version of the Bible,[13] but since the Bible became unfamiliar nothing equally excellent has taken its place.

In the teaching of history as opposed to literature a smattering can be of great utility. For those who are not going to be professional historians the sort of thing that in America is called a survey course[14] can, if it is rightly done, give a valuable sense of the larger process within which things which are near and familiar take place. Such a course should deal with the history of man, not with the history of this or that country, least of all one's own. It should begin with the oldest facts known through anthropology and archaeology, and should give a sense of the gradual emergence of those things in human life which give man such a place in our respect as he may deserve. It should not present as the world's heroes those who have slaughtered the greatest number of "enemies," but rather those who have been most notable in adding to the world's capital of knowledge and beauty and wisdom. It should show the strange resurgent power of what is valuable in human life, defeated time and again by savagery and hate and destruction, but nevertheless, at the very first possible opportunity, emerging again like grass in the desert after rain. It should, while youth leaves

---

[10]Chaucer — English poet (1340?–1400). Author of *The Canterbury Tales*.

[11]Examiners — people who compose and judge student examinations at school or university.

[12]Shakespeare — English dramatist and poet (1564–1616). Author of *Hamlet, King Lear, Macbeth*, etc.

[13]Authorized Version of the Bible — translation of the Bible from Hebrew and Greek into English, carried out under the direction of King James I of England and first published in 1611.

[14]Survey course — a comprehensive view of literature or other arts, studied in historical context.

hopes and desires still plastic,[15] fix those hopes and desires not upon victory over other human beings, but upon victory over those forces which have hitherto filled the life of man with suffering and sorrow—I mean, the forces of nature reluctant to yield her fruits, the forces of militant ignorance, the forces of hate, and the deep slavery to fear which is our heritage from the original helplessness of mankind. All this a survey of history should give and can give. All this, if it enters into the daily texture of men's thoughts, will make them less harsh and less mad.

One of the great things that education can and should give is the power of seeing the general in the particular, the power of feeling that this, although it is happening to *me,* is very like what happens to others, what has happened through many ages, and may continue to happen. It is very difficult not to feel that there is something quite special and peculiar about one's own misfortunes, about the injustices that one suffers, and the malevolence of which one is the object, and this applies not only to oneself as an individual but to one's family, one's class, one's nation, and even one's continent. To see such matters with impersonal justice is possible as the result of education, but is scarcely possible otherwise.

All this education can do, all this education should do, very little of it education does do.

[15]Plastic — capable of being shaped or formed.

☆ FOLLOW-UP QUESTIONS

I. Bertrand Russell believes that a "suitable education" could help young people deal with the problems of the modern world. He states, however, that there are several reasons why these problems are "difficult to solve, if not to understand." He then discusses two of these reasons in detail.
    A. What are these reasons?
    B. Why is it that few people understand the skills that govern modern society and modern politics?
    C. Why does Russell think of the man of science as the "modern medicine man"? What can't the "modern medicine man" guarantee?
    D. According to Russell, why have technical developments made a new social psychology necessary?
    E. Why is the psychology of competition no longer satisfactory in the modern world? Russell states, "To the British, who are enduring the results of complete victory in two great wars, this is fairly obvious." Why is this sentence ironic? Which word draws attention to the tone?

II. Russell states, "Our *feelings* are those appropriate to warlike nomads in rather empty regions, but our technique is such as must bring disaster unless our feelings become more co-operative."

A. How do most educational systems emphasize competitiveness rather than cooperativeness? In your own schooling, what part did competitiveness play?

B. If grades and examinations were universally abolished, what do you think would be the effect on the students? On the educational system? On the world in general?

III. Russell says that the goals of education are skill and wisdom.

A. What is the difference between skill and wisdom? Which is easier to attain? Why is it easier to define any given skill than to define wisdom?

B. Which goal does modern education emphasize, according to Russell? Do you agree? Can you think of any personal experiences that might lead you to disagree with the writer?

C. Why does Russell claim that "a dictatorship of men of science would very soon become horrible"? What does he feel science fails to teach us?

IV. Russell believes that understanding, patience, sympathy, and a sense of human destiny "in so far as they can be taught in formal education, are most likely to emerge from the learning of history and great literature."

A. Why does he object to teaching literature or history by emphasizing information? What example does he give from his own childhood?

B. Why does he feel that children acting a play of Shakespeare acquire what is valuable in a literary education? How, according to the writer, is this more effective than reading all the plays? Do you agree?

C. Describe Russell's conception of a valuable survey course in history. What would it begin with? What would it emphasize? How would it make men "less harsh and less mad"?

D. What does Russell mean when he says what "education can and should give is the power of seeing the general in the particular"?

V. "Education for a Difficult World" ends with the statement, "All this education can do, all this education should do, very little of it education does do."

A. Why has Russell chosen to devote a separate paragraph to this sentence?

B. What is he referring to by "All this . . ."?

C. Do you feel the last phrase "very little of it education does do" is an appropriate way of ending the essay? Why?

☆ THEME TOPICS

1. Russell states that "Men are not all equal in congenital capacity, and any system of education which assumes that they are involves a possibly disastrous waste of good material." Discuss.

2. Competition is necessary to motivate the student and maintain high standards. Defend or criticize the above statement.

3. Discuss whether your education, up to this time, has equipped you to deal with the modern world. In what ways has it succeeded in doing this? In what ways has it failed?

The New Nihilists*
Herbert A. Deane

INTRODUCTION

Historically, the term *nihilism* goes back to the program of a nineteenth century Russian party which advocated revolutionary reform, using terrorism and assassination. Today, nihilism is thought of as being the viewpoint that all traditional values and beliefs are worthless, and that existence is senseless and useless. This is an extreme, negative way of judging life. Most people who question accepted beliefs and institutions are not nihilists. For example, many women today are critically examining their traditional roles in society. They are, however, interested in substituting roles that are more acceptable to them.

A. Are there any groups in your country that are seeking some kind of change? How are they trying to achieve this? What forms of resistance do they face? Do you agree with their goals?

B. What traditions and values do you have faith in? How do they affect your life?

C. Are there any traditions and values that you find worthless? If you were able to, how would you abolish them?

D. If the institution of marriage were abolished, what do you think the results would be? Would society be changed radically? In what ways?

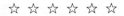

I have been increasingly concerned in the last year or so about an attitude—or, perhaps, collection of attitudes—among some students in the present generation of rejection and hostility toward many, if not all, established institutions, organizations, and standards. The hostility which alarms me is demonstrated by only a small minority of students, and it may be that it has not yet appeared at all campuses.[1] Nevertheless, I fear that this attitude of rejection of organizations and traditional patterns of behavior will probably spread. It has, for youth, all the attraction of a highly moral and principled refusal to compromise in any way with the world, the flesh, and the devil.[2] And our contemporary society does

---

[1]Campus — the grounds and buildings of a university, college, or school.

[2]The world, the flesh, and the devil — In some forms of the Christian ceremony of Baptism, the clergyman offers a prayer that the infant will triumph over the world, the flesh, and the devil. In other words, he prays that the child will lead a pure spiritual and moral life, uncorrupted by worldly ways.

indeed contain hypocrisy, vulgar materialism, expensive ugliness, addiction to high-sounding ideals that are rarely permitted to interfere with shrewd, cold pursuit of narrow self-interest, and widespread indifference to those who are not successful in the competitive race—the poor, the elderly, the handicapped, the disinherited minorities at home, and the "stupid" and impoverished masses of Asia, Africa, and Latin America abroad. All these obvious aspects of contemporary American life provide, I believe, a fertile soil for further growth of an attitude of total rejection.

Yet, to this negative reaction there may be a hopeful complement. To an extent perhaps unequaled in history, conscientious self-examination is denying us the comfort of pretenses; there is great idealism, which is by no means confined to the young, and new striving to break through the accumulated parochialisms of ages. What is necessary, I think, is to distinguish sharply between negative attitudes and this radical critique of existing standards.

The new student attitude—and for want of a better term I will call it the "nihilistic" attitude—seems to reject all existing institutions and patterns of behavior. It is better, I think, to speak of the new nihilism than, say, the "new Left,"[3] for the attitude I am concerned with is not confined to any one ideological position. It seems to reject the state, the legal system, political parties, churches, colleges, and universities, and seems to deny objective standards of excellence in literature, the arts, and morals. I want, however, to distinguish between the attitude and the students. Although I cautiously use the term "nihilism," I do not wish to describe any of the students as outright nihilists. A few of them seem to speak and behave as if they thought destruction were the only suitable solution for existing ills; but others are less dogmatic, and still others have more limited targets for their hostility.

There is much talk about how individuals in the present, complex world find themselves in a state of "alienation" (a word which has become so amorphous and vague as its use has become popular that we would all do well to avoid it). Organizations, institutions, norms are condemned, root and branch,[4] because they stifle the expression of the free, creative impulses of the individuals caught up in their toils and turn them into gray, faceless, conforming automata.[5] In particular, our nonrational impulses—our capacities for pleasure, anger, sexual enjoyment, domination—are said to be in danger of being stamped out by the rationalism and conformity that are supposed to be characteristic of organizational and institutional life today.

Civilization—for that is the short-hand term for the whole complex of institutions, norms and standards—is the enemy. In the new anarchist gospel, preached, for example, by Norman O. Brown in his book, *Life against Death,*

---

[3] "New Left" — term used for radical political movements, especially among students, that developed during the 1960s.

[4] Root and branch — in every part (as of a tree); completely.

[5] Automata — self-operating machines; robots.

civilization and all its appurtenances must be smashed, or at least radically simplified, in order to liberate the primal human urges and capacities that are now being stifled or blunted by it. A corollary is that no activity should be organized, planned, or directed—that action (indeed even art) should follow the dictates of momentary impulse and "feeling," and that spontaneity, "genuineness," and the satisfaction of impulse should be the only guides to conduct.

So, for example, we are now asked to go to the theater, the concert hall, or the art gallery to see and hear spontaneous "happenings," whose authors and performers proudly proclaim that they do not know in advance what is going to happen and, after the event, are unable to tell us what has happened and what it all meant. Of course, some of these "happenings" are not as spontaneous as they are claimed to be. But the terms in which they are rationalized are highly significant. This mood in the world of the arts is not confined to a small fringe group; it has made its way even into the commercial theater of Broadway; and we in New York have had "happenings" of this sort for the edification of the public in Central Park under the patronage of an energetic high-priest of "culture," ex-Parks Commissioner Thomas Hoving.

Students who have become converted to this new doctrine now tell us that colleges and universities in the present form are not fulfilling their true function of liberating and developing the potentialities of human beings. Indeed, organized courses and seminars, even regular, organized extra-curricular activities,[6] to say nothing of elaborately organized administrative apparatuses—committees, department chairmen, cold-faced deans, provosts, and presidents—constitute an elaborate contrivance to repress all real curiosity, imagination, and individuality that may still survive within the student.

In the nihilist vision the only meaningful education would be found in a deeply personal, sustained, unorganized, and spontaneous relation between a single student and his teacher, who would presumably be available at any hour, day or night, when the student felt the urge to "communicate." There would be no courses, no structured curriculum, certainly no requirements and no grades to mar this ideal relationship.

While this dream is obviously a fantasy, it—or something close to it—is sometimes seriously advanced by students who like to consider themselves radical. Not too long ago one of my College students complained bitterly about the lack of "personal contact" of students with faculty and administration at Columbia—a perennial complaint on most campuses and one that is sometimes justified. I reminded him of the conversations that he and I had had after class, of the office hours during which members of the faculty made themselves available to students, and of the series of informal "fireside chats" which the Dean of the College and members of the faculty had been holding with reasonably small

---

[6]Extracurricular activities — organized student activities outside of regular academic work: for example, working on a college magazine or newspaper, or participating in a drama group or in a political or social club. There are usually many extracurricular activities at American colleges.

groups of undergraduates in the dormitories. He dismissed all these "contacts" as "phony"[7] because they were not spontaneous and "free" but were in some degree organized and planned. When I pushed him a bit, he finally admitted that the only "communication" with the Dean or a teacher that he would regard as satisfactory would be a meeting that occurred without plan and that led to an hour or so of conversation about life, love, death, war and peace, and basic values.

A weaker but more popular version of this same ideal is the Paul Goodman[8]–supported vision of "participatory democracy" in the university. In this new world, there is still a university and there are still courses and seminars, but students share with the faculty the decisions about what shall be taught, how it shall be taught, how the university shall be administered, and how faculty should be chosen and promoted to tenure posts. A few such "universities" have been started in make-shift[9] ways, and provide us with examples of what the "students" and "faculties" have in mind. It might be added that many who attend these have not seen fit to cut themselves off completely from traditional education.

Lest I seem to be an unreconstructed Bourbon reactionary,[10] let me say that I have no objection at all to student concern with college and university administrative decisions. Administrators who consult student representatives on a variety of issues are likely to make wiser decisions and rules than those who never make any effort to discover what students want or what is troubling them. But I am concerned when some students spend far more of their time in discussions of the problems of university administration than they do on their academic pursuits.

The main responsibility of students, after all, is still studying, just as the primary task of teachers is teaching and of administrators is administering. If students do not want their teachers to decide what courses shall be taught and what should be included in them, if a course is only a sustained conversation or "bull-session,"[11] why should the student and his parents waste their time and money on a college education? Why should I (or anyone else) be paid for teaching if all I do is to go into a classroom and ask, "Well, fellows, what do you think about all this?" and if what follows is an unstructured conversation to which I contribute no more than any of the students?

Another facet of this problem is the refusal of some students to admit that there are any valid, objective criteria for determining the worth of an idea or an

[7]"Phony" — slang term meaning false, dishonest, intending to deceive.

[8]Paul Goodman — radical American writer and social critic whose books (especially *Growing Up Absurd*) written in the 1950s and 1960s became very popular among American students. These books were highly critical of established institutions in the United States.

[9]Make-shift — temporary; insubstantial.

[10]Unreconstructed Bourbon reactionary — unchangingly conservative; holding obstinately to the past (like the French Bourbon kings before the French Revolution).

[11]"Bull session" — slang term meaning an aimless discussion.

interpretation of an event or a piece of writing. Personal reaction, sincerity, what one feels deeply—these are said to be the real criteria. One of my students said to me last year, "This is what I felt when I was reading Freud.[12] Since I am reporting honestly and sincerely my emotional reactions to the work, you should accept my report as a valid account of what Freud really means." "This," he said, "is 'my Freud.'" "You are entitled," he acknowledged with great magnanimity, "to 'your Freud,' but don't force me to accept 'your Freud.'" When I asked whether despite all the problems of interpreting and understanding any text, we could not agree that there was a "real Freud" "out there," to whose writings we could both go to see whether his interpretation could be justified, he insisted that there was no such independent entity and that only his (or my) personal, emotional reactions to the words were real. Down this road, of course, lie absolute chaos and nihilism; the "communication" that these students value so highly becomes a total impossibility when nothing except subjective, emotional reactions are recognized as real and legitimate. Each of us ends up as a totally isolated self, locked in a soundproof room, and unable to communicate with any other human being.

One of the greatest ironies involved in the whole nihilistic critique of civilization and all its works is that the opponents of institutions and standards often rely, as Norman Brown does, on Freud as the basis for their condemnation of artifice, organization, and civilization and for their glorification of individual impulse and instinctual urges. It is clear that in *Civilization and Its Discontents* and in other works Freud argued that the fabric of increasingly complex institutions has been built up in large part on the basis of the renunciation of instinct, and especially on the repression or redirection of erotic[13] and aggressive impulses. He urged that, precisely to preserve the fragile fabric of civilization and rationality, excessive and unnecessary restraints on impulses be lightened or removed so as to minimize the danger of an explosion of repressed instincts which might destroy civilization. But this is a far cry[14] from arguing that the restraints imposed on instincts by civilization, by institutions, and by accepted standards of behavior should be smashed in order to liberate the full force of instinctual energy.

Freud, like Augustine,[15] was far too much the sad-eyed realist to agree with the 19th century anarchist view that human beings were by nature predominantly altruistic, cooperative, and reasonable, and that this essentially good human nature would exhibit itself in conduct once the distorting and warping influences of the political, economic, and legal orders were removed. He would, I am certain, be equally appalled by the views of the contemporary nihilists who see in institutions and standards of behavior nothing but forces

[12]Freud — Sigmund Freud (1856–1939). Austrian psychologist, founder of analytic psychiatry.

[13]Erotic — relating to sexual desire.

[14]A far cry — very different from; a long way from. Usually refers to distinct differences in situation, personality, or political position; seldom refers to physical distance.

[15]Augustine — Roman Catholic philosopher and saint (354–430).

repressing basically good and cooperative human impulses. For it was Freud who regarded the limited, hard-won gains of human reason in individual and social life as the most valuable achievement of men.

Nothing I have said in criticism of the nihilist view should be taken as opposition to radical criticism of existing political, educational, religious, and other institutions, especially on the part of the young. There is always need for vigorous and fundamental criticism of existing norms and institutions; given the fact that most of us normally tend to become more conservative and fearful of change as we grow older, such criticism must come primarily from the young. Without critical assaults, institutions and standards tend to become ossified and decadent; the spirit that originally motivated them—the concern, ultimately, for the well-being of the individuals who make up the organization or the group—is gradually forgotten or relegated to a position of inferiority to the demands of the organizational machinery. We are left with the dry husks[16] of external forms from which life has departed. So society needs its radical critics, along with its ess radical reformers, and its intelligent conservataives, in order to prosper, even if the young radicals sometimes appear to their elders to be naive, utopian, and simplistic.

The attitude of the radical, however, differs sharply from the nihilist attitude that I have been discussing; no matter how vigorous and fundamental his criticisms may be, his view is essentially a constructive one, since he always believes that he can propose a new set of institutions or standards that will serve human needs and aspirations better than do existing arrangements.

He may be wrong in this judgment, and he is often mistaken in his too-easy assumption that it is possible to move directly and smoothly from where we now are to where he would have us be (as Marx forcefully pointed out in his criticisms of the Utopian Socialists of his day). But the radical does recognize the need for some structure or order to give meaning and direction to human life, and his own positive proposals are presented for examination and criticism by those who are more satisfied with existing institutions or who would change them only gradually and slowly. Even if his proposals turn out to be utopian or visionary, statement and discussion of them sometimes help to clarify a present situation and to suggest reforms that were not part of the radical's intention. The young radical does not propose to smash the existing order of institutions and standards without giving any thought to what shall be put in its place or what the disastrous consequences may be if the fabric of civilization is ripped apart and nothing is or can be substituted for it.

To the members of my generation who have seen the incredible barbarity and destructiveness of which men are capable if the restraining forces of the artifice we call civilization are destroyed, the nihilistic program—smash the constraints of civilization so that blind, spontaneous impulse and instinct may be unhindered and men may be "free"—is an open invitation to destruction,

---

[16]Dry husks — external or outer covering, as of corn.

and, finally, to tyranny, for men will not long endure the misery of anarchy, and they will prefer even the tyrant's order to no order at all.

☆ FOLLOW-UP QUESTIONS

I.   The writer of this essay expresses his concern about "the rejection and hostility" some students have directed against "many . . . established institutions, organizations and standards."
  A.   What examples does Deane give which seem to justify criticism of contemporary life?
  B.   What is the positive "complement" to the negative reaction?
  C.   Why does he speak of new nihilism rather than of the "new left"?
  D.   How does he "distinguish between the attitude and the students"?

II. In discussing what he believes is an attack on civilization, Deane refers to fears held by the attackers.
  A.   In what ways do the attackers regard civilization as "the enemy"?
  B.   Why do some students condemn "organizations, institutions and norms"?
  C.   What are "nonrational impulses"? Why are they said to be in particular danger of "being stamped out"?

III. Giving Norman O. Brown's book, *Life against Death,* as an example, Deane claims that there is a "new anarchistic gospel."
  A.   Why does he use the word "gospel," which is generally related to religious teaching?
  B.   According to this "gospel," what must be liberated?
  C.   How have "the dictates of momentary impulse" affected art?
  D.   Referring to New York "happenings," Deane calls the ex-Parks Commissioner "an energetic high priest of culture." How does this description reveal Deane's feelings about the official? What is ironic about his use of the term "high priest"?
  E.   What is the writer's impression of happenings?

IV. Deane states that students who have "converted to this new doctrine" of nihilism are dissatisfied with colleges and universities.
  A.   What are their main complaints?
  B.   In what ways do they feel the educational institution is stifling creativity and individuality?
  C.   What, according to the writer, is the "nihilistic vision" of a "meaningful education"? Why does he feel this vision is impractical?
  D.   Why does one of Deane's students dismiss the informal "fireside chats" as "phony"? What kind of "communication" is he in favor of?
  E.   How does the writer describe "participatory democracy" in the university?

V.   According to Deane, the main responsibility of students "is still studying, just as the primary task of teachers is teaching and of administrators is administering."
  A.   Why does he object to a course that is only "a sustained conversation"?
  B.   Describe the problem Deane has in dealing with students who refuse to recognize "valid, objective criteria for determining the worth of an idea or an

interpretation of an event or a piece of writing." What do these students claim are the real criteria?

C.   In the example Deane gives, how does the student justify his interpretation of Freud?

D.   Why does the writer feel that "communication" will become impossible when "emotional, subjective reactions are recognized as legitimate"? Do you agree? Why?

VI.   Deane states that "there is always need for vigorous and fundamental criticism of existing norms and institutions."

A.   Why does he claim that "most of us" tend to become more conservative as we grow older? Do you agree?

B.   Why, according to the writer, does society need radical critics?

C.   What distinctions does he make between the attitudes of the nihilist and the radical?

VII.   Deane concludes by reminding the reader of the nihilist program—"Smash the constraints of civilization so that blind, spontaneous impulse and instinct may be unhindered and men may be free."

A.   How do the words "smash" and "blind" reveal the writer's attitude?

B.   Why does he feel that anarchy ultimately leads to tyranny?

C.   Do you agree with Deane's statement on man's need for order? Why or why not?

VIII.   "The New Nihilists" is essentially an argument against a way of thinking.

A.   What examples of "nihilism" does the writer focus on? How specific is he?

B.   Does he cite particular actions that he feels constitute "nihilism"?

C.   Who does he actually name in this essay?

D.   Is Deane too general in presenting his argument? For example, would his attitude about "spontaneity" in art have been more convincing if he had focused on a specific "happening"? Why?

E.   Why does he include the two specific discussions with dissatisfied students? How does he use their attitudes against them?

F.   Why does he first provide some justification for criticism of contemporary society before going on to argue against the "nihilistic" attitude?

☆ THEME TOPICS

1.   Discuss one aspect of contemporary life that you are critical of. Try to include specific examples which show the harm (or annoyance) it causes.

2.   Select a particular point that Mr. Deane makes, and discuss why you agree or disagree with it. Include specific examples.

3.   Discuss your attitude toward a political, social, educational, or artistic institution or idea. Try to explain how you have acquired this attitude.

Love among the Old Folk*
George P. Elliott

INTRODUCTION

I.   When we apply the word *old* to someone, we do not always limit our meaning to chronological age. Obviously, two seventy-year-old people may be very different in health, personality, intelligence, and appearance. One may think of himself as old; the other may not: moreover, their attitudes will be reflected in their behavior.

   A. At what age do you think one is no longer young?

   B. Why is the term "middle-aged" often used in a negative sense?

   C. Why are some people afraid of losing their youth? Why do they fear old age?

   D. What are some of the advantages of old age?

   E. Admittedly, age changes a person physically. Is character necessarily changed by the same process?

II. The problem of old age is universal. However, different societies, reflecting their distinctive attitudes, values, customs, and traditions, regard the phenomenon in different ways. In some cultures, the elderly are an inevitable part of family and community life, treated with respect and even veneration. In other cultures, their role is less certain and old age becomes a serious problem.

   A. What is the general attitude toward the elderly in your native country?

   B. Does the government provide institutions for old people who cannot live with their families and cannot live alone?

   C. What problems might arise from two or three generations of the same family living together?

   D. How would an elderly person in your country feel about living in an institution for the aged?

   E. What are some of the advantages and disadvantages of living among people one's own age?

   F. In the United States, elderly people are sometimes called "Senior Citizens," a term used to dignify old age.

     1. Do any comparable phrases exist in your native language? If so, what are they?

     2. If you were seventy years old and someone applied the term "senior citizen" to you, what would your reaction be?

*Reprinted by permission of Georges Borchardt, Inc., Copyright © 1952, George P. Elliott.

☆ ☆ ☆ ☆ ☆ ☆

It was Case's regular practice to call on Hattie every morning at eleven o'clock after she had finished listening to the *Luster-lene Variety Hour.*[1] All the other radios in the house would be tuned to *The Saga of Wanda Ryan;*[2] part of Case's motive in calling on Hattie was to seek sanctuary with someone who also disliked *Wanda Ryan.* Moreover it was a pleasure to talk to somebody who wanted to hear what he had to say and who did not talk back.

He announced his visit by a rap on the door before he entered.

"Well Hattie," he said as he closed the door behind him, "it's a nice clear day out. I think the green ought to be dry enough now for a game this afternoon."

She smiled and waved her left hand a little in greeting. She had had a stroke[3] two months before, and she would never recover the use of her right side.

"Well, was it a good program this morning?" She nodded. "Those radio fellows," he said shaking his head. "Five days a week and always something new. *Ja.* Well, give me a good boxing match any time." He started to laugh, a laugh caked dry with age but still warm, still human. "Or a football game." He laughed harder, rocking his round little body back and forth on the straight chair. "Or the world series,"[4] and he laughed so hard that he broke down in phlegmy coughing.

Hattie looked worried and patted his knee with her left hand. She made certain sounds—low, howling, unsteady sounds—which were not quite English and which seemed badly combined with her frail features and melancholy eyes; she was trying to tell Case to read the paper to her. "*Ja, ja,*" he said after he had quit coughing. "I read now." He adjusted his spectacles on his nose and opened to the editorial page.[5] He never understood what she said, but there was nothing else that she would have been likely to say and this was what he had been going to do anyway. She thought that he had understood her, and was pleased with this sign of improvement.

Hattie did not care a hoot[6] for the daily opinions of the *Examiner* editorial writers; what she cared for was that Case wanted to read them to her. She had had a year-old competition with Melissa, the other roomer in the Hooks' house, for the attentions of Case, and it was clear now that Hattie had won.

---

[1]*Luster-lene Variety Hour* — a commercial radio program, probably sponsored by a soap company.

[2]*The Saga of Wanda Ryan* — also a radio program, probably a melodramatic or sentimental serial story.

[3]Stroke — a sudden illness, usually involving some damage to the brain and loss of control of some part of the body.

[4]The world series — the final professional baseball championships in the United States.

[5]Editorial page — page of the newspaper where the editors express their opinions, usually about political or social matters.

[6]Not to care a hoot for — not to care at all about something. To be wholly uninterested.

Melissa was quite grand in a palsied way.[7] She had been something of a singer fifty or sixty years before, a glory she had not forgotten. Melissa scorned the favors of a fat little old Dutch butcher like Case Hook, but she could not scorn the lack of these favors.

Today at 11:30, after the passions of *Wanda Ryan* had been harrowed again and quelled again, Melissa came to the door of Hattie's room. "Oh," she said standing in the doorway, "I hope I am not intruding."

Hattie howled a little and motioned with her hand. Case laid down his paper, settled his glasses back on his head as he always did when he had finished reading something, and told Melissa to come in.

"Quite a good program today," said Melissa. "Of course it is nothing beside what I was accustomed to in better days. Duse, Bernhardt.[8] Ah." She flourished her handkerchief a little and gave her wobbling head a toss of pure panache.[9] "Nothing. Still, one must make the best of what one has. Case, I find it very surprising that you do not enjoy the *Wanda Ryan* thing."

"Ney," he said, "I like better the paper."[10]

"There are good things in it. Hattie, my dear, did you have a good night?"

Hattie signified by a smile and a nod that she had had a good night.

"My poor dear," said Melissa taking Hattie's slack right hand for a moment, "my poor dear. At least you are not in pain. It is a blessing for those who can be comfortable in their affliction."

Now Melissa herself was in no pain; her worst problem was getting food into her mouth without spilling it. Hattie, on the other hand, had a permanent sense of pressure and prickling in her paralyzed members, but she would have had more trouble explaining to the others what she felt than their sympathy was worth—the endless sympathizing, the daily questions to which there must always be the same, same answers. She preferred to fall in with[11] their comfortable view: that since like a plant a paralyzed limb cannot move, then like a plant it also cannot feel. She nodded and smiled at Melissa again.

"How she needs," said Melissa to Case, "all the love and companionship she can get now."

"*Ja*," said Case uneasily.

"I spent last evening with Carrie Pellissière," said Melissa pronouncing the surname in a perfect—a very pluperfect[12]—French manner.

---

[7]In a palsied way — in a shaky way, as with someone who suffers from the disease, palsy.

[8]Duse, Bernhardt — Eleanora Duse and Sarah Bernhardt. Famous actresses of the late 19th and early 20th century.

[9]Pure panache — flamboyant or showy style.

[10]"I like better the paper." — Many of Case's and Katrina's remarks are grammatically or idiomatically incorrect, reflecting the Hooks' Dutch language background. The standard English word order here would be, "I like the paper better."

[11]To fall in with — to agree with or to pretend to agree with other people's views or actions when your own views were originally, and perhaps still are, different.

[12]Pluperfect — usually refers to the past perfect tense. Here the word simply means, "more than perfect," an impossibility, of course. The author is gently mocking Melissa here.

"Ney," said Case, who had not understood her, "I don't know."

"Carrie," said Melissa dropping Hattie's hand, "Carrie Pellissière, Hattie's sister."

"Ney," said Case, "I seen her once or twice."

"She is a fine woman," said Melissa, "a woman of refinement and culture."

"*Ja,*" said Case, "Hattie's sister."

"She would be a valuable addition to any community," said Melissa. "I think I could persuade her to join us."

"*Ja,*" said Case beginning to laugh. "Trinka tell me Carrie save a theater program she see in Paris where you sing." He laughed himself into a cough again. "I remember she tell me. We laugh."

Josephine Melissa Froumier, contralto, in Beethoven's *Ninth Symphony,* 1897, Paris École des Études Musicales—her big role. Carrie, the Michigan girl on a tour, had saved the program of that concert because that very evening Jean-Jacques Pellissière, a dashing young lawyer from Lyons, had asked her to marry him.

That same year Melissa had married a rich American lawyer, who had thereupon immured[13] her in Sacramento, where he had begot[14] three children upon her. It was clear enough to Melissa which of them had come off with the better husband.

"An amusing coincidence," said Melissa smiling at her memories, at the tricks of chance.

"*Ja,* well," said Case, "I think I go bowling pretty soon now."

"It seems a fine day," said Melissa. "Think over our opportunity."

"What?"

"Our opportunity to add Carrie Pellissière to our group."

"Ney," he said arising. "All the rooms are full."

"There is the guest room."

"Well, that's for guests, Trinka says. You see Trinka."

"But if you say she comes, Katrina will agree."

"I don't know," he said at the doorway. "I send her up now." He went downstairs.

"I am doing what I can for you, dearest," said Melissa taking up Hattie's spoiled hand again. "Your darling sister is such a cultured woman. Our only problem will be to persuade her to come live in a house with such people as this. Not that the Hooks are inferior in any real way, oh no, but they are certainly lacking in refinement." She smiled knowingly at Hattie. Her vision was not good; she did not see the distaste in Hattie's eyes behind the weak smile. "The refinements which a person of Carrie's cosmopolitan background is so accustomed to. She is handsomely situated now of course. The Lakecliff gives the best of service; there isn't a finer hotel in Oakland. And her room has a fine

---

[13]Immured — confined; imprisoned.

[14]To beget — to father children.

view of Lake Merritt; transportation is so accessible. But I know you have told
her of our family. That's something not even money can buy. I am so sorry for
those who live alone or with ungrateful children." Melissa reached into her
bosom for a scented handkerchief with which she wiped her eyes under their
glasses. "My eyes are watering so much these days. Excuse me. It's so fortunate
for you, dearest, that your eyes are still good. You have a great deal to thank your
lucky stars for.[15] It's so terrible to have to impose yourself upon your children,
inconveniencing them. Or a home—a home." She shuddered. "Really, Hattie, I
think we are doing Carrie a service to bring her here with us. A hotel is so cold, so
impersonal. I am sure my sons are very happy to have me come to live here.
They insisted so much that I shouldn't go to a hotel, and I know it was not a
question of money. They are both doing so well in their careers. Real successes.
But they simply hadn't the room in their homes for me. Such active people, both
of them. No, no, a family, Hattie, a family is the best solution. We must bring
Carrie here with us."

Hattie acquiesced because it would have exhausted her to communicate
her disagreement. But she did not rejoice in this plan, for Carrie looked down on
her, and outshone her completely and always had, and had much more money
than she. All Hattie had was her stroke; it was not enough. Besides, though
Hattie had a son in Boston who paid her board and room, Carrie had a daughter
right down in San Jose who invited her to dinner four or five times a year and who
had produced two grandchildren for her to show pictures of and to brag about.

Downstairs Case put on his hat and his sweater and looked about for his
wife. She was in the kitchen making bread.

"Trinka," he said, "they want to bring Hattie's sister to live too. I tell them
you come up and talk about it. I don't care."

"Carrie Pellissière," she said punching the dough vigorously. "Oh ho,
what airs she has.[16] We got no room."

"Okay. You go talk."

"Unless, Kees Hoek"—she would not English[17] his name any more than
she had ever Englished her own—"you get that Hattie to go to a hospital. What
you think, we're a hospital? Thelma a nurse?"

"Neen!" he cried. "She's okay. We take her in well, we keep her sick. *Ja.*
You do with Carrie anything, okay. Hattie stay."

Katrina turned her back on him and muttered, "Dutchhead,"[18] mostly to
herself.

"*Ja,*" he said angrily, "Dutchhead Hoek, okay. She has stroke? Too bad,
we keep her. Thelma don't have to bathe her, her nurse does that. Twice a week.
We get twenty dollars a month extra. Okay. Maybe she like to see her sister."

---

[15] To thank your lucky stars — to be grateful for your good fortune.

[16] "What airs she has" — "What a haughty, superior manner she has."

[17] To English — to anglicize.

[18] Dutchhead — Here Katrina uses this term insultingly, implying that he is stubborn.

"You go bowling," said Katrina. "Leave me alone."

"I think we have Carrie live here."

"You think, you think! I don't think. Go on."

He went up the hall toward the front door, muttering to himself. Thelma came out of the parlor where she had been vacuuming the rug. Thelma was unmarried and very strong. She did most of the work in the house, which meant that she was busy a good sixty hours a week—more if one of the old folk was sick. But she was no servant, for she got no pay. She was the Hooks' daughter.

"Papa," she said smiling, "are you going out now?"

"Dutchhead," he muttered, not even looking at her.

"What Papa?"

He shook his head.

"Tonight I'm going to the show. You ought to come along too. You don't get much entertainment."

"Ney," he said at the door, "I go bowling."

She looked after him wondering what was wrong, whether she had done something to offend him. She was worried but she forgot to quit smiling. Adjusting her hair beneath her bandanna she went into the kitchen.

"Hello Mama. How's the bread coming?"

"You like anybody more come live here?" Katrina demanded.

"Oh it all depends," said Thelma smiling more than ever.

"Hattie's sister. You know that Carrie Pellissière."

From her mother's snappish tone of voice it was obvious that this had been the cause of some quarrel with her father. Thelma avoided quarrels.

"What do you think, Mama?"

"What do I think? Who cares what I think? That old Dutchhead, he don't care."

"It would be a lot of trouble. But it would be nice for Hattie."

"Nice for Hattie," said Katrina with scorn. "A nice hospital nice for Hattie, nicer too."

"Then there's the guest room."

"*Ja*, what we do for a guest room with that Carrie in it?"

"Of course, Mama. Still, we don't have any guests."

"You can never tell, Thelma, we might someday. It's a good thing to have a guest room."

"Sure, Mama, for emergencies."

"*Ja*. Besides you work enough already. Plenty to do without no fancy lady too."

"More money though, Mama."

"*Ja*, more money." She lapsed into silence while she shaped the loaves. "Well, we get along okay now. That Dutchhead, he don't care how many people die here. She'll die, you'll see. Bad stroke. He don't care. Well I care."

"Maybe it's a good idea to have Carrie here when Hattie dies, Mama. She'll pay good too. We need the money. Everything costs so much."

"Neen!" said Katrina. "In that family they die all the time. Neen, see?"

"All right, sure Mama. Maybe I'll win something tonight."

"Eh?"

"Sure, at the show they're having a big drawing.[19] A hundred prizes with a mammoth[20] first prize. A fully mechanized home."

"Eh?"

"Sure, fully mechanized home on a view lot. Brand new with two bedrooms and a garage. If I win that then we can rent this house, Mama, and live there in peace."

"*Ja.* Does it have a hot water heater?"

"Mama, fully mechanized. Automatic water heater and electric stove and refrigerator and washing machine and furnace. Everything the heart could desire."

"Well, you go win it, Thelma." She laughed. "What the old Dutchhead do then?" She laughed hard.

"Mama!"

"You clean the rug. I go up to see them upstairs. Those two old ones."

But by the time Katrina had got to the top of the stairs Hattie was dead of another stroke. Melissa gave a very piercing shriek and came banging out against the door of Hattie's room.

"Katrina! Katrina! My God, what has happened?"

Katrina mumbled a curse under her breath in Dutch. "Dead?" she said to Melissa at the door.

Melissa, her handkerchief at her trembling mouth, could only nod.

"Stroke," said Katrina flatly, and went in to look at the body.

Thelma came running up the stairs, not smiling.

"My dearest," said Melissa grabbing one of Thelma's hands, "I was holding her hand just like this, just so, talking to her. Suddenly she made a little sound. I can't explain. Not a strange sound. But my intuition told me look at her. Oh Thelma, we must trust our intuition." Melissa buried her face in her hands. "Too shocking, too much for me. Help me to my room."

Katrina came out into the hall.

"What should I do, Mama?" said Thelma on the point of tears herself.

"Put her to bed."

"You, Mama?" said Thelma over her shoulder as she was supporting Melissa into her room.

"I call the coroner."[21]

"Thelma!" cried Melissa straightening up suddenly. "Thelma, we must call her next of kin."[22]

"*Ja*," said Katrina on her way downstairs.

---

[19] Drawing — the pulling of a lottery ticket, for a prize.

[20] Mammoth — huge.

[21] Coroner — a public officer in charge of investigating the cause of a person's death.

[22] Next of kin — closest relatives.

"Katrina," cried Melissa leaning over the banisters, "you must call Carrie immediately. She must come be with us. She needs us."

"*Ja,* I call her."

"Oh, poor Carrie, the poor delicate creature. My heart goes out to her."

"She can have Hattie's room," said Katrina. "Same price."

"You must come lie down," said Thelma.

"How close death is. We are surrounded by it."

"You never can tell," said Thelma.

"Cover her, Thelma. Cover her poor old face."

"Yes," said Thelma, and at the thought of it easy tears brimmed from her eyes.

Melissa took off her glasses and lay back on her satin chaise longue. "My spirits,"[23] she said with a large gesture, her left hand held to her eyes. "My spirits, then leave me."

Thelma put the bottle into her trembling hand, pulled the dress down over her knees, and went to cover Hattie.

Downstairs, Katrina sat by the telephone with a sour expression on her face.

"I'd better go get Papa," said Thelma trying to smile through her tears.

"Why?"

"Well, he ought to know. You know . . ."

"Ney. Let him play. He's just in the way here."

"I'll make you some soup, Mama. We need to keep up our strength."

"Why not?"

"Do you think I ought to take some up to Melissa?"

"She has words, don't she? Let her use them."

"I'll go now, Mama. You rest awhile."

"Let me alone," snapped Katrina. She went over to a couch and for a moment hesitated whether to lie on it. She decided it would be too much trouble to get up again for soup in ten minutes and sat leaning sidewise against a pillow. She was small and slack, and her hands were gnarled. "Old Dutchhead," she mumbled. "She could die just as good in a hospital. Too many people dying around here. Dying, dying, dying." She closed her eyes and napped.

At two o'clock the men came for Hattie. At three o'clock Case came home. At three-thirty Carrie arrived in a taxi.

Carrie was of medium height and held herself upright. She wore a fur coat; it was a squirrel coat and not new, but she wore it as though it were a fine chinchilla. Her hair was carefully and frequently dyed to match the fur. She had cancer of the liver, which is incurable, but she had never told anybody about it. She had had her last lover when she was sixty-five, before her face had quite disappeared behind a mask of wrinkles.

Thelma, as the maid, went to the door to answer Carrie's ring. Katrina, as the hostess of the house, leaned against the jamb of the door to the parlor.

---

[23] Spirits — either alcoholic spirits or spirits of ammonia, used as a remedy for faintness.

Melissa, as friend, bumped, blinking and tragic, right past Katrina to get to Carrie first. Case, as Case, sat drinking his coffee.

"My dear!" cried Carrie to Melissa when the door opened.

"Carrie!" cried Melissa opening her arms.

"Isn't it dreadful," said Carrie depositing her umbrella on Thelma as she went past her. It was one of Carrie's peculiarities always to take an umbrella when she went out in case the weather should turn against her.

"I must tell you about her last moments," said Melissa as they embraced. "She passed so quietly. I am so grateful that I could be with her."

"Hlo," said Katrina.

"It is so sad," said Thelma with fresh tears ready in her eyes.

"Dear Mrs. Hook," said Carrie disengaging herself from Melissa. "I am so happy that my sister was surrounded by such an atmosphere of friendliness in her last days."

"*Ja,*" said Katrina, "friendly."

"Mrs. Pellissière," said Thelma tentatively.

"Yes Thelma?" Carrie said in a cool voice, half-turning.

Thelma had intended to say something comforting, as Carrie had guessed from the tone of her voice. But Carrie liked having at least one servant about her and she was testing to see whether, in case she wanted to move in here, Thelma was thrall[24] enough. She was.

"Mrs. Pellissière, may I take your coat?"

"Thank you, Thelma. Will you help me? Please hang it up on a wide hanger. I'm careful with the shoulders."

"I'll try."

"And my dear Mr. Hook," said Carrie advancing upon him.

"*Ja,*" said Case grinning on his way up from his chair. He was stiff from bowling.

"How often," said Carrie taking one of his hands in both of hers, "how often Harriet had told me how much your companionship meant to her."

"Well, I read the paper to her."

"You know," she said rather intimately to him though the others were about them, "there is not a man in our family—my family now, I should say. My brother is dead, my daughter's husband has left her. My son is in New York. Harriet's son is far away. Mr. Hook, I am going to ask you to do me the greatest favor I could ask of any man. I am going to ask you to escort me at Hattie's funeral."

"*Ja,*" he said grinning more than ever, "well, I don't know."

"I had rather thought," said Melissa sniffing a bit, "that since I have a little difficulty sometimes Case would walk by my side."

"What's that?" cried Katrina catching on. "What's that? He walk by me. Sure. He's my man."

"Oh dear," said Thelma, "would you like some coffee, Mrs. Pellissière?"

---

[24]Thrall — slave.

"Thank you Thelma. With cream and two lumps of sugar."

"You will stay to dinner with us too, won't you," asked Thelma.

"I would like nothing so much as to be with you all today. Hattie's family!" Carrie opened her arms to them.

"I hope you like lamb stew," said Thelma.

"It doesn't matter at all. Anything."

Thelma left for the kitchen.

"Now," said Carrie, "I must hear about Hattie's end."

"It was so peaceful," said Melissa fishing in her bosom for her handkerchief again. "I was sitting beside her, just chatting about the future and her good fortune in not suffering. How inspiring to think that she went with her thoughts on higher things. What a difference it makes to those left behind."

"She want you to come live here," said Case.

Melissa was very annoyed at his blurting it out so crassly. She had been going to lead up to it gradually when she had Carrie by herself.

"That was in her mind," said Melissa. "She was thinking of others."

"*Ja,*" said Katrina. "Well, you can come if you want to."

"Thank you so much," said Carrie going over to her. "I am so moved by your generosity."

"Same price," said Katrina.

"I would need more room. I must think about it."

"Carrie my dearest," said Melissa taking her by the elbow, "you must come up with me and see her bed."

"You aren't in any hurry are you?" said Carrie to Katrina.

"Ney, any time before Sunday."

"Come dearest."

"I must," said Carrie.

Thelma entered with coffee. "Don't you want your coffee?"

"Just bring it up after us," said Carrie, and she did.

Carrie was not very interested in Melissa's story about Hattie's death. She kept looking shrewdly about the room. When Melissa had exhausted her subject, Carrie spoke. "The furniture is quite agreeable. I would have the mattress changed, of course."

"The mattress? Poor Hattie said it was very comfortable. Innerspring."

"A superstition. I'm superstitious, Melissa. I could never sleep on the same mattress someone died on."

"Especially not your own sister."

"That has nothing to do with it." She made an odd clicking sound in her mouth. "My damned upper plate is giving me trouble." She took it out and began wiping it with a handkerchief. "I've got to have more room than this! That's why I have to leave the Lakecliff. No room."

"We have a guest room too," said Melissa. "Right adjoining this. Perhaps you could have it too."

"Splendid. We must look at it."

She was putting her teeth back in as they opened the door. Thelma was standing in the hall waiting to see if they needed anything, but Carrie thought she was eavesdropping.

"Thelma," she said severely, "show me the guest room."

"Certainly, certainly, Mrs. Pellissière. It's not used very often. Would you like to stay here tonight? I can make it up[25] for you." Thelma saw that Carrie was displeased with her, and tried to make up for it[26] as best she could.

Carrie did not answer her but strode into the room and looked about. She approved of it. "That will be enough, Thelma. Our coffee cups are in the other room."

"Thank you," said Thelma, and went in for the cups.

"I hope you will join us dearest," said Melissa in a rather shaky voice. "They are a warmhearted family."

"These are airy rooms and very pleasantly done up. I would save a good deal of money over the Lakecliff. Still, what a view." The windows gave on 55th Street back yards. "I must think about it." But she had already made up her mind to come here, because it would be the pleasantest place she knew of in which to spend her months dying. "I am going to lie down."

"And think of poor dear Hattie," said Melissa. "I will leave till dinnertime."

"How long will that be?"

"About an hour."

"Tell me, how often is the guest room used?"

"I really can't say, dearest. I can't remember that it has ever been used since I have been here. Now you lie quietly if you can."

The house fell quiet for an hour. All those in it lay quiet, except for Thelma in the kitchen, who was busy preparing dinner. Out of respect for Hattie they did not even listen to the radio, as they usually did during this time.

At quarter to six Thelma rang the triangle in the front hall. The old folk bestirred themselves. At six all five sat down. The meal consisted of mustard greens, lamb stew, very soft white bread, honey, coffee, and for dessert a heavy turnip pudding with an orange sauce. Everything was put on the table at the beginning of the meal. As in a progressive school[27] everybody went at his own speed without much regard for the speed of the others. Carrie took displeased note of all this and wondered how she could use her displeasure to strengthen her bargaining position.

"Papa," said Thelma to Case, who was already on the last lap, "how is the pudding?"

"All right Thelma. Not like it used to be in the old country."

"You always say that."

---

[25]To make it up — to make the bed; to put clean sheets on it and make it tidy.

[26]To make up for it — to atone for something.

[27]A progressive school — a school where children are allowed more freedom to follow their own activities or to proceed at their own pace of learning.

"Well," said Katrina, "he's right. I can't even make it the same myself." She was still eating stew.

"I think," said Melissa, who in her care to avoid dribbling on herself was lagging far behind, "that it is very commendable of you, Thelma, to try to make the old dishes for your parents."

Thelma turned rosy with gratitude.

Carrie, perceiving in what coin this servant was paid,[28] took a few pennies out of her pocket. "You're a very good daughter, Thelma," she said. "I am sure it must give you a wonderful sense of satisfaction to think of how marvelously you have stood by[29] your parents."

"She's a good girl," said Case.

"*Ja,*" said Katrina.

"There aren't many children as devoted as you," said Melissa.

"Your parents must be proud of themselves every time they look at you," said Carrie. "There are so few in this world who can, particularly nowadays. *Cette grosse-là, Melisse, elle n'a pas de mari, hein? Qu'en dites-vous?*"

"*Non, pas de mari.*"

"*Jamais?*"

"*Jamais,*"[30] said Melissa. She was embarrassed to be talking about Thelma in front of her thus, though Thelma, suffused with happiness, had not noticed the shift into French, and neither Case nor Katrina was paying enough attention to care. "Tell me, my dear, what parlor[31] is going to handle the services?"

"What?" said Carrie.

"I mean Hattie's services."

"Oh, the Cloister of Harmony."

"Eh?" said Katrina.

"She just said, Mama," said Thelma, "that she's going to have Hattie buried by the Cloister of Harmony."

"That's all right," said Katrina, "we'll go."

"Such a lovely columbarium[32] too," said Melissa. "Are you having her interred,[33] dearest, or preserved in a crypt?"[34]

---

[28]"In what coin this servant was paid" — how this servant was rewarded.

[29]To stand by — to be loyal to.

[30]"Cette grosse-là," etc. — "That heavy one there, Melissa, she isn't married, is she? What do you say?"

"No, she isn't married."
"Never?"
"Never."

[31]Parlor — funeral parlor. House which makes all arrangements for a funeral.

[32]Columbarium — a vault with places for urns containing the ashes of the dead.

[33]Interred — buried.

[34]Crypt — a chamber wholly or partly underground, often under the main floor of a church.

"I think cremation," said Carrie, having got to the turnip pudding and getting no further.

"It's cheaper," said Katrina.

"It's so distressing," said Melissa, "to think of these matters at this time, but we must." She smiled, but only Thelma smiled in return. "Who are you having to conduct the services?"

"The man the Cloister has, whoever he is. Hattie was no church-goer."

"If you would like, dearest, I could ask Dr. Peabody to officiate.[35] He's very capable, so cultured."

"What's the difference," said Katrina.

"I'll just have the Cloister of Harmony," said Carrie impatiently. She pushed her pudding away as though it was food that revolted her, not the turnips, and spoke decisively. "I have thought about coming to live with you," she said to Case.

"*Ja.* Good."

"I would bring my own mattress and curtains, and I would have to have some special services."

"What's the difference," said Katrina.

"*Ja,* well," said Case, "you pay extra for special things."

"Certainly. And I need the guest room along with the other one."

"Neen!" cried Katrina.

"Trinka!" said Case. Then he turned to Carrie, "You pay extra for that too."

"Naturally."

"Thirty dollars a month for that."

"No, too much."

"She can't have!" cried Katrina. "We need a guest room."

"I'll tell you," said Carrie, "I'll take it for twenty dollars a month and let you have it for any guest you have."

"All right," said Case.

"Who does the work?" said Katrina to him. "Who wants things nice here?"

"Ney," said Case, "what guest we ever have?"

"I have not decided," said Carrie, "absolutely to take it. I just want to see if we could come to terms."

"A family is *so* nice," said Melissa. "So much nicer. And ours is a superior family. Case is so helpful with me when I go out. I sometimes have trouble at the street corners." She smiled at Case.

"You will walk with me at the funeral?" said Carrie to Case. "I have no other man at all."

"Well," said Melissa tossing her head.

"Ney," said Katrina flatly.

"If you will excuse me," said Thelma and left the table precipitously for the front hall.

---

[35]To officiate — to conduct a service or ceremony, in this case the funeral service.

"Where are you going?" asked Carrie.

"Out," said Thelma. "Just out."

"To a movie," said Katrina.

"I hope you don't mind," said Thelma at the door to Carrie, smiling nervously. "On such a day as this."

"What movie is it that's so good?" said Carrie.

"Oh it's a drawing, a mammoth drawing. I have eighty-five tickets saved up for it."

"Yes," said Carrie, "yes, go."

She turned back to the others. Case was lighting a cigar, Katrina was pouring herself a third cup of coffee, Melissa was trying to pour orange sauce onto the pudding. Carrie had much more money than she had time left in which to spend it, and there were at least half-a-dozen men she could get to escort her at Hattie's funeral; nevertheless she drove her bargain.[36]

"I would pay forty dollars a month extra, for the room and for breakfast in bed and a few other little extras."

"Okay?" said Case to Katrina.

"Forty dollars. Okay."

"Oh Carrie . . ." Melissa began.

"*If* I decide to come."

"You couldn't!" Melissa cried. "Not come?"

"About the funeral," Carrie began.

"Ney," said Katrina. "Nothing to say."

"Hattie was so fond of you," said Carrie to Case. "You meant so much to her in her last days. I would hate to think of anyone but you there."

"Well," he said, "I read the paper to her. Poor woman."

"It means so much to me and I am sure it would have meant so much to her."

"Kees, neen!" said Katrina.

As it did every once in a while Carrie's liver fluttered; she felt pressed for time.

"I would like so very much to come live with you," said Carrie in a final tone of voice, "but I could not bear to if I didn't have complete faith in your loyalty."

"You must pardon me, dearest," said Melissa. "Katrina. Case." She went to the door. "So painful to hear." With a sniff she went upstairs.

"Well," said Case indecisively.

Katrina angrily stirred her coffee, muttering to herself in Dutch. "How old are you?" she said sharply to Carrie.

"Seventy-six," said Carrie, understanding perfectly the drift of her question and relishing the way she would take the answer.

"No noise after nine o'clock," said Katrina.

"Just the radio if I can't sleep?"

---

[36]To drive a bargain — to press hard for your own wishes in coming to an agreement with someone.

"No noise!" cried Katrina. "No radio."

"Oh all right."

Case coughed.

Katrina stirred her coffee some more, drank it down, and mumbling, "Forty dollars, *ja,*" stood up. "Okay, Kees," she said and started out of the room.

Case grinned at Carrie. "Okay, she say."

"Dear Case," said Carrie moving toward him and taking one of his hands, "I can't tell you how much your support means to me at a time like this."

Case began to laugh, rocking back and forth in his chair and finally choking up. Carrie laughed too, merrily and youthfully.

"What's the difference," said Katrina, and went cackling with laughter into the parlor to lie down.

☆ FOLLOW-UP QUESTIONS

I. There are six characters in this story, five of whom are old. But the "old folk" of the title do not behave in ways that reflect age exclusively. They are individuals, and they are written about as such.

    A. Hattie, paralyzed and unable to speak, listens to Case Hook read to her.

        1. Why is his kindness a source of triumph to her?

        2. Why does she avoid attempting to explain her pain and discomfort to the others?

        3. Why is she unhappy about the plan to persuade her sister to move into the Hooks' home?

    B. Katrina and Case Hook are an elderly couple who quarrel a great deal of the time.

        1. What are the reasons for their disputes?

        2. What nationality were they originally?

        3. What does Katrina mean by calling her husband "Dutchhead?"

        4. What is Katrina's predominant interest?

        5. How do they treat their daughter Thelma?

    C. We are told that Melissa "scorned the favors of a fat little old Dutch butcher like Case Hook, but she could not scorn the lack of these favors."

        1. How does this statement explain her connection with Hattie?

        2. Why does Melissa want Carrie to join the household?

    D. How do Carrie and Melissa differ in temperament? Which of the two seems stronger, perhaps more honest?

    E. Why does Carrie consider moving in with the Hooks? Will it be a long-term arrangement?

    F. Why does Carrie insist that Case escort her at Hattie's funeral?

II. "Love among the Old Folk" is concerned with old age, loneliness, jealousy, illness, imminent death, and death itself. Nevertheless, the writer has chosen to deal with these elements in what is essentially a comic story. His attitude toward the characters has resulted in a tone that may make it difficult for the reader to be emotionally moved.

A. Describing Melissa, he states, "Melissa was grand in a palsied way." Do you find this an unsympathetic, even cruel, description?

B. Revealing Hattie's thoughts, he writes that "Carrie looked down on her, and outshone her completely and always had, and had much more money than she. All Hattie had was her stroke." Do you think the last sentence is shockingly cold? Do you find it at all funny?

C. Describing Thelma, he writes, "Thelma was unmarried and very strong. She did most of the work in the house, which meant that she was busy a good sixty hours a week—more if one of the old folk was sick. But she was no servant, for she got no pay. She was the Hooks' daughter." If the last sentence were interchanged with the first, would this description be less effective? Why?

D. What does the description—"She was worried but she forgot to quit smiling"—tell us about Thelma's personality?

E. What is Elliott's purpose in abruptly informing the reader of Hattie's death? Would a long, painful description of her death have changed the reader's reaction? How?

F. How does each of the characters react to Hattie's death? Who is the most emotional of the five?

G. Why is the description of the meal cruel and comic at the same time?

III. Elliott reveals his characters by narrative description and dialogue.

A. How does the manner in which they speak reveal the kind of people they are?

B. For instance, Carrie, while speaking about the impossibility of sleeping on a mattress someone has died on, states, "My damned upper plate is giving me trouble." Is it likely that Melissa would ever refer to a similar condition? Why?

IV. Although Elliott's treatment of his characters is comic, the situation is essentially sad.

A. How do you interpret the title, "Love among the Old Folk"? Do you find any examples of loving relationships in the story?

B. Though the author does not give the reasons, can we infer why Hattie, Melissa, and Carrie don't live with their children?

C. How does Melissa react to the thought of a home (a private institution for the aged)?

D. What do Hattie's envious thoughts about Carrie having a daughter who invited her to dinner four or five times a year reveal about her conception of family ties?

E. Why does the story end in laughter? What does this reveal about the kind of situation the characters find themselves in?

F. If the writer's somewhat distant attitude to his characters were replaced by a more sympathetic one, would the story seem different? How?

☆ *THEME TOPICS*

1. Discuss the attitude toward old age in your native country. What is the role of the elderly person in the family and the community? Is old age a social problem? Has the state passed laws concerning the welfare of old people? If so, what kind of laws?
2. Imagine yourself seventy or eighty years old, and describe your vision of a perfect old age.
3. Select one of the five elderly characters in the story and describe how they would have behaved in a specific situation fifty years earlier. For example: Melissa reacting to a proposal of marriage.

A Provincial in New York:
Living in the Big Cave*
Willie Morris

INTRODUCTION

I.   Originally, the word *province* referred to a country or region brought
       under the control of the ancient Roman government. Today, a
       province is thought of as any section of a country that is not a large
       city or close to a large city. A provincial is someone living in or
       coming from a province. If one's ideas or attitudes are called
       provincial, it generally implies lack of sophistication, narrowness.
       A. What are some reasons people might give for wanting to leave
           the provinces?
       B. Why is it an economic necessity for many to leave?
       C. What kinds of fulfillment may one find in a big city that are
           difficult or impossible to attain in the provinces?
       D. Is it likely that a young writer, artist, or musician would want to
           stay in the small town or village of his birth? Why or why not?
       E. What are some of the problems a young man or woman from the
           provinces confronts in a big city?
       F. Some people say that New Yorkers are the most provincial
           people in the world. How can one interpret this irony?

II.   The author of "A Provincial in New York" was born in Mississippi,
       a large, mostly rural state in the "Deep South." Mississippi is one of
       those states that fought against the federal government of the United
       States in the Civil War during the 1860s. One of the basic issues
       leading to the Civil War was Negro slavery. More than one hundred
       years after the defeat of the South and the abolition of slavery,
       deeply rooted attitudes toward the North still exist. Willie Morris
       considers himself a "liberated Mississippian," who has broken from
       the old emotional attitudes and perhaps from the Southern culture
       itself.
       A. What might influence a person to reject the culture he has grown
           up in?
       B. Is it possible to grow up in a particular culture without sharing at
           least some of the attitudes and values of that culture?
       C. Why is it often difficult for someone to adapt to a new culture
           even after he has rejected a very different one?

Our literature is filled with young people like myself who came from the provinces to the Big Cave, seeking involvement in what one always thought from the outside was a world of incomparable wonder, hoping for some vague kind of literary "fulfillment." In the 1960s, as always since New York became our literary and journalistic marketplace, there would be thousands of them clustered around the great axis of publishing, newspapering, and broadcasting, starting out at minuscule salaries, living in unfamiliar, claustrophobic walk-ups, fighting the dread and alien subways twice a day, coming to terms with the incredible noise and crowdedness. Most of them would not "make it";[1] the more resourceful and talented might.

Why did we come? Not because the materials for our work did not exist in those places we knew best. Not merely for fame and money and success, for these also some of us could have had, and perhaps in more civilized ways, in places far removed from New York. Not even because we wanted to try ourselves in the big time,[2] and out of curiosity to see how good the competition was. We had always come, the most ambitious of us, because we *had* to, because the ineluctable pull of the cultural capital when the wanderlust was high was too compelling to resist.

Yet there were always secret dangers for these young people from the provinces in the city. It became dangerously easy to turn one's back on his own past, on the isolated places that nurtured and shaped him into maturity, for the sake of some convenient or fashionable "sophistication." There were temptations to be not merely careless, but dishonest, with the most distinctive things about one's self. The literary and publishing worlds of the city were perilous vantage points from which to understand the rest of America. There was a marked sense of superiority, amounting to a kind of distrust, toward other American places. This had always been true, and it was likely to become more so, as the older regionalism died in America and as the cities of the East became more and more the center of an engaged and argumentative intellection. Coming to the Big Cave for the first time, the sensitive outlander might soon find himself in a subtle interior struggle with himself, over the most fundamental sense and meaning of his own origins. It was this struggle, fully comprehended, which finally could give New York its own peculiar and wonderful value as a place, for it tested who you are, in the deepest and most contorted way.

I spent that first night with an old friend from Mississippi, in a cramped apartment high above Washington Square. He was teaching now at the New York University law school. The last time I had seen him had been the previous summer, at the Ole Miss[3] law school, to which he had returned from Oxford, England, to finish three courses; outside class that summer, he had spent his whole time getting drunk in front of an electric fan, either that or indulging

---

[1] To make it — to become a success.

[2] The big time — the top level of any competitive field, as in sports, theater, etc.

[3] Ole Miss — nickname for the University of Mississippi.

himself in wild, uncontrollable outbursts against the young middle-class racists who were his fellow students. He was a "liberated Mississippian" who had just joined New York's burgeoning and implacable Southern expatriate community; he was the first of many Mississippi "exiles" I would see in the city—for, in truth, as I would come to understand, Mississippi was almost the only state in the Union (certainly one of a mere half-dozen) which had produced a genuine set of exiles, almost in the European sense: alienated from home yet forever drawn back to it, seeking some form of personal liberty elsewhere yet obsessed with the texture and the complexity of the place from which they had departed as few Americans from other states could ever be. We sat talking until midnight about people we had known, about old forgotten high-school football games in the Delta,[4] about Ross Barnett[5] and James Meredith,[6] Paul Johnson and Hodding Carter, about unusual weekend celebrations at country clubs in the hills. Then, groggy from the transcontinental Greyhound,[7] I went off to bed.

The next morning I arose early to set out to find a job. On the recommendation of a mutual acquaintance I had made an appointment with a well-known editor—he was described to me as "tough-minded," a glowing description for anyone in those days—in a distinguished publishing firm. I strolled through Washington Square, walking past those sepulchral warehouses of New York University, the magnificent old town houses on the north side which had yet to give in to the wrecker's hammer, the red-brick apartment towers to the west. Then I sat on a bench to while away[8] an hour, watching the old men playing chess on the concrete tables, and the bums[9] and the beats[10] who congregated in agitated little circles making activity out of nothing. Two young men with sandals and long hair appeared from nowhere and accosted me on my bench. "Could I have fifteen cents for a cup of coffee?" one of them asked. I handed over fifteen cents. Then the other said, "Could I have fifty cents for a *Partisan Review*?"[11] When I declined, he shrugged his shoulders, whispered *square,*[12] and he and his running mate ambled off.

I sat there counting out my private responsibilities. Besides having to get a job to support a family, I needed to find an apartment, one with enough room for a three-year-old boy to roam around in, next to a big park perhaps, and preferably overlooking some body of water: a place with a study, and dark oak

---

[4]The Delta — the area near the mouth of a river; in this case, the delta of the Mississippi River.

[5]Ross Barnett — former Governor of Mississippi.

[6]James Meredith — first black person to attend the University of Mississippi, in 1962.

[7]Greyhound — a major bus company in the United States.

[8]To while away — to spend leisure so that one is not bored.

[9]Bums — tramps; people, often dressed in ragged clothes, who try to avoid taking regular jobs.

[10]Beats — people who, in dress, manner, and attitude, reject the values of the mainstream of society. From the term "beat generation," after the Second World War.

[11]*Partisan Review* — an American magazine dealing with political, social, and intellectual matters.

[12]Square — conformist, accepting the values of the society. Slang.

paneling, and within walking distance of my office. I started feeling again, as I had not since my sophomore year at the University of Texas in Austin, as Thomas Wolfe[13] had felt, coming north to this Rock.[14] *Only the dead know Brooklyn,* he said, and he got a book published, and he went to literary cocktail parties in Park Avenue penthouses;[15] he stood on their terraces and heard the tinkling of the ice in the glasses of those critics and editors and authors, and watched the lights of Manhattan come on. At that point he always felt he would never die.

All of a sudden, in the middle of these harmless recollections, a slightly familiar figure came out from the corner of my eye, from the arch at the north side of Washington Square. Be damned if it wasn't Mr. DeMent Warren, who ran the men's clothing store at the corner of Jefferson and Main in Yazoo City, Mississippi, during my boyhood. I stood up to go and greet him, but I saw it wasn't Mr. DeMent at all—only a big balding man in a topcoat uncommonly heavy for that time of year. A few minutes later the same thing happened. Over near the fountain I saw, of all people, Earlene Whitt, a fine well-constructed beauty queen from the University of Texas in 1955. But it wasn't Earlene—only a big blonde Village girl taking her beagle on a morning's walk. Within the next fifteen minutes I spotted four people I had once known: "Jap," the old yellow-skinned Negro man who had cut our yard for us when I was in grammar school; A. J. "Buddy" Reeves, an American Legionnaire[16] from Yazoo County, who used to go out with us when we played taps for the military funerals; Bibb Falk, the baseball coach at Texas;[17] and Wallace Miller, a rotund conservative in the Texas legislature—all apparitions! They were my first experience, all of them, of what would become my own peculiar New York eyesight. With my mind on the past, only haphazardly thinking of long-ago things, just basking lazily in old events as is my wont[18] (even something as ephemeral as a touch football[19] game in Lintonia Park in Yazoo twenty years ago, or the funeral of a friend's father in 1948), people all around me—on the sidewalks of Broadway or in a subway—would take on known shapes, tangible recognitions. All they had to do, when these moods were upon me, was to bear some vague resemblance to someone who once had had a meaning for me, in a period of my past I was thinking about, and my dastardly subconscious would toss up for me a real person! I believe the

---

[13]Thomas Wolfe — American novelist (1900–1938).

[14]Rock — Manhattan Island, New York City.

[15]Park Avenue penthouses — luxury apartments situated on the roof or top floor of apartment houses on Park Avenue, known for its many elegant and expensive buildings.

[16]American Legionnaire — person who belongs to the American Legion, an organization of American war veterans.

[17]At Texas — at the University of Texas.

[18]"As is my wont" — "as I am accustomed to doing." Morris is deliberately using archaic style here.

[19]Touch football — American football, often played informally, where the person carrying the ball is stopped by being touched instead of tackled.

crowds did it, and the awful and unfamiliar isolation of the city when thousands of human beings are around you and none knows you or cares. I later grew accustomed to this phenomenon that the Cave worked on me, and even to enjoy it, but on that day it struck me as passing strange;[20] it made me fear the extent to which my rambling imaginings of past places that had intimately shaped me could, in this unknown and uncaring city, produce forms so tangible as to make the very present itself incongruous and ghostlike. I had returned, among the smog pelts[21] and pollution indices,[22] to my childhood's land of seething mirages.

II

The apartment I found was in the East Twenties,[23] between Madison and Park.[24] The other places that I had seen and liked, airy places with parks nearby, never rented for less than $250 or $300 a month. This one rented at $125, and it occupied the third floor of a narrow gray building next to a parking lot. The exposed side was pocked with holes and ridges, and someone had written on it in white enamel: "The Dukes." Looking at this unusual structure from a block down the street, one was struck by its lean-to[25] quality; it seemed to have no business existing at all. It rose from the west side of the parking lot, gaunt and improvised. Someone walking down the street with the address almost always walked right past it, not thinking that the place might be inhabited. One reason may have been that there was a red canopy over the sidewalk at the front door advertising the short-order take-home service[26] which shared the entrance off to the left.

One walked up the three flights through several padlocked doors, often past the garbage which the landlord had neglected to remove for two or three days. Once inside our place, things were not bad at all. There was a big front room with an old floor, a little alcove for a study, and to the back a short corridor opening up into a tiny bedroom for my son and a larger bedroom behind it. The kitchen was in the back bedroom near the bed. I had not been able to find a view of an extensive body of water at popular prices, but from the rear window, about forty yards out, there *was* a vista of a big tank, part of some manufacturing installation in the building under it, and the tank constantly bubbled with some

---

[20]Passing strange — extremely strange. This use of *passing* is deliberately archaic, going back to *surpassing,* meaning "very" or "great."

[21]Smog pelts — layers of smoke; air pollution.

[22]Pollution indices — measurements of levels of air pollution.

[23]East Twenties — many of the streets running east and west in Manhattan are numbered. The term "East Twenties" refers to the twenties east of Fifth Avenue, which runs north and south.

[24]Madison and Park — avenues, running north and south.

[25]Lean-to — a shelter, often enclosed on three sides and with a one-slope roof. Usually located in wilderness areas.

[26]Short-order take-home service — a store which quickly prepares food to be eaten at home or outside.

unidentified greenish substance. From this window one could also see the tarred
rooftops of the surrounding buildings, and off to the right a quiet stretch of God's
earth, this being the parking lot next door.

From the front room the view was more animated. Across the street there
was a large bar, which remained open twenty-four hours a day, and in front of
this, on the corner, one could look down at any hour and see the little circles of
people, just standing, watching the mad traffic on lower Madison. We were
without sunlight, which was unable to penetrate down from the tall office building across the street; and when it rained, which was often that first year, I
remembered the hard cold rainfalls in the Mississippi Delta of my childhood,
and how they encompassed the green earth and fields and trees in such a torrent
that one seemed at the mercy of nature itself; here, from the front window, the
rain merely kicked up little pools of dirt and debris on East Twenty-sixth, and
sent people under the canopy of the corner bar. My old *Texas Observer*[27]
friends, Ronnie Dugger and Larry Goodwyn, came to New York for a visit, and
one gray Saturday morning during a blizzard we sat here talking of old times and
places. Suddenly Goodwyn opened the window, and stuck his head out. Then he
slammed the window down, turned to us, and said, "Well, boys, they got us all
up here together . . . and then they *snowed* on us." The subway was also difficult to get used to. There was a station twenty yards from the building; every five
minutes the building rocked and groaned at its very foundation.

I was only seven blocks from my office at *Harper's,*[28] and in the mornings I
could walk up Madison to work. On a fine day, carrying my black briefcase with
poems from housewives in the Midwest, or stream-of-consciousness prose[29]
from the graduate schools,[30] I enjoyed making my way up the avenue through
the bustling crowds on the sidewalks, feeling very much the cosmopolite. But on
some grim foggy morning, when the steam came out of the sewers in the streets
as if the earth beneath were on fire, the city had a dreadful claustrophobic
quality, like death itself: closed-in, blind, and airless, compressed by the endless
concrete and asphalt exteriors. The horns from the cabs, the cursing of the
drivers, the harsh violence of the street workers dodging the already clogged
traffic, caused a new arrival to feel that humanity here was always at war with its
machines and with itself. In the course of a year, walking seven blocks to work
and back over the same route, I saw three people killed by cars and four others
badly hurt. The most likely place for this mayhem was the curious intersection of
Park and Thirty-third. Here there was a tunnel which came suddenly out of

---

[27] *Texas Observer* — a Texas newspaper.

[28] *Harper's* — a national monthly magazine, published in New York. It was designed to have broad
appeal to a well-educated audience.

[29] Stream-of-consciousness prose — the written record of thoughts and impressions as they come to
the mind of one of the characters in a work of fiction. This technique was developed by the Irish
novelist, James Joyce (1882–1941), in *A Portrait of the Artist as a Young Man* and in *Ulysses.*

[30] Graduate schools — divisions of a university in which one can study for an advanced degree
beyond the Bachelor of Arts.

nowhere. Cars whipped out of it at terrific speeds, catching pedestrians crossing against the red light on Park. There was no sign suggesting the existence of this tunnel, which added somewhat to the spirit of adventure. At first it would be disrupting to see the white sheet covering an unfortunate pedestrian caught by surprise by some taxicab coming out of the tunnel, the crowds milling around with that sullen big-city curiosity looking at the blood, the cop or two waiting perfunctorily for the ambulance to arrive. After a time I grew used to the spectacle, however, and would walk gingerly past the broken body and its spectators as if it were all in the morning's walk.

Many times, walking home from work, I would see some unknowing soul venture across that intersection against the light and then freeze in horror when he saw the cars ripping out of the tunnel toward him. For a brief instant the immobile human would stand there, transfixed by the vehicle bearing down upon him, the contrast of desperate vulnerable flesh and hard chrome never failing to send a horrible tremor through an onlooker's being. Then, suddenly, the human reflex would take over, and the pedestrian would jackknife first one way, then another, arms flaying the empty air, and often the car would literally *skim* the man, brushing by him so close it would touch his coat or his tie. If another car coming behind did not nail him[31] then, much the way a linebacker moves in for the kill after the tackle or end[32] merely slows down a ball-carrier, the pedestrian would stand there briefly, all the blood drained from his face, oblivious to the curses from the driver of the car which had just missed him. If there was a cop[33] on the corner he would wait while the man staggered in his shock to the sidewalk beyond, there to accost him: "Ya crazy, hah? Ya stupid? Walkin' against the light! Hah! Ya almost got killed, ya know it? Ya *know* it?" On one occasion, feeling sorry for the person who had brushed against the speeding car, I hurried across the intersection after him to cheer him up a little. Catching up with him down by Thirty-second I said, "That was good legwork, sir. Excellent moves for a big man!" but the man looked at me with an empty expression in his eyes, and then moved away mechanically and trancelike, heading for the nearest bar.

On a number of occasions on my peregrinations from Thirty-third to Twenty-sixth there would be some bum sprawled out on the sidewalk, and the people would walk right past him or sometimes step over him, glancing back a little nervously, usually saying to their companions, "Somebody should call a cop." The first time I saw a man lying prone on the concrete, blood trickling slightly from his nose, I bent over and asked him if he was all right, and he moaned a little, and I went into a restaurant and phoned the police to report his distress. But after a while, like the others when confronted with such a sight, I would keep going too, though always a little guiltily, wishing a cop would come by soon. Why should people in such a city be *expected* to stop and do something

---

[31]To nail someone — to tackle or hit someone, as in American football.

[32]Linebacker; tackle; end — positions of players on an American football team.

[33]Cop — slang term for a policeman.

about their fallen wounded, not knowing them or caring? The existence involved in moving daily to and from work in the immense and faceless crowds inevitably hardens one's senses to violence and despair. I came to feel it perfectly natural, this isolated callousness of the city dweller. Anyone who expected valor or compassion in everyday acts in a monstrous American city in these times expected too much of human nature, and would sooner or later be disappointed. The cops became the guardians of benevolence; they were our salaried Samaritans.[34]

III

Along the sidewalks in our neighborhood roamed two old walkers who made their mark on the area. One was a bent-over old man who wore a pince-nez;[35] he carried an American flag, a Bible, and a megaphone. At almost any hour of the day you could hear him, standing on some street corner nearby, delivering a feverish sermon on sin, redemption, and patriotism, or moving along the sidewalk with his dragging gait shouting vengeance on every moving object in the vicinity, animal or vegetable. He was just as content trying to convert a Chevrolet pickup truck as he was in shouting his evangelical threats to the little Italian boys who congregated at the fruit stand on Lexington. There was a horror to this old man, to the echo of his grating voice coming down the narrow streets between the big buildings. Thin trickles of saliva would form on his mouth and drip to the pavement; his moist, insane proselytizing seemed as inexorable and illogical as the city itself, as its insane flow of vehicles and people. On Christmas morning, as my son played with his toys in the front room of our apartment, I heard him from down the block, and through a drab December mist I saw him shuffling along on Twenty-sixth Street, solitary and mad; suddenly I felt sorry for him, alone on this Christmas Day. I picked up a couple of cans of fancy sardines and rushed down the stairs, catching up with him on the sidewalk. "Merry Christmas," I said, the first words I had ever spoken to his face. He took the gift and said, "What is your religion, young man?" "I'm an old Mississippi Methodist," I replied. "Ah . . . Methodist," he said. "Then you don't believe in Jesus. Pity on you, young man." And he walked away, gingerly putting the sardines in his coat pocket.

The other neighborhood apparition was a woman of about sixty, a gaunt old specter who worked regularly as clockwork. She was a junkie,[36] and every afternoon from three to five she roamed the streets shouting some demented gibberish, a considerable tumult for such a scrawny old woman. Once I saw the evangelist and the drug addict meet by chance in front of a shabby building on Lexington with a plaque on it explaining that Chester A. Arthur had been sworn in here as President of the U.S.A. after Garfield was assassinated; they shouted

---

[34]Samaritans — helpers. From the Bible story of the Good Samaritan who helped a traveler.

[35]Pince-nez — eyeglasses that are clipped to the bridge of the nose.

[36]Junkie — slang term for a drug addict.

at one another as if mortal enemies, and the old man walked away, whispering through his megaphone, "*Doomed, Doomed!*" The woman's shouts were even more disrupting than the man's, however, because they were self-inflicted, and because she worked on a schedule, coming out of God knows what place every day to exercise her private perspectives. Both were always alone and always ignored. Except when taunted by the neighborhood kids they seemed quite self-sufficient.

In our apartment my son walked and crawled around the front room, exploring the edges of his new existence. There was nowhere to take him to run. Running him down the sidewalks of Madison or Park or Lexington in early evening was like taking a nighttime trot in the Carlsbad Caverns.[37] Once the traffic had thinned out at night, traffic lights for the taxis were as physically efficacious as a resolution of the U.N.[38] General Assembly; I had never seen red lights ignored with such disdain. Madison Square Park, the closest piece of earth in the vicinity, was a good place to watch the drunks and the old men sleeping under shrubs, but no likely retreat for a three-year-old child. Finally I took to playing with him in the parking lot next door, throwing a tennis ball against our apartment house and letting him retrieve it, until the man who owned the lot came by one bright fall evening and said, "Cancha see that *sign*; it says *private property*. If ya can't read, mistuh, go back to trainin' school."

We missed the easy, open life of Texas, the impromptu beer parties, the casual way people had of dropping by on friends, the old German beer hall, and the tables under the trees in back. The only person we knew in the neighborhood was Nick, who sold newspapers at a little stand on Madison. I could leave my son with him for half an hour or so while I went off on an errand, and come back and find the child behind the counter, helping to sell the *Journal-American* and the *World-Telegram*. Returning to the newsstand one night, I sidled up to the papers and saw my son selling a *Post* to a cabdriver, who gave him a nickel tip; Mississippi seemed far, far away.

We decided our third month there to give a cocktail party for some of the people I had dealt with on *Harper's Magazine*: a few editors, a writer or two, some reporters. The day of the party I noticed that the garbage had not been collected from the hall outside our door. There was three or four days of it, tomato peels and eggshells trickled out on the floor, and coffee grinds poured out of a hole in a sack. I phoned the landlord.

"We're having an important social occasion in Apartment Three tonight," I said, "and there's garbage in the hall."

"What's that? What?"

"There's garbage in the hall outside Apartment Three. Please send the janitor to get it right away. We're entertaining tonight."

"The janitor's off. He'll be back tomorrow. Wait till tomorrow."

---

[37] Carlsbad Caverns — huge caves in southern New Mexico.

[38] U.N. — United Nations.

"We can't do that. Important people are coming. Some of the most important people who ever came to this apartment. And the stuff stinks. It's fetid."

"It's what?" the voice said.

"It's *fetid.*"

"I tell ya we can't get it till tomorrow. The janitor's *off.*"

"Look," I said, "we've got some unusual people coming."

"Fellah, I'll try to get one of the boys up there, but I can't promise, see? We're busy, *understand*? Okay?"

"Okay," I said. "Then just send somebody up before six." By six o'clock, however, no one had come. I went to the dime store[39] on Lexington Avenue and got two big cardboard boxes, filled them up with the garbage, and when no one was looking put them under a Chrysler in the parking lot.

IV

The narrow old building which housed our walk-up apartment[40] was attached not only to the short-order take-out shop, but to a corner delicatessen and to a huge cafeteria which stayed open until 4:00 A.M. every day of the year. All these, including our building, were owned by a man and his two sons, whose offices were in the building. They were Lower East Side[41] people, but now they owned most of the entire block.

The cafeteria had large plate-glass windows, and displayed there under the cellophane were the specialties of the day: a shank of ham, perhaps, or some greasy fried chicken, or an apple pie. Inside, the place was brilliantly lit, a sharp glaring light that gave to the tables and the floor and the great rows of food behind the counter a sterile, antiseptic look, much like the cafeterias one sees in hospitals. It was always crowded, even in the early hours of the morning, with cabbies, truck drivers, newspaper vendors, drunks who wandered in for coffee— the night people. It was a harsh, driven place, lacking in even the smallest courtesies: a ragged, hard place, filled with muted violence and petty cruelties. Behind the counters the men in their starched white uniforms shouted to the line of people waiting to be served: "Move it, move it! Whatta ya *want*? Ya think we got all night? Come on, come on, make up your damned mind, *will ya*?" Every so often someone would be tossed out on the sidewalk, for not having enough money to pay, or for being a little too drunk. Two of the men behind the counter would rush out to the floor and take some pathetic old reprobate by the elbows, dragging him through the front door and giving him a little push, shouting, "Outta here, ya bum!" Once my wife and I were getting lunch at the counter; as she hesitated between the meat loaf and the lamb the man serving up the meats shouted, "Come on, sister, get a move on. Whatta ya want, hah? *Hah*?"

---

[39]Dime store — also called Five-and-Ten-Cent store, where things can be bought cheaply.

[40]Walk-up apartment — an apartment in a building that has no elevator.

Standing across the counter from this angular, glint-eyed son of the city I shouted back at him, "Don't you know how to treat a *lady,* friend? This is a Southern belle from Texas. Or did you grow up without any *manners.* You got any *decency?* Hah?" I felt the Mississippi boil rising; the people around us were staring hard, eager for an incident; customers never shouted back like that in this place. The man behind the counter looked at me; he was taken by surprise. Then he laughed, apparently a form of apology: "Mister, I ain't *seen* no lady. What makes ya think I know a *lady?*" And he dished out the meat loaf, shaking his head in mock bewilderment.

The owner, who was our landlord, was a big pot-bellied man with a great shock of gray hair; he spoke in a croaking bullfrog's voice. He wandered in and out of the cafeteria and the hardware store next door, dressed in his starched white intern's suit, even wearing white shoes and socks. His two sons, both in their thirties, wore the same uniforms, policing the place from time to time to supervise the treatment of the bums and derelicts. They shouted orders to the employees from across the big room, or stood off in a corner, their arms crossed, looking out expressionlessly at the customers gobbling down their food at the long aluminum tables.

Several times a month I came into the cafeteria, to bring a check for the monthly rent or to complain about the service in the building on Twenty-sixth Street. The old man had a small office with a big padded door in the hardware store adjoining the cafeteria. There was a buzzer next to the door, and when I pushed it I would hear the voice from inside, "Who the hell is it?" I would identify myself, and he would push a buzzer inside automatically opening the door. "Here's the check for Apartment Three," I would say, handing it to him. He would take it, hardly looking up, saying, "Yah, okay, okay," in a kind of grumble, never once exchanging pleasantries, not hellos or goodbyes, and then go back to his paper work. My complaints, however, began to mount. His workers continued to go for three or four days without taking away the garbage in the hallways. The heating system in our apartment was controlled from the furnace in the cafeteria, and when the cold season began there was sometimes no heat at all. The other tenants in the building, a German girl who dated an editor of *The National Enquirer* and a Japanese artist who barely spoke English, were too frightened to complain; having lived there for some time, they were intimidated by the landlord and his sons. I took to phoning the landlord more persistently, or going to see him. Often it would take three or four calls before they would turn on the heat. The landlord and his two offspring treated every complaint with a hurried, exasperated crudity. I had known Mississippi rednecks,[42] mother-killers, grandmother-killers, sixth-year graduate students, and spitballers[43] who threw at your head; I had never run up against people so lacking in the human graces.

---

[41] Lower East Side — a section of New York City where many poorer people live.

[42] Rednecks — white rural laborers in the Southern United States. A disparaging term.

[43] Spitballers — schoolchildren who throw small rolled-up balls of paper wetted with their saliva (spitballs).

One Sunday in the winter the thermometer in our apartment registered 42. I began calling down to the cafeteria at ten in the morning. Four calls proved fruitless. Finally I burst down to the cafeteria and asked for the landlord or his boys. They were all away. I found the assistant manager and buttonholed him in a corner. "I want that furnace turned on!" I shouted. He shouted back, "We can't get to da furnace!" I returned to my apartment and phoned the landlord at his home on the Upper East Side. "I'm tired of your bitchin', ya *punk,"* he said, and hung up. The next day I advertised in the *Times* for someone to take over the lease. We had a taker within three hours of the first day, and I went off and found a place on the Upper West Side.

The next-to-the-last day in our apartment, the telephone was still ringing from the ad in the *Times*: $125 a month rent got takers in New York City. I had turned down the offer of three bribes. I had rejected callers who pleaded for preferential treatment. Shortly before the telephone was disconnected, there was another call.

"I've seen your ad about the apartment," a man's voice said. "I understand it's only $125."

"That's right," I said.

"Has it been taken?"

"Well, yes and no. It has been, but I'm open to discussion."

There was a pause at the other end. "I see," the man finally said, for New Yorkers understood these things. "Can you tell me about the apartment?"

"It has four large rooms, a modern kitchen, air-conditioning, and a nice system for heat. Very comfortable in all seasons."

"What floor is it on?"

"Well, you see, it's in the subway."

"In the *subway!"*

"That's right. It's about ten yards or so from the track, right in the station."

I could hear the man mumbling to someone else, his wife, perhaps. "It's in a *subway* station," he was whispering. "Yeah, right in it." Then he addressed me again. "That sounds pretty inconvenient to me. I never heard of an apartment right in the *subway.*"

"It's not inconvenient at all. It's very convenient to the subway. And the noise isn't the least bit bad, except during the rush hours."

"Is it built into the concrete, or what?"

"Well actually, the kitchen goes out over the tracks a few feet."

"Over the *tracks*! I never heard of such a thing."

"It's part of the agreement, you see. You don't expect a nice apartment for $125 for nothing, do you? During rush hours my wife or I have to open the kitchen door to let the express through."

"What?"

"Yes, but not on weekends. It's actually quite colorful, being a part of the transit system. It's only three minutes from Grand Central. It's not nearly so bad as it sounds."

The caller paused. "Well, it's certainly unusual. When can I come to look at it?"

"Let me call you," I said.

"Fine, I'll be here all tomorrow." He gave me his number. "How do I get there?"

"Take the Lexington Avenue express," I said, "and get off when you see a red kitchen overhanging the tracks," and hung up. The next day I moved my family to the Upper West Side.

V

The Big Cave in the 1960s lived frenetically in the present, bereft of the tangible reminders of its own history. The ubiquitous pavement drills—"New York music"—relentlessly destroyed even many of the settled places. A crowded and noisy city almost totally lacking in landscape, full of fumes and smog, without open spaces and growing things, encouraged a certain desolation of the senses; after a time a man who was not born to this environment accepted the rattled edges of daily existence in the same way he might grow to live with pain, hunger, or unhappiness. One wondered most of all about the children, growing up with no local *belonging,* no feel for place or of generations gone. The massive office buildings where people worked, the elbowing for position in the elevators taking them up to their work, the windows opening out onto other office buildings equally massive and impersonal—all this was part of a way of living unknown to me, uprooted from the earth and its sources. On some gray and rainy day in the winter solstice, when the sun began to set in late morning, with the wind rattling at the panes of the window, one's office seemed less a place to work than a cell, without the relief of something more *open* a few minutes away from it. Leaving work each late afternoon, having spent a day reading sober or responsible, or wild and imaginative, prose by writers who seemed to matter to America, one went down into the claustrophobic crowds, and jostled against people who had never heard of your writers, and cared less. Occasionally, on the night of a heavy snow, before the filth of a workday turned the snow into a sooty mush, the city was slow and quiet under the winter stars, out of character in its strange loveliness. The night all the lights went out in 1965,[44] after the first panic, one could actually see the moon; the whole city was enveloped in an elemental blackness, and nine months later the births were more numerous.

I would take the subway to work every morning—the Seventh Avenue IRT from the Upper West Side. I bought the *New York Times* at the newsstand on Broadway and 94th, and headed downstairs to get the express to Penn Station. As soon as I got to the platform in the stale, airless place I folded the *Times* to the news-index section, then I started my preliminary jousts[45] for

---

[44]"The night all the lights went out in 1965" — November 9, 1965, when there was an electric power failure in the northeastern United States. The lights went out for several hours.

[45]Jousts — battles, as in a medieval tournament.

position near the track in order to be closer to the door of the train when it arrived. In three years of waiting on this platform I had yet to hear one "Good Morning" exchanged among any of my fellow passengers, for human communication was normally restricted to atavistic grumbles and more direct early-morning obscenities. Far down the track, in an eerie dark, the light of the express glared and winked, and then in a terrible roar and screech of brakes it was upon us. The crowds at the platform waited for the people to emerge from the car; then there would be one solid mass of flesh pushing forward through the doors, somewhat like the scrum-heap in English Rugby football, though larger, more motley, and less sporting. There was a loudspeaker in the station, and the voice would say: "Step lively, folks, step lively." And after a pause, "Get that arm out of the door, buddy!" or "Pull in that leg, sister!" Once this mass was crammed into the subway car, two or three hardy souls, holding back the doors when they were closing, would literally squeeze themselves in, which served to push the mass even closer upon itself.

At this moment, if I had three or four inches of elbow room and a reasonably secure position, I would bring out the paper and read the news-index section three or four times during the fifteen-minute trip south. If this elbow room was not available, however, I read the advertisements on the wall of the train, about quick cash loans, employment agencies, Miss Subway contests, and Preparation H for shrinking hemorrhoids without surgery. Then I would stare sullenly at the other passengers, who sullenly stared back, seeking diversion as much as I. Once I spent the full fifteen minutes examining a peculiar wart under the nose of a neighbor three or four inches away—a strange yellow wart that might have benefited considerably from Preparation H. At other times I would close my eyes and think about such items as green fields in the springtime, or the vast desolate terrain of West Texas, or Five Mile Lake in Yazoo County during a summer thunderstorm. There was a certain identifiable expression on the faces of New Yorkers in these moments. It was "subway glaze"; their eyes might be open but they were not looking; they were *obliterating,* which required great practice and an extraordinary will. The train rocked and moaned, sometimes knocking a few passengers against one another in a sudden multiracial jumble. The juxtaposition of human matter was so intimate, one feared that a sneeze, or an obnoxious cough, might set off an urban epidemic like the Black Plague.[46] I wish John Donne[47] could have taken the Seventh Avenue IRT during the morning rush hour, before sitting down to write about islands, clods, promontories, and bells.

I discovered most of all in these trips to work each morning that they brought out in one his old, latent, controlled hostility toward people of other races—an inevitable battle, if one speaks honestly, that requires the total application of a man's civilized acquisitions.

---

[46]Black Plague — bubonic plague; epidemics which killed millions in Europe in the Middle Ages.

[47]John Donne — English churchman and poet (1573–1631) who wrote that "No man is an island unto himself."

One morning on the IRT the passengers at 94th Street were crammed into the subway car even more closely than usual. I was unable to get a grip on the holding-pole or on one of the dangling handles; I stood there at the mercy of motion. Halfway between 94th and 72nd the train suddenly lurched, and I felt myself flying helplessly into the other passengers. Instinctively I grabbed for something, and it turned out to be the arm of a Negro next to me; he was about my age. When the train steadied again, reverting to my old Mississippi accent as I always do under stress, I told him I was sorry. He gave me a cold stare, and then he sneered.

"I'm sorry," I said. "I didn't have anything to hold on to. This is a hell of a way to live."

"It beats them hills, don't it?" the man said, in a strong Southern Negro accent.

"What hills?" I asked.

"Them hills you come from with that cracker accent."

"If I wasn't a liberal I'd hit you for that," I said.

At this point the other human matter standing face-to-face with us started looking away and grinning.

"Hell, ain't *nobody* liberal," the man said. "Who's liberal?"

"Well, I'm not from the hills, I'm from Mississippi."

"The *mud* then. Don't this beat the mud?"

"The mud's dried."

"Wait till spring," he said. "Then it'll be mud again."

We stared wordlessly at each other, two sons of the South on the IRT. Finally, at the next stop, ashamed and a little guilty, I clawed my way out, into the dusty glare of the subway platform.

☆ FOLLOW-UP QUESTIONS

I.   Willie Morris opens this autobiographical piece by explaining the attraction of New York to people from the provinces. As "A Provincial in New York" develops, he also describes his initial feelings about the city that has become his new home.

A.   What point does Morris emphasize by beginning his article with a reference to "young people like myself" and by using the personal pronoun *we* in asking, "Why did we come?"

B.   What reasons does he give for "the most ambitious of us coming to New York, the cultural capital"?

C.   What feeling does he convey by describing himself as a Mississippian "exiled" in New York City?

D.   Why does the confrontation between the provincial and New York result in a "subtle interior struggle with himself over the most fundamental sense and meaning of his origins?"

E. While sitting in Washington Square Park, Morris suddenly begins seeing familiar Southern faces, who turn out to be total strangers. What does this reveal about his state of mind concerning the home he has left?

II. This excerpt from Morris's memoirs is entitled "A Provincial in New York: Living in the Big Cave," which immediately conveys to the reader a strong sense of what this section is going to be about. The reference to New York as a "Big Cave" introduces the tone and attitude Morris will take toward the city.

A. Describe the layout of the apartment Morris rents and how it differed from his original "dream" of what his New York City apartment would be like.

B. Why does he react so strongly to the city's "claustrophobic quality"?

C. What does he mean when he claims that "humanity here was always at war with its machines and with itself"?

D. Describe the danger, violence, even death, he observes walking to and from work.

E. In describing the reaction of a pedestrian caught in the middle of the street by incoming traffic, he draws a comparison, using football terminology. What does the pedestrian have in common with the football player?

F. What does Morris convey by reproducing the sub-English spoken by the policeman ("ya crazy, hah, ya stupid?")?

G. How does Morris react at first to the callousness shown by New Yorkers toward the "fallen wounded"? How does he think of it after he has lived in the city for several months?

H. When his friend looks out the window during the blizzard and says, "they got us all up here together . . . and then they *snowed* on us," what feeling for the city is he expressing? Who or what is referred to as *they*?

I. On the night of his cocktail party, how does he manage to dispose of his garbage? Although his method seems comical, what does it show about how Morris is perhaps blending in with the ways of the city? How does this action resemble his acceptance of the callousness New Yorkers often show toward fallen victims?

III. Morris is fascinated by the "two old walkers," eccentrics who inhabit his neighborhood.

A. Why do they seem strange?

B. What is the old man's reaction to the gift of sardines?

C. Describe the encounter between the drug addict and the evangelist.

D. These two people, lost in their own fantasies, don't affect Morris's life in New York very strongly. Why, then, has he chosen to include them in his memoir?

IV. The American South is noted for its courtesy, particularly toward women.

A. How does Morris react when the serving man in the cafeteria is rude to his wife?

B. Is there any recognition on the man's part that he has insulted a lady?

C. Why does the writer again reproduce the sub-English speech patterns of the man? ("Mister, I ain't *seen* no lady. What makes ya think I know a *lady*?")

D. In describing his landlord and his two sons, Morris compares them with mother-killers, grandmother-killers, and sixth-year graduate students, examples of types of people "lacking in the human graces." What is ironic about placing sixth-year graduate students in the same category as mother-killers?

E.   Why does he finally have to find another apartment?

F.   What does his conversation with the man who still considers subleasing the apartment after being told it is located in the subway reveal about housing conditions in New York? What does it reveal about New Yorkers?

V.   In the last section, Morris describes an encounter in the subway. Again he uses an analogy with a tough sport, this time English rugby football. He states about his daily trips on the subway: "They brought out in one his old latent, controlled hostility toward people of other races—an inevitable battle, if one speaks honestly, that requires total application of a man's civilized acquisitions."

A.   Why does he feel guilty after his encounter with the Southern Negro?

B.   Why does he tell the Negro, "If I wasn't a liberal, I'd hit you for that."? What conflict does this reveal in Morris?

C.   What effect does this incident have on Morris's conception of himself as a "liberated Mississippian"?

VI.   This excerpt from Morris's memoir is written in a very personal, emotional style.

A.   The first three paragraphs provide a generalized introduction to the subject of young people from the provinces seeking their fortune in New York.

1. Why has Morris included it before describing his personal experiences?

2. Does this introduction strengthen the effect of Morris's own impressions of New York?

3. How do we know immediately in the fourth paragraph that he has made the transition from the general to the particular?

B.   Throughout the excerpt, the writer blends his descriptions and impressions of his experiences with analyses of those experiences. For example, after explaining the phenomenon of his "peculiar eyesight" (mistaking strangers for people he had known in the South), he writes, "it made me fear the extent to which my rambling imagination of past places that had intimately shaped me could, in this unknown and uncaring city, produce forms so tangible as to make the very present itself incongruous and ghostlike." Give some other examples of a description of a sequence of events followed by some kind of analytical remark.

C.   Although Morris has probably been very honest about his impressions of New York, should one accept them as the definitive description of life in the city?

☆ THEME TOPICS

1.   Discuss the advantages of living in the provinces (a village or small town). What fulfillment could be attained by remaining in the place of one's birth?

2.   Describe an eccentric person whose manner or way of life seems strange to you or to the society in which he or she lives. (He need not be as strange as the evangelist or the junkie Morris describes.)

3.   Morris calls New York the "Big Cave." Give a similar epithet to a place you have known and tell why that epithet is appropriate.

Figure over the Town
William Goyen

INTRODUCTION

I.   In this story, the narrator remembers an important event from his childhood. He tells us that the memory of that event has remained a dominant force in his life.

    A. What was your most important childhood experience? What does this experience reveal about you as a child? As an adult?

    B. How would your description of the event probably differ from the way you would have described it a day after it had taken place? Which description would be more accurate?

    C. What might the description lose if it were written years after the event? What might it gain?

II.   In "Figure over the Town," the narrator's dreams are described in detail.

    A. When is it more likely you will remember a dream in detail? Upon waking, or a few hours later?

    B. Are nightmares easier to recall than pleasant dreams?

    C. Have you ever had the same dream again and again over a period of weeks, months, or years?

    D. Have any of your dreams influenced your life in some way?

    E. Why do many psychiatrists place a great deal of emphasis upon the significance of dreams?

    F. If a dream reflects a situation disturbing to the dreamer when he is awake, how can remembering it in detail help him?

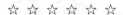

In the town of my beginning[1] I saw this masked figure sitting aloft. It was never explained to me by my elders, who were thrilled and disturbed by the figure too, who it was, except that he was called Flagpole Moody. The days and nights he sat aloft were counted on calendars in the kitchens of small houses and in troubled minds, for Flagpole Moody fed the fancy of an isolated small town of practical folk whose day's work was hard and real.

    Since the night he was pointed out to me from the roof of the little shed where my father sheltered grain and plowing and planting implements, his shape has never left me; in many critical experiences of my life it has suddenly

---

---

[1]"Town of my beginning" — where the author was born and grew up.

appeared before me, so that I have come to see that it is a dominating emblem of my life, as often a lost lover is, or the figure of a parent, or the symbol of a faith, as the scallop shell was for so many at one time, or the Cross.[2]

It was in the time of a war I could not understand, being so very young, that my father came to me at darkening, in the beginning wintertime, and said, "Come with me to the Patch, Son, for I want to show you something."

The Patch, which I often dream about, was a mysterious fenced-in plot of ground, about half an acre, where I never intruded. I often stood at the gate or fence and looked in through the hexagonal lenses of the chicken wire and saw how strange this little territory was, and wondered what it was for. There was the shed in it where implements and grain were stored, but nothing was ever planted nor any animal pastured here; nothing, not even grass or weed, grew here; it was just plain common ground.

This late afternoon my father took me into the Patch and led me to the shed and hoisted me up to the roof. He waited a moment while I looked around at all the world we lived in and had forgotten was so wide and housed so many in dwellings quite like ours. (Later, when my grandfather, my father's father, took me across the road and railroad tracks into a large pasture—so great I had thought it, from the window of our house, the whole world—where a little circus had been set up as if by magic the night before, and raised me to the broad back of a sleepy elephant, I saw the same sight and recalled not only the night I stood on the roof of the shed, but also what I had seen from there, that haunting[3] image, and thought I saw it again, this time on the lightning rod[4] of our house . . . but no, it was, as always, the crowing cock that stood there, eternally strutting out his breast and at the break of crowing.)

My father waited, and when he saw that I had steadied myself, he said, "Well, Son, what is it that you see over there, by the Methodist church?"

I was speechless and could only gaze; and then I finally said to him, not moving, "Something is sitting on the flagpole on top of a building."

"It is just a man," my father said, "and his name is Flagpole Moody. He is going to sit up there for as long as he can stand it."

When we came into the house, I heard my father say to my mother, lightly, "I showed Son Flagpole Moody and I think it scared him a little." And I heard my mother say, "It seems a foolish stunt,[5] and I think maybe children shouldn't see it."

All that night Flagpole Moody was on my mind. When it began raining, in the very deepest night, I worried about him in the rain, and I went to my window and looked out to see if I could see him. When it lightninged, I saw that he was

---

[2] The Cross — cross on which Jesus Christ was put to death.

[3] Haunting — staying in the memory.

[4] Lightning rod — metal rod set up on a building and connected with the ground in order to reduce danger of destruction by lightning.

[5] Stunt — trick performed in order to attract attention.

safe and dry under a little tent he had raised over himself. Later I had a terrible dream about him, that he was falling, falling, and when I called out in my nightmare, my parents came to me and patted me back to sleep, never knowing that I would dream of him again.

He stayed and stayed up there, the flagpole sitter, hooded (why would he not show his face?), and when we were in town and walked under him, I would not look up as they told me to; but once, when we stood across the street from the building where he was perched, I looked up and saw how high he was in the air, and he waved down at me with his cap in his hand.

Everywhere there was the talk of the war, but where it was or what it was I did not know. It seemed only some huge appetite that craved all our sugar and begged from the town its goods, so that people seemed paled and impoverished by it, and it made life gloomy—that was the word. One night we went into the town to watch them burn Old Man Gloom, a monstrous straw man with a sour, turned-down look on his face and dressed even to the point of having a hat—it was the Ku Klux Klan[6] lit him afire—and above, in the light of the flames, we saw Flagpole Moody waving his cap to us. He had been up eighteen days.

He kept staying up there. More and more the talk was about him, with the feeling of the war beneath all the talk. People began to get restless about Flagpole Moody and to want him to come on down. "It seems morbid," I remember my mother saying. What at first had been a thrill and an excitement— the whole town was there every other day when the provisions basket was raised up to him, and the contributions were extravagant: fresh pies and cakes, milk, little presents, and so forth—became an everyday sight; there he seemed ignored and forgotten by the town except for me, who kept a constant, secret watch on him; then, finally, the town became disturbed by him, for he seemed to be going on and on; he seemed an intruder now. Who could feel unlooked at or unhovered over in his house with this figure over everything? (It was discovered that Flagpole was spying on the town through binoculars.) There was an agitation to bring him down and the city council met to this end.

There had been some irregularity in the town which had been laid to the general lawlessness and demoralizing effect of the war: robberies; the disappearance of a beautiful young girl, Sarah Nichols (but it was said she ran away to find someone in the war); and one Negro shot in the woods, which could have been the work of the Ku Klux Klan. The question at the city-council[7] meeting was, "Who gave Flagpole Moody permission to go up there?" No one seemed to know; the merchants said it was not for advertising, or at least no one of them had arranged it, though after he was up, many of them tried to use him to advertise their products—Egg Lay or Red Goose shoes or Have a Coke at Robbins Pharmacy—and why not? The Chamber of Commerce had not brought him, nor

[6]Ku Klux Klan — a secret society organized in the American South after the Civil War of 1861–1865. Aim of the organization was to promote supremacy of the white race.

[7]City council — the elected legislative or governing body of a city.

the Women's Club; maybe the Ku Klux had, to warn and tame the Negroes, who were especially in awe of Flagpole Moody; but the Klan was as innocent as all the others, it said. The pastor was reminded of the time a bird had built a nest on the church steeple, a huge foreign bird that had delighted all the congregation as well as given him subject matter for several sermons; he told how the congregation came out on the grounds to adore the bird, which in time became suddenly savage and swooped to pluck the feathers from women's Sunday hats and was finally brought down by the fire department, which found the nest full of rats and mice, half devoured, and no eggs at all—this last fact the subject of another series of sermons by the pastor, drawing as he did his topics from real life.

As the flagpole sitter had come to be regarded as a defacement of the landscape, an unsightly object, a tramp, it was suggested that the Ku Klux Klan build a fire in the square and ride round it on their horses and in their sheets, firing their guns into the air, as they did in their public demonstration against immorality, to force Flagpole down. If this failed, it was suggested someone should be sent up on the firemen's ladder to reason with Flagpole. He was regarded now as a *danger* to the town, and more, as a kind of criminal. (At first he had been admired and respected for his courage, and desired, even: many women had been intoxicated by him, sending up, in the provisions basket, love notes and photographs of themselves, which Flagpole had read and then sailed down for anyone to pick up and read, to the embarrassment of this woman and that. There had been a number of local exposures.[8])

The town was ready for any kind of miracle or sensation, obviously. A fanatical religious group took Flagpole Moody for[9] the Second Coming.[10] The old man called Old Man Nay, who lived on the edge of the town in a boarded-up house and sat at the one open window with his shotgun in his lap, watching for the Devil, unnailed his door and appeared in the square to announce that he had seen a light playing around Flagpole at night and that Flagpole was some phantom representative of the Devil and should be banished by a raising of the Cross; but others explained that what Old Man Nay saw was St. Elmo's fire,[11] a natural phenomenon. Whatever was given a fantastical meaning by some was explained away by others as of natural cause. What was right? Who was to believe what?

An evangelist[12] who called himself "The Christian Jew" had, at the beginning, requested of Flagpole Moody, by a letter in the basket, the dropping of

---

[8]Exposures — public revelation of immorality or corruption.

[9]To take . . . for — in this case: to interpret his presence as . . .

[10]The Second Coming — in Christian belief, the return of Jesus Christ as judge on the last day; the millennium.

[11]St. Elmo's fire — flames sometimes seen in stormy weather at sharp points on ships, planes, or land. Believed to be from the discharge of electricity. Name derives from Elmo, patron saint of sailors.

[12]Evangelist — a preacher or missionary.

leaflets. A sample was pinned to the letter. The leaflet, printed in red ink, said in huge letters across the top: WARNING! YOU ARE IN GREAT DANGER! Below was a long message to sinners. If Flagpole would drop these messages upon the town, he would be aiding in the salvation of the wicked. "The Judgments of God are soon to be poured upon the Earth! Prepare to meet God before it is too late! Where will you spend Eternity? What can you do to be saved? How shall we escape if we neglect so great salvation! (Heb. 2:3)."

But there was no reply from Flagpole, which was evidence enough for the Christian Jew to know that Flagpole was on the Devil's side. He held meetings at night in the square, with his little group of followers passing out the leaflets.

"Lower Cain!"[13] he bellowed. "You sinners standing on the street corner running a long tongue about your neighbors;[14] you show-going, card-playing, jazz-dancing brothers—God love your soul—you are a tribe of sinners and you know it and God knows it, but He loves you and wants you to come into His tabernacle and give up your hearts that are laden with wickedness. If you look in the Bible, if you will turn to the chapter of Isaiah, you will find there about the fallen angel, Lucifer was his name, and how his clothing was sewn of emeralds and sapphires, for he was very beautiful; but friends, my sin-loving friends, that didn't make any difference. 'How art thou fallen from Heaven, O Lucifer, son of the morning!' the Bible reads. And it says there that the Devil will walk amongst us and that the Devil will sit on the rooftops; and I tell you we must unite together to drive Satan from the top of the world. Listen to me and read my message, for I was the rottenest man in this world until I heard the voice of God. I drank, I ran with women, I sought after the thrills of the flesh . . . and I admonish you that the past scenes of earth *shall be remembered in Hell.*"

The old maid,[15] Miss Hazel Bright, who had had one lover long ago, a cowboy named Rolfe Sanderson who had gone away and never returned, told that Flagpole was Rolfe come back, and she wrote notes of poetic longing to put in the provisions basket. Everybody used Flagpole Moody for his own purpose, and so he, sitting away from it all, apparently serene in his own dream and idea of himself, became the lost lover to the lovelorn, the saint to the seekers of salvation, the scapegoat of the guilty, the damned to those who were lost.

The town went on tormenting him; they could not let him alone. They wished him to be their own dream or hope or lost illusion, or they wished him to be what destroyed hope and illusion. They wanted something they could get their hands on; they wanted someone to ease the dark misgiving[16] in themselves, to take to their deepest bosom, into the farthest cave of themselves where they would take no other if he would come and be for them alone. They plagued him with love letters, and when he would not acknowledge these professions of love,

[13]Cain — murderer of his brother, Abel, in the Old Testament of the Bible.

[14]"Running a long tongue about your neighbors" — gossiping about them maliciously.

[15]Old maid — older, unmarried woman; spinster.

[16]Misgiving — doubt.

they wrote him messages of hate. They told him their secrets, and when he would not show himself to be overwhelmed, they accused him of keeping secrets of his own. They professed to be willing to follow him, leaving everything behind, but when he would not answer "Come," they told him how they wished he would fall and knock his brains out. They could not make up their minds and they tried to destroy him because he had made up his, whatever it was he had made his mind up to.

Merchants tormented him with proposals and offers—would he wear a Stetson hat all one day, tip and wave it to the people below? Would he hold, just for fifteen minutes every hour, a streamer[17] with words on it proclaiming the goodness of their bread, or allow balloons, spelling out the name of something that ought to be bought, to be floated from the flagpole? Would he throw down Life Savers?[18] Many a man, and most, would have done it, would have supplied an understandable reason for his behavior, pacifying the general observer, and in the general observer's own terms (or the general observer would not have it), and so send him away undisturbed, with the feeling that all the world was really just as he was, cheating a little here, disguising a little there. (Everybody was, after all, alike, so where the pain, and why?)

But Flagpole Moody gave no answer. Apparently he had nothing to sell, wanted to make no fortune, to play no jokes or tricks; apparently he wanted just to be let alone to do his job. But because he was so different, they would not let him alone until they could, by whatever means, make him quiet like themselves, or cause him, at least, to recognize them and pay *them* some attention. Was he camping up there for the fun of it? If so, why would he not let them all share in it? Maybe he was there for the pure devilment[19] of it, like a cat on a chimney top. Or for some very crazy and not-to-be-tolerated reason of his own (which everyone tried to make out, hating secrets as people do who want everything in the clear, where they can attack it and feel moral dudgeon[20] against it).

Was it Cray McCreery up there? Had somebody made him another bet? One time Cray had walked barefooted to the next town, eighteen miles, because of a lost bet. But no, Cray McCreery was found, as usual, in the Domino Parlor. Had any crazy people escaped from the asylum? They were counted and found to be all in. The mind reader, Madame Fritzie, was importuned: There seemed, she said, to be a dark woman in the picture; that was all she contributed: "I see a dark woman . . ." And as she had admonished so many in the town with her recurring vision of a dark woman, there was either an army of dark women tormenting the minds of men and women in the world, or only one, which was Madame Fritzie herself. She could have made a fortune out of the whole affair if

[17]Streamer — cloth banner, on which a message can be inked or sewed.

[18]Life Savers — name of a popular hard candy.

[19]Devilment — mischief.

[20]Dudgeon — resentment.

she had had her wits about her.[21] More than one Ouija board[22] was put questions to, but the answers were either indistinguishable or not to the point.

Dogs howled and bayed at night and sometimes in the afternoons; hens crowed; the sudden death of children was laid to the evil power of Flagpole Moody over the town.

A masked buffoon came to a party dressed as Flagpole Moody and caused increasing uneasiness among the guests until three of the men at the party, deciding to take subtle action rather than force the stranger to unmask, reported to the police by telephone. The police told them to unmask him by force and they were coming. When the police arrived they found the stranger was Marcus Peters, a past president of the Lions Club and a practical joker with the biggest belly laugh[23] in town, and everybody would have known all along who the impostor was if he had only laughed.

A new language evolved in the town: "You're crazy as Moody," "cold as a flagpole sitter's ———," "go sit on a flagpole" and other phrases of that sort.

In that day and time there flourished, even in that little town, a group of sensitive and intellectual people, poets and artists and whatnot, who thought themselves quite mad and gay — and quite lost, too, though they would turn their lostness to a good thing. These advanced people needed an object upon which to hinge their loose and floating cause, and they chose Flagpole Moody to draw attention, which they so craved, to themselves. They exalted him with some high, esoteric meaning that they alone understood, and they developed a whole style of poetry, music and painting, the echoes of which are still heard, around the symbol of Flagpole Moody. They wrote, and read aloud to meetings, critical explanations of the Theory of Aloftness.

Only Mrs. T. Trevor Sanderson was bored with it all, shambling restlessly about the hospital in her Japanese kimono, her spotted hands (liver trouble, the doctors said) spread like fat lizards on the knolls of her hips. She was there again for one of her rest cures, because her oil-money worries were wearing her to death, and now the Catholic Church was pursuing her with zeal to convert her — for her money, so she said. Still, there was something to the Catholic Church; you couldn't get around that, she said, turning her spotted hands to show them yellow underneath, like a lizard's belly; and she gave a golden windowpane illustrating *The Temptation of St. Anthony* to St. Mary's Church, but would do no more than that.

There were many little felonies and even big offenses of undetermined origin in the police records of the town, and Flagpole was a stimulus to the fresh inspection of unsolved crimes. He drew suspicions up to him and absorbed them like a filter, as though he might purify the town of wickedness. If only he would

---

[21] To have your wits about you — to be clever or resourceful at a particular moment.

[22] Ouija board — marked board that some people believe can be used to seek out and receive messages from the dead or from people far away.

[23] Belly laugh — deep, hearty laugh.

send down some response to what had gone up to him. But he would not budge; and now he no longer even waved to the people below as he had during the first good days. Flagpole Moody had utterly withdrawn from everybody. What the town finally decided was to put a searchlight on him at night, to keep watch on him.

With the searchlight on the flagpole sitter, the whole thing took a turn, became an excuse for a ribald attitude. When a little wartime carnival came to the town, it was invited to install itself in the square, and a bazaar was added to it by the town. The spirit of Flagpole had to be admired, it was admitted; for after a day and night of shunning the gaiety and the mockery of it all, he showed his good nature and good sportsmanship — even his daring — by participating! He began to do what looked like acrobatic stunts, as though he were an attraction of the carnival.

And what did the people do, after a while, but turn against him again and say he was, as they had said at first, a sensationalist? Still, I loved it that he had become active; that it was not a static, fastidious, precious and Olympian[24] show, that Flagpole did not take on a self-righteous or pompous or persecuted air, although my secret conception of him was still a tragic one. I was proud that my idea fought back — otherwise he was like Old Man Gloom, a shape of straw and sawdust in man's clothing, and let them burn him, if only gloom stood among the executioners, watching its own effigy and blowing on the flames. I know now that what I saw was the conflict of an idea with a society; and I am sure that the idea was bred by the society — raised up there, even, by the society — in short, society was the flagpole sitter and he was in the society of the town.

There was, at the little carnival, one concession called "Ring Flagpole's Bell." It invited customers to try to strike a bell at the top of a tall pole resembling his — and with a replica of him on top — by hitting a little platform with a rubber-headed sledgehammer; this would drive a metal disk up toward the bell. There was another concession where people could throw darts at a target resembling a figure on a pole. The Ferris wheel was put so close to Flagpole that when its passengers reached the top they could almost, for a magical instant, reach over and touch his body. Going round and round, it was as if one were soaring up to him only to fall away, down, from him; to have him and to lose him; and it was all felt in a marvelous whirling sensation in the stomach that made this experience the most vaunted of the show.

This must have tantalized Flagpole, and perhaps it seemed to him that all the beautiful and desirable people in the world rose and fell around him, offering themselves to him only to withdraw untaken and ungiven, a flashing wheel of faces, eyes, lips and sometimes tongues stuck out at[25] him and sometimes a thigh shown, offering sex, and then burning away. His sky at night was filled with voluptuous images, and often he must have imagined the faces of

---

[24]Olympian — superior; above the crowd. The gods of ancient Greece were believed to live on Mt. Olympus.

[25]To stick one's tongue out at someone — to show derision and contempt.

those he had once loved and possessed, turning round and round his head to torment him. But there were men on the wheel who made profane signs to him, and women who thumbed their noses.[26]

Soon Flagpole raised his tent again and hid himself from his tormentors. What specifically caused his withdrawal was the attempt of a drunken young man to shoot him. This young man, named Maury, rode a motorcycle around the town at all hours and loved the meaner streets and the women who gave him ease, especially the fat ones, his mania. One night he stood at the hotel window and watched the figure on the pole, who seemed to flash on and off, real and then unreal, with the light of the electric sign beneath the window. He took deep drags of his cigarette and blew the smoke out toward Flagpole; then he blew smoke rings as if to lasso Flagpole with them, or as if his figure were a pin he could hoop with the rings of smoke. "You silly bastard, do you like what you see?" he had muttered, and, "Where have I seen you before?" between his half-clenched teeth, and then he had fired the pistol. Flagpole turned away then, once and for all.

But he had not turned away from me. I, the silent observer, watching from my window or from any high place I could secretly climb to, witnessed all this conflict and the tumult of the town. One night in my dreaming of Flagpole Moody—it happened every night, this dream, and in the afternoons when I took my nap, and the dreaming had gone on so long that it seemed, finally, as if he and I were friends, that he came down secretly to a rendezvous with me in the little pasture, and it was only years later that I would know what all our conversations had been about—that night in my dream the people of the town came to me and said, "Son, we have chosen you to go up the flagpole to Flagpole Moody and tell him to come down."

In my dream they led me, with cheers and honors, to the top of the building and stood below while I shinnied[27] up the pole. A great black bird was circling over Flagpole's tent. As I went up the pole I noticed crowded avenues of ants coming and going along the pole. And when I went into the tent, I found Flagpole gone. The tent was as if a tornado had swept through the whole inside of it. There were piles of rotten food; shreds of letters torn and retorn, as small as flakes of snow; photographs pinned to the walls of the tent were marked and scrawled over so that they looked like photographs of fiends and monsters; corpses and drifts of feathers of dead birds that had flown at night into the tent and gone so wild with fright that they had beaten themselves to death against the sides. And over it all was the vicious traffic of insects that had found the remains, in the way insects sense what human beings have left, and come from miles away.

What would I tell them below, those who were now crying up to me, "What does he say, what does Flagpole Moody say?" And there were whistles and an increasingly thunderous chant of "Bring him down! Bring him down!

[26]To thumb one's nose at someone — like footnote 25, to show derision and contempt.

[27]To shinny — to climb, especially a rope, pole, or tree by gripping alternately with one's hands or arms and legs.

Bring him down!" What would I tell them? I was glad he had gone; but I would not tell them that—yet. In the tent I found one little thing that had not been touched or changed by Flagpole; a piece of paper with printed words, and across the top the huge red words: WARNING! YOU ARE IN GREAT DANGER!

Then, in my dream, I went to the flap of the tent and stuck out my head. There was a searchlight upon me through which fell a delicate curtain of light rain; and through the lighted curtain of rain that made the people seem far, far below, under shimmering and jeweled veils, I shouted down to the multitude, which was dead quiet now, "He is not here! Flagpole Moody is not here!"

There was no sound from the crowd, which had not, at first, heard what I said. They waited; then one voice bellowed up, "Tell him to come down!" And others joined this voice until, again, the crowd was roaring, "Tell him that we will not harm him; only tell him he has to come down!" Then I waved down at them to be quiet, in Flagpole Moody's gesture of salute, as he had waved down at people on the sidewalks and streets. Again they hushed to hear me. Again I said, this time in a voice that was not mine, but large and round and resounding, "Flagpole Moody is not here. His place is empty."

And then, in my magnificent dream, I closed the flap of the tent and settled down to make Flagpole Moody's place my own, to drive out the insects, to erase the marks on the photographs, and to piece together, with infinite and patient care, the fragments of the letters to see what they told. It would take me a very long time, this putting together again what had been torn into pieces, but I would have a very long time to give to it, and I was at the source of the mystery, removed and secure from the chaos of the world below that could not make up its mind and tried to keep me from making up my own.

My dream ended here, or was broken, by the hand of my mother shaking me to morning; and when I went to eat breakfast I heard them saying in the kitchen that Flagpole Moody had signaled early, at dawn, around six o'clock, that he wanted to come down; that he had come down in his own time, and that he had come down very, very tired, after forty days and nights, the length of the Flood. I did not tell my dream, for I had no power of telling then, but I knew that I had a story to one day shape around the marvel and mystery that ended in a dream and began in the world that was to be mine.

☆ FOLLOW-UP QUESTIONS

I.   A symbol stands for or suggests something else because of relationship, association, or possible resemblance to it. In "Figure over the Town," Goyen uses symbolism in telling the story of how a strange event affected the citizens of a small southern town in the United States. The story is told by a narrator whose life has been greatly influenced by the event. He states, "I have come to see that it is a dominating emblem of my life, as often a lost lover is, or the figure of a parent, or the symbol of a faith as the scallop shell was for so many at one time, or the Cross."

    A.   What is the essential symbol of the story?

    B.   Who shows Flagpole Moody to the boy?

    C.   How does the boy's mother feel about Flagpole Moody's stunt?

    D.   How does the boy react when it begins raining?

    E.   What happens in his first dream about Flagpole Moody?

II.   As the figure continues to sit on the pole, the town's feelings toward him shift.

    A.   How does the town feel about him at first?

    B.   What does the first feeling change to, and why?

    C.   Why is there a special meeting of the city council?

    D.   What parallel does the pastor draw between the bird that had built a nest on the church steeple and the act of Flagpole Moody?

    E.   How does the fanatical religious group interpret Flagpole's presence?

    F.   What does the evangelist who calls himself "the Christian Jew" ask of Flagpole?

    G.   How does Flagpole react to the provision baskets, love notes, and photographs sent up to him?

    H.   What do these varied requests and interpretations of Flagpole Moody reveal about how the townspeople are using him?

III.   Analyzing the phenomenon of Flagpole Moody, the narrator states, "I know now that what I saw was the conflict of an idea with a society—in short, society was in the flagpole sitter and he was in the society of the town."

    A.   What idea does Flagpole Moody embody?

    B.   When he sets himself off from the town and at the same time functions as the focal point for everyone, what element in society does he seem to represent?

    C.   Throughout the story, Flagpole never conforms to anyone's wishes. He remains an individualist. How does the society represented in the story react to his individualism?

IV.   The author gives satirical descriptions of some of the people's reactions to Flagpole Moody. In making fun of these reactions, Goyen criticizes some elements of the society.

    A.   How do the merchants attempt to enlist Flagpole's aid in advertising their products?

    B.   How do the religious people interpret the figure?

    C.   How does the rich, hypochondriac Mrs. T. Trevor Sanderson respond to Flagpole?

    D.   How do the poetic and intellectual citizens honor him?

V.   The narrator tells this story, which took place during his childhood, from the perspective of maturity.

    A.   How does his first dream relate to the climactic dream at the end of the story?

    B.   What do these dreams reveal about the narrator?

    C.   In his dream, the narrator is chosen as the representative of society to tell Flagpole Moody to come down. How does this symbolically illuminate the previous statement, ". . . society was in the flagpole sitter and he was in the society of the town"?

D.   What does he find in Flagpole's tent?

E.   Taking Flagpole Moody's place, the narrator proceeds to drive out the insects and piece together the fragments of letters that had been torn to pieces. Why does he feel that by taking the role of Flagpole Moody, he is "at the source of the mystery, removed and secure from the chaos of the world." What mystery is he referring to?

VI.   Starting with the first phrase, "In the town of my beginning . . ." the narrator sets the poetic tone that prevails throughout the story. Although we know that "Figure over the Town" is set in a small southern town in the United States during the Second World War, the writer does not attempt to tell a realistic story. He is more concerned with presenting an imaginative version of a particular event. Describing the various reactions to Flagpole Moody, he emphasizes the variety of interpretations applied to Flagpole's "stunt." By confronting the reader with the central symbol, with the varied reactions of the townspeople, and with the narrator's dreams, Goyen encourages the reader to form certain interpretations.

A.   Why does the figure over the town seem godlike? What kind of god-figure does Flagpole Moody appear to be?

B.   Does he ever respond to the people below?

C.   Why does he become more remote as the story progresses?

D.   Is the author criticizing the god-figure or the people who attempt to believe in him?

E.   In the last paragraph, the narrator tells us that the figure came down after 40 days and 40 nights, the length of the Biblical Flood. Moreover, Lent, a period of penitence and fasting observed by the Roman Catholic and some other Christian churches, also extends over a period of 40 days. What does the symbolic significance of the time span suggest about the effect Flagpole has had on the town?

F.   Does Flagpole Moody's significance have to be interpreted religiously? If we left aside religious meaning to the story, what significance would he and his actions have?

☆ THEME TOPICS

1.   Describe an event that affected you in some way as a child. Discuss your reactions at the time and then comment on the event and your remembered reactions from the perspective of the present.

2.   Describe a dream you have had; then attempt to interpret it.

3.   Discuss a controversial event in the area of politics, religion, science, or the arts. Try to include several different attitudes which people have taken toward the event.

Everything That Rises Must Converge*
Flannery O'Connor

INTRODUCTION

I.   This story takes place in the American South just after the 1954 Supreme Court ruling that segregation of black people and white people was illegal and unconstitutional. Under segregation, which had been legal in many southern states before 1954, there were, for example, separate schools, restaurants, hotels, and living areas for blacks and whites, and blacks had to ride in the rear sections of trains and buses.

   A.   Is any type of racial segregation legal in your country? Has it ever been legal?

   B.   Do you approve of segregation of any kind? Why or why not? On what grounds do you oppose or support it?

   C.   Do you think it is possible for segregated facilities to ever be truly equal?

   D.   What effects do you think segregation would have upon the people who live in a segregated society?

II.   Flannery O'Connor was a white southerner who wrote many stories and short novels in which she explored the mentality of white people under the pressure of rapid social changes that they could not always understand. For many white southerners, who had been brought up to believe they were the guardians of genteel values and civilization, the changes came as a severe shock.

   A.   Has your country undergone any rapid social changes which certain groups of people had difficulty adjusting to? If so, what were the changes, and what kinds of adjustments did people have to make?

   B.   Does the relationship between generations become closer or more in conflict during a time of rapid social change? Why?

Her doctor had told Julian's mother that she must lose twenty pounds on account of her blood pressure, so on Wednesday nights Julian had to take her downtown on the bus for a reducing class at the Y.[1] The reducing class was designed for working girls[2] over fifty, who weighed from 165 to 200 pounds. His mother was one of the slimmer ones, but she said ladies[3] did not tell their age or weight. She would not ride the buses by herself at night since they had been integrated,[4] and because the reducing class was one of her few pleasures, necessary for her health, and *free,* she said Julian could at least put himself out[5] to take her, considering all she did for him. Julian did not like to consider all she did for him, but every Wednesday night he braced himself and took her.

She was almost ready to go, standing before the hall mirror, putting on her hat, while he, his hands behind him, appeared pinned to the door frame, waiting like Saint Sebastian[6] for the arrows to begin piercing him. The hat was new and had cost her seven dollars and a half. She kept saying, "Maybe I shouldn't have paid that for it. No, I shouldn't have. I'll take it off and return it tomorrow. I shouldn't have bought it."

Julian raised his eyes to heaven. "Yes, you should have bought it," he said. "Put it on and let's go." It was a hideous hat. A purple velvet flap came down on one side of it and stood up on the other; the rest of it was green and looked like a cushion with the stuffing out. He decided it was less comical than jaunty and pathetic. Everything that gave her pleasure was small and depressed him.

She lifted the hat one more time and set it down slowly on top of her head. Two wings of gray hair protruded on either side of her florid face, but her eyes, sky-blue, were as innocent and untouched by experience as they must have been when she was ten. Were it not that she was a widow who had struggled fiercely to feed and clothe and put him through school and who was supporting him still, "until he got on his feet,"[7] she might have been a little girl that he had to take to town.

"It's all right, it's all right," he said. "Let's go." He opened the door himself and started down the walk to get her going. The sky was a dying violet

---

[1] The Y — probably the YWCA (Young Women's Christian Association), a social and athletic club offering courses and organized activities at a reasonable price.

[2] Working girls — The term "working girls," which was especially common before the 1970s, refers to working women of any age.

[3] Ladies — women of gentle and refined manners, often from leading social families.

[4] "Since they had been integrated" — reference to the court-ordered integration of public buses in the American South by which black people (here called "Negroes") were permitted to ride in the same sections of the bus as white people. Previously, in most Southern states, blacks had to ride in a separate area to the rear of the bus.

[5] To put oneself out — to make a special effort.

[6] Saint Sebastian — a Roman who became a Christian martyr in the third century A.D. His body was pierced with arrows.

[7] To get on one's feet — to become financially self-supporting.

and the houses stood out darkly against it, bulbous liver-colored monstrosities of a uniform ugliness though no two were alike. Since this had been a fashionable neighborhood forty years ago, his mother persisted in thinking they did well to have an apartment in it. Each house had a narrow collar of dirt around it in which sat, usually, a grubby child. Julian walked with his hands in his pockets, his head down and thrust forward and his eyes glazed with the determination to make himself completely numb during the time he would be sacrificed to her pleasure.

The door closed and he turned to find the dumpy figure, surmounted by the atrocious hat, coming toward him. "Well," she said, "you only live once and paying a little more for it, I at least won't meet myself coming and going."[8]

"Some day I'll start making money," Julian said gloomily—he knew he never would—"and you can have one of those jokes whenever you take the fit."[9] But first they would move. He visualized a place where the nearest neighbors would be three miles away on either side.

"I think you're doing fine," she said, drawing on her gloves. "You've only been out of school a year. Rome wasn't built in a day."[10]

She was one of the few members of the Y reducing class who arrived in hat and gloves and who had a son who had been to college. "It takes time," she said, "and the world is in such a mess. This hat looked better on me than any of the others, though when she brought it out I said, 'Take that thing back. I wouldn't have it on my head,' and she said, 'Now wait till you see it on,' and when she put it on me, I said, 'We-ull,' and she said, 'If you ask me, that hat does something for you and you do something for the hat, and besides,' she said, 'with that hat, you won't meet yourself coming and going.' "

Julian thought he could have stood his lot[11] better if she had been selfish, if she had been an old hag[12] who drank and screamed at him. He walked along, saturated in depression, as if in the midst of his martyrdom he had lost his faith. Catching sight of his long, hopeless, irritated face, she stopped suddenly with a grief-stricken look, and pulled back on his arm. "Wait on me,"[13] she said. "I'm going back to the house and take this thing off and tomorrow I'm going to return it. I was out of my head. I can pay the gas bill with that seven-fifty."

He caught her arm in a vicious grip. "You are not going to take it back," he said. "I like it."

---

[8]"Paying a little more for it, I at least won't meet myself coming and going." — If she buys a fairly expensive hat, she believes she won't meet other people wearing the same one.

[9]To take the fit — to get a crazy, impulsive idea.

[10]"Rome wasn't built in a day." — Great things weren't accomplished in a short time. This, like many of her other statements, is a cliché, an expression that has been used too often, though it may try to sound fresh and new.

[11]To stand one's lot — to bear a difficult situation.

[12]Hag — unpleasant and bad-tempered old woman.

[13]"Wait on me." — In many regions of the United States, this expression would be, "Wait for me." It means, "Wait until I catch up with you."

"Well," she said, "I don't think I ought . . ."

"Shut up and enjoy it," he muttered, more depressed than ever.

"With the world in the mess it's in," she said, "it's a wonder we can enjoy anything. I tell you, the bottom rail is on the top."[14]

Julian sighed.

"Of course," she said, "if you know who you are, you can go anywhere." She said this every time he took her to the reducing class. "Most of them in it are not our kind of people," she said, "but I can be gracious to anybody. I know who I am."

"They don't give a damn for your graciousness," Julian said savagely. "Knowing who you are is good for one generation only. You haven't the foggiest idea[15] where you stand now or who you are."

She stopped and allowed her eyes to flash at him. "I most certainly do know who I am," she said, "and if you don't know who you are, I'm ashamed of you."

"Oh hell," Julian said.

"Your great-grandfather was a former governor of this state," she said. "Your grandfather was a prosperous landowner. Your grandmother was a Godhigh."

"Will you look around you," he said tensely, "and see where you are now?" and he swept his arm jerkily out to indicate the neighborhood, which the growing darkness at least made less dingy.

"You remain what you are," she said. "Your great-grandfather had a plantation and two hundred slaves."

"There are no more slaves," he said irritably.

"They were better off[16] when they were," she said. He groaned to see that she was off on that topic.[17] She rolled onto it every few days like a train on an open track. He knew every stop, every junction, every swamp along the way, and knew the exact point at which her conclusion would roll majestically into the station: "It's ridiculous. It's simply not realistic. They should rise, yes, but on their own side of the fence."[18]

"Let's skip it,"[19] Julian said.

"The ones I feel sorry for," she said, "are the ones that are half white. They're tragic."

"Will you skip it?"

"Suppose we were half white. We would certainly have mixed feelings."

---

[14]"The bottom rail is on the top."—People once considered on a low social level are now dominant.

[15]"The foggiest idea" — the vaguest idea.

[16]"*They* were better off . . ." — *They* here refers to the blacks, or Negroes.

[17]To go off on a topic — to speak at length on one's favorite subject, often on a favorite complaint.

[18]"Their own side of the fence" — in their own area. She is arguing here against the integration of blacks and whites.

[19]"Let's skip it." — "Let's move on to another topic."

"I have mixed feelings now," he groaned.

"Well let's talk about something pleasant," she said. "I remember going to Grandpa's when I was a little girl. Then the house had double stairways that went up to what was really the second floor—all the cooking was done on the first. I used to like to stay down in the kitchen on account of the way the walls smelled. I would sit with my nose pressed against the plaster and take deep breaths. Actually the place belonged to the Godhighs but your grandfather Chestny paid the mortgage and saved it for them. They were in reduced circumstances,"[20] she said, "but reduced or not, they never forgot who they were."

"Doubtless that decayed mansion reminded them," Julian muttered. He never spoke of it without contempt or thought of it without longing. He had seen it once when he was a child before it had been sold. The double stairways had rotted and been torn down. Negroes were living in it. But it remained in his mind as his mother had known it. It appeared in his dreams regularly. He would stand on the wide porch, listening to the rustle of oak leaves, then wander through the high-ceilinged hall into the parlor that opened onto it and gaze at the worn rugs and faded draperies. It occurred to him that it was he, not she, who could have appreciated it. He preferred its threadbare elegance to anything he could name and it was because of it that all the neighborhoods they had lived in had been a torment to him—whereas she had hardly known the difference. She called her insensitivity "being adjustable."

"And I remember the old darky[21] who was my nurse, Caroline. There was no better person in the world. I've always had a great respect for my colored friends," she said. "I'd do anything in the world for them and they'd . . ."

"Will you for God's sake get off that subject?" Julian said. When he got on a bus by himself, he made it a point to sit down beside a Negro, in reparation as it were for his mother's sins.

"You're mighty touchy tonight," she said. "Do you feel all right?"

"Yes I feel all right," he said. "Now lay off."[22]

She pursed her lips. "Well, you certainly are in a vile humor,"[23] she observed. "I just won't speak to you at all."

They had reached the bus stop. There was no bus in sight and Julian, his hands still jammed in his pockets and his head thrust forward, scowled down the empty street. The frustration of having to wait on the bus as well as ride on it began to creep up his neck like a hot hand. The presence of his mother was borne in upon him as she gave a pained sigh. He looked at her bleakly. She was holding herself very erect under the preposterous hat, wearing it like a banner of her imaginary dignity. There was in him an evil urge to break her spirit. He suddenly unloosened his tie and pulled it off and put it in his pocket.

---

[20]In reduced circumstances — a polite term for being poor.

[21]"The old darkey" — term used by some whites to refer to black people. Patronizing in tone.

[22]"Lay off" — "stop bothering me."

[23]In a vile humor — in a bad mood.

She stiffened. "Why must you look like *that* when you take me to town?" she said. "Why must you deliberately embarrass me?"

"If you'll never learn where you are," he said, "you can at least learn where I am."

"You look like a—thug,"[24] she said.

"Then I must be one," he murmured.

"I'll just go home," she said. "I will not bother you. If you can't do a little thing like that for me . . ."

Rolling his eyes upward, he put his tie back on. "Restored to my class," he muttered. He thrust his face toward her and hissed, "True culture is in the mind, the *mind*," he said, and tapped his head, "the mind."

"It's in the heart," she said, "and in how you do things and how you do things is because of who you *are*."

"Nobody in the damn bus cares who you are."

"I care who I am," she said icily.

The lighted bus appeared on top of the next hill and as it approached, they moved out into the street to meet it. He put his hand under her elbow and hoisted her up on the creaking step. She entered with a little smile, as if she were going into a drawing room[25] where everyone had been waiting for her. While he put in the tokens,[26] she sat down on one of the broad front seats for three which faced the aisle. A thin woman with protruding teeth and long yellow hair was sitting on the end of it. His mother moved up beside her and left room for Julian beside herself. He sat down and looked at the floor across the aisle where a pair of thin feet in red and white canvas sandals were planted.

His mother immediately began a general conversation meant to attract anyone who felt like talking. "Can it get any hotter?" she said and removed from her purse a folding fan, black with a Japanese scene on it, which she began to flutter before her.

"I reckon it might could,"[27] the woman with the protruding teeth said, "but I know for a fact my apartment couldn't get no hotter."

"It must get the afternoon sun," his mother said. She sat forward and looked up and down the bus. It was half filled. Everybody was white. "I see we have the bus to ourselves," she said. Julian cringed.

"For a change," said the woman across the aisle, the owner of the red and white canvas sandals. "I come on one the other day and they were thick as fleas[28]—up front and all through."

---

[24]Thug — a tough, low-grade criminal.

[25]Drawing room — a formal reception room found only in more elegant houses.

[26]Tokens — pieces of stamped metal that are often used instead of coins on buses and subways.

[27]"I reckon it might could." — "I guess it could." The speaker's faulty grammar indicates her lower social standing and education.

[28]"They were thick as fleas" — "Many Negroes were on the crowded bus." Describing the Negroes as fleas indicates the contempt with which the speaker regards them.

"The world is in a mess everywhere," his mother said. "I don't know how we've let it get in this fix."[29]

"What gets my goat[30] is all those boys from good families stealing automobile tires," the woman with the protruding teeth said. "I told my boy, I said you may not be rich but you been raised right and if I ever catch you in any such mess, they can send you on to the reformatory.[31] Be exactly where you belong."

"Training tells," his mother said. "Is your boy in high school?"

"Ninth grade," the woman said.

"My son just finished college last year. He wants to write but he's selling typewriters until he gets started," his mother said.

The woman leaned forward and peered at Julian. He threw her such a malevolent look that she subsided against the seat. On the floor across the aisle there was an abandoned newspaper. He got up and got it and opened it out in front of him. His mother discreetly continued the conversation in a lower tone but the woman across the aisle said in a loud voice, "Well that's nice. Selling typewriters is close to writing. He can go right from one to the other."

"I tell him," his mother said, "that Rome wasn't built in a day."

Behind the newspaper Julian was withdrawing into the inner compartment of his mind where he spent most of his time. This was a kind of mental bubble in which he established himself when he could not bear to be a part of what was going on around him. From it he could see out and judge but in it he was safe from any kind of penetration from without. It was the only place where he felt free of the general idiocy of his fellows. His mother had never entered it but from it he could see her with absolute clarity.

The old lady[32] was clever enough and he thought that if she had started from any of the right premises, more might have been expected of her. She lived according to the laws of her own fantasy world, outside of which he had never seen her set foot. The law of it was to sacrifice herself for him after she had first created the necessity to do so by making a mess of things. If he had permitted her sacrifices, it was only because her lack of foresight had made them necessary. All of her life had been a struggle to act like a Chestny without the Chestny goods, and to give him everything she thought a Chestny ought to have; but since, said she, it was fun to struggle, why complain? And when you had won, as she had won, what fun to look back on the hard times! He could not forgive her that she had enjoyed the struggle and that she thought *she* had won.

What she meant when she said she had won was that she had brought him up successfully and had sent him to college and that he had turned out so well—good looking (her teeth had gone unfilled so that his could be straightened),

---

[29]Fix — predicament. Difficult situation.

[30]To get one's goat — to annoy one very much.

[31]Reformatory — a penal institution for young people who have broken the law. Often called "reform school."

[32]"The old lady" — disrespectful term for Julian's mother.

intelligent (he realized he was too intelligent to be a success), and with a future ahead of him (there was of course no future ahead of him). She excused his gloominess on the grounds that he was still growing up and his radical ideas on his lack of practical experience. She said he didn't yet know a thing about "life," that he hadn't even entered the real world—when already he was as disenchanted[33] with it as a man of fifty.

The further irony of all this was that in spite of her, he had turned out so well. In spite of going to only a third-rate college, he had, on his own initiative, come out with a first-rate education; in spite of growing up dominated by a small mind, he had ended up with a large one; in spite of all her foolish views, he was free of prejudice and unafraid to face facts. Most miraculous of all, instead of being blinded by love for her as she was for him, he had cut himself emotionally free of her and could see her with complete objectivity. He was not dominated by his mother.

The bus stopped with a sudden jerk and shook him from his meditation. A woman from the back lurched forward with little steps and barely escaped falling in his newspaper as she righted herself. She got off and a large Negro got on. Julian kept his paper lowered to watch. It gave him a certain satisfaction to see injustice in daily operation. It confirmed his view that with a few exceptions there was no one worth knowing within a radius of three hundred miles. The Negro was well dressed and carried a briefcase. He looked around and then sat down on the other end of the seat where the woman with the red and white canvas sandals was sitting. He immediately unfolded a newspaper and obscured himself behind it. Julian's mother's elbow at once prodded insistently into his ribs. "Now you see why I won't ride on these buses by myself," she whispered.

The woman with the red and white canvas sandals had risen at the same time the Negro sat down and had gone further back in the bus and taken the seat of the woman who had got off. His mother leaned forward and cast her an approving look.

Julian rose, crossed the aisle, and sat down in the place of the woman with the canvas sandals. From this position, he looked serenely across at his mother. Her face had turned an angry red. He stared at her, making his eyes the eyes of a stranger. He felt his tension suddenly lift as if he had openly declared war on her.

He would have liked to get in conversation with the Negro and to talk with him about art or politics or any subject that would be above the comprehension of those around them, but the man remained entrenched behind his paper. He was either ignoring the change of seating or had never noticed it. There was no way for Julian to convey his sympathy.

His mother kept her eyes fixed reproachfully on his face. The woman with the protruding teeth was looking at him avidly as if he were a type of monster new to her.

---

[33]Disenchanted — disillusioned.

"Do you have a light?" he asked the Negro.

Without looking away from his paper, the man reached in his pocket and handed him a packet of matches.

"Thanks," Julian said. For a moment he held the matches foolishly. A NO SMOKING sign looked down upon him from over the door. This alone would not have deterred him; he had no cigarettes. He had quit smoking some months before because he could not afford it. "Sorry," he muttered and handed back the matches. The Negro lowered the paper and gave him an annoyed look. He took the matches and raised the paper again.

His mother continued to gaze at him but she did not take advantage of his momentary discomfort. Her eyes retained their battered look. Her face seemed to be unnaturally red, as if her blood pressure had risen. Julian allowed no glimmer of sympathy to show on his face. Having got the advantage, he wanted desperately to keep it and carry it through. He would have liked to teach her a lesson that would last her a while, but there seemed no way to continue the point. The Negro refused to come out from behind his paper.

Julian folded his arms and looked stolidly before him, facing her but as if he did not see her, as if he had ceased to recognize her existence. He visualized a scene in which, the bus having reached their stop, he would remain in his seat and when she said, "Aren't you going to get off?" he would look at her as at a stranger who had rashly addressed him. The corner they got off on was usually deserted, but it was well lighted and it would not hurt her to walk by herself the four blocks to the Y. He decided to wait until the time came and then decide whether or not he would let her get off by herself. He would have to be at the Y at ten to bring her back, but he could leave her wondering if he was going to show up. There was no reason for her to think she could always depend on him.

He retired again into the high-ceilinged room sparsely settled with large pieces of antique furniture. His soul expanded momentarily but then he became aware of his mother across from him and the vision shriveled. He studied her coldly. Her feet in little pumps dangled like a child's and did not quite reach the floor. She was training on him an exaggerated look of reproach. He felt completely detached from her. At that moment he could with pleasure have slapped her as he would have slapped a particularly obnoxious child in his charge.

He began to imagine various unlikely ways by which he could teach her a lesson. He might make friends with some distinguished Negro professor or lawyer and bring him home to spend the evening. He would be entirely justified but her blood pressure would rise to 300. He could not push her to the extent of making her have a stroke,[34] and moreover, he had never been successful at making any Negro friends. He had tried to strike up an acquaintance on the bus with some of the better types, with ones that looked like professors or ministers

---

[34]Stroke — a sudden illness that affects part of the brain, causing speech disturbances and minor or major paralysis of the body.

or lawyers. One morning he had sat down next to a distinguished-looking dark brown man who had answered his questions with a sonorous solemnity but who had turned out to be an undertaker. Another day he had sat down beside a cigar-smoking Negro with a diamond ring on his finger, but after a few stilted pleasantries, the Negro had rung the buzzer and risen, slipping two lottery tickets[35] into Julian's hand as he climbed over him to leave.

He imagined his mother lying desperately ill and his being able to secure only a Negro doctor for her. He toyed with that idea for a few minutes and then dropped it for a momentary vision of himself participating as a sympathizer in a sit-in demonstration.[36] This was possible but he did not linger with it. Instead, he approached the ultimate horror. He brought home a beautiful suspiciously Negroid woman. Prepare yourself, he said. There is nothing you can do about it. This is the woman I've chosen. She's intelligent, dignified, even good, and she's suffered and she hasn't thought it *fun*. Now persecute us, go ahead and persecute us. Drive her out of here, but remember, you're driving me too. His eyes were narrowed and through the indignation he had generated, he saw his mother across the aisle, purple-faced, shrunken to the dwarf-like proportions of her moral nature, sitting like a mummy beneath the ridiculous banner of her hat.

He was tilted out of his fantasy again as the bus stopped. The door opened with a sucking hiss and out of the dark a large, gaily dressed, sullen-looking colored woman got on with a little boy. The child, who might have been four, had on a short plaid suit and a Tyrolean hat with a blue feather in it. Julian hoped that he would sit down beside him and that the woman would push in beside his mother. He could think of no better arrangement.

As she waited for her tokens, the woman was surveying the seating possibilities—he hoped with the idea of sitting where she was least wanted. There was something familiar-looking about her but Julian could not place what it was. She was a giant of a woman. Her face was set not only to meet opposition but to seek it out. The downward tilt of her large lower lip was like a warning sign: DON'T TAMPER[37] WITH ME. Her bulging figure was encased in a green crepe dress and her feet overflowed in red shoes. She had on a hideous hat. A purple velvet flap came down on one side of it and stood up on the other; the rest of it was green and looked like a cushion with the stuffing out. She carried a mammoth red pocketbook that bulged throughout as if it were stuffed with rocks.

To Julian's disappointment, the little boy climbed up on the empty seat beside his mother. His mother lumped all children, black and white, into the common category, "cute," and she thought little Negroes were on the whole cuter than little white children. She smiled at the little boy as he climbed on the seat.

---

[35]Lottery tickets — tickets for a game of chance in which winning tickets are selected and prizes awarded.

[36]Sit-in demonstration — organized movement in which blacks would enter a restaurant reserved only for whites and sit down at tables or at the lunch counter. This "sit-in movement" led to the integration of many formerly segregated restaurants.

[37]To tamper — to interfere.

Meanwhile the woman was bearing down upon[38] the empty seat beside Julian. To his annoyance, she squeezed herself into it. He saw his mother's face change as the woman settled herself next to him and he realized with satisfaction that this was more objectionable to her than it was to him. Her face seemed almost gray and there was a look of dull recognition in her eyes, as if suddenly she had sickened at some awful confrontation. Julian saw that it was because she and the woman had, in a sense, swapped sons. Though his mother would not realize the symbolic significance of this, she would feel it. His amusement showed plainly on his face.

The woman next to him muttered something unintelligible to herself. He was conscious of a kind of bristling[39] next to him, a muted growling like that of an angry cat. He could not see anything but the red pocketbook upright on the bulging green thighs. He visualized the woman as she had stood waiting for her tokens—the ponderous figure, rising from the red shoes upward over the solid hips, the mammoth bosom, the haughty face, to the green and purple hat.

His eyes widened.

The vision of the two hats, identical, broke upon him with the radiance of a brilliant sunrise. His face was suddenly lit with joy. He could not believe that Fate had thrust upon his mother such a lesson. He gave a loud chuckle so that she would look at him and see that he saw. She turned her eyes on him slowly. The blue in them seemed to have turned a bruised purple. For a moment he had an uncomfortable sense of her innocence, but it lasted only a second before principle rescued him. Justice entitled him to laugh. His grin hardened until it said to her as plainly as if he were saying aloud: Your punishment exactly fits your pettiness. This should teach you a permanent lesson.

Her eyes shifted to the woman. She seemed unable to bear looking at him and to find the woman preferable. He became conscious again of the bristling presence at his side. The woman was rumbling like a volcano about to become active. His mother's mouth began to twitch slightly at one corner. With a sinking heart, he saw incipient signs of recovery on her face and realized that this was going to strike her suddenly as funny and was going to be no lesson at all. She kept her eyes on the woman and an amused smile came over her face as if the woman were a monkey that had stolen her hat. The little Negro was looking up at her with large fascinated eyes. He had been trying to attract her attention for some time.

"Carver!" the woman said suddenly. "Come heah!"[40]

When he saw that the spotlight was on him at last, Carver drew his feet up and turned himself toward Julian's mother and giggled.

"Carver!" the woman said. "You heah me? Come heah!"

Carver slid down from the seat but remained squatting with his back against the base of it, his head turned slyly around toward Julian's mother, who was smiling at him. The woman reached a hand across the aisle and snatched

---

[38]To bear down upon — to walk toward someone or something in a menacing manner.

[39]To bristle — to be on guard, like an animal whose hair is standing on end.

[40]"Heah" — Southern dialect for "here."

him to her. He righted himself and hung backwards on her knees, grinning at Julian's mother. "Isn't he cute?" Julian's mother said to the woman with the protruding teeth.

"I reckon he is," the woman said without conviction.

The Negress yanked him upright but he eased out of her grip and shot across the aisle and scrambled, giggling wildly, onto the seat beside his love.

"I think he likes me," Julian's mother said, and smiled at the woman. It was the smile she used when she was being particularly gracious to an inferior. Julian saw everything lost. The lesson had rolled off her like rain on a roof.

The woman stood up and yanked the little boy off the seat as if she were snatching him from contagion. Julian could feel the rage in her at having no weapon like his mother's smile. She gave the child a sharp slap across his leg. He howled once and then thrust his head into her stomach and kicked his feet against her shins. "Be-have," she said vehemently.

The bus stopped and the Negro who had been reading the newspaper got off. The woman moved over and set the little boy down with a thump between herself and Julian. She held him firmly by the knee. In a moment he put his hands in front of his face and peeped at Julian's mother through his fingers.

"I see yooooooooo!" she said and put her hand in front of her face and peeped at him.

The woman slapped his hand down. "Quit yo' foolishness," she said, "before I knock the living Jesus out of you!"

Julian was thankful that the next stop was theirs. He reached up and pulled the cord. The woman reached up and pulled it at the same time. Oh my God, he thought. He had the terrible intuition that when they got off the bus together, his mother would open her purse and give the little boy a nickel.[41] The gesture would be as natural to her as breathing. The bus stopped and the woman got up and lunged to the front, dragging the child, who wished to stay on, after her. Julian and his mother got up and followed. As they neared the door, Julian tried to relieve her of her pocketbook.

"No," she murmured, "I want to give the little boy a nickel."

"No!" Julian hissed. "No!"

She smiled down at the child and opened her bag. The bus door opened and the woman picked him up by the arm and descended with him, hanging at her hip. Once in the street she set him down and shook him.

Julian's mother had to close her purse while she got down the bus step but as soon as her feet were on the ground, she opened it again and began to rummage inside. "I can't find but a penny,"[42] she whispered, "but it looks like a new one."

"Don't do it!" Julian said fiercely between his teeth. There was a streetlight on the corner and she hurried to get under it so that she could better

---

[41] Nickel — five cents. One-twentieth of a United States dollar.

[42] Penny — One cent. One one-hundredth of a United States dollar; the smallest denomination coin in United States currency.

see into her pocketbook. The woman was heading off rapidly down the street with the child still hanging backward on her hand.

"Oh little boy!" Julian's mother called and took a few quick steps and caught up with them just beyond the lamppost. "Here's a bright new penny for you," and she held out the coin, which shone bronze in the dim light.

The huge woman turned and for a moment stood, her shoulders lifted and her face frozen with frustrated rage, and stared at Julian's mother. Then all at once she seemed to explode like a piece of machinery that had been given one ounce of pressure too much. Julian saw the black fist swing out with the red pocketbook. He shut his eyes and cringed as he heard the woman shout, "He don't take nobody's pennies!" When he opened his eyes, the woman was disappearing down the street with the little boy staring wide-eyed over her shoulder. Julian's mother was sitting on the sidewalk.

"I told you not to do that," Julian said angrily. "I told you not to do that!"

He stood over her for a minute, gritting his teeth. Her legs were stretched out in front of her and her hat was on her lap. He squatted down and looked her in the face. It was totally expressionless. "You got exactly what you deserved," he said. "Now get up."

He picked up her pocketbook and put what had fallen out back in it. He picked the hat up off her lap. The penny caught his eye on the sidewalk and he picked that up and let it drop before her eyes into the purse. Then he stood up and leaned over and held his hands out to pull her up. She remained immobile. He sighed. Rising above them on either side were black apartment buildings, marked with irregular rectangles of light. At the end of the block a man came out of a door and walked off in the opposite direction. "All right," he said, "suppose somebody happens by and wants to know why you're sitting on the sidewalk?"

She took the hand and, breathing hard, pulled heavily up on it and then stood for a moment, swaying slightly as if the spots of light in the darkness were circling around her. Her eyes, shadowed and confused, finally settled on his face. He did not try to conceal his irritation. "I hope this teaches you a lesson," he said. She leaned forward and her eyes raked his face.[43] She seemed trying to determine his identity. Then, as if she found nothing familiar about him, she started off with a headlong movement in the wrong direction.

"Aren't you going on to the Y?" he asked.

"Home," she muttered.

"Well, are we walking?"

For answer she kept going. Julian followed along, his hands behind him. He saw no reason to let the lesson she had had go without backing it up[44] with an explanation of its meaning. She might as well be made to understand what had happened to her. "Don't think that was just an uppity[45] Negro woman," he said.

---

[43] To rake with one's eyes — to examine thoroughly.

[44] To back something up — to offer evidence in support of one's argument or position.

[45] Uppity — slang term for someone who is overambitious, trying to rise higher than he or she should.

"That was the whole colored race which will no longer take your condescending pennies. That was your black double. She can wear the same hat as you, and to be sure," he added gratuitously (because he thought it was funny), "it looked better on her than it did on you. What all this means," he said, "is that the old world is gone. The old manners are obsolete and your graciousness is not worth a damn." He thought bitterly of the house that had been lost for him. "You aren't who you think you are," he said.

She continued to plow ahead,[46] paying no attention to him. Her hair had come undone on one side. She dropped her pocketbook and took no notice. He stopped and picked it up and handed it to her but she did not take it.

"You needn't act as if the world had come to an end," he said, "because it hasn't. From now on you've got to live in a new world and face a few realities for a change. Buck up,"[47] he said, "it won't kill you."

She was breathing fast.

"Let's wait on the bus," he said.

"Home," she said thickly.

"I hate to see you behave like this," he said. "Just like a child. I should be able to expect more of you." He decided to stop where he was and make her stop and wait for a bus. "I'm not going any farther," he said, stopping. "We're going on the bus."

She continued to go on as if she had not heard him. He took a few steps and caught her arm and stopped her. He looked into her face and caught his breath. He was looking into a face he had never seen before. "Tell Grandpa to come get me," she said.

He stared, stricken.

"Tell Caroline to come get me," she said.

Stunned, he let her go and she lurched forward again, walking as if one leg were shorter than the other. A tide of darkness seemed to be sweeping her from him. "Mother!" he cried. "Darling, sweetheart, wait!" Crumpling, she fell to the pavement. He dashed forward and fell at her side, crying, "Mamma, Mamma!" He turned her over. Her face was fiercely distorted. One eye, large and staring, moved slightly to the left as if it had become unmoored. The other remained fixed on him, raked his face again, found nothing and closed.

"Wait here, wait here!" he cried and jumped up and began to run for help toward a cluster of lights he saw in the distance ahead of him. "Help, help!" he shouted, but his voice was thin, scarcely a thread of sound. The lights drifted farther away the faster he ran and his feet moved numbly as if they carried him nowhere. The tide of darkness seemed to sweep him back to her, postponing from moment to moment his entry into the world of guilt and sorrow.

---

[46]To plow ahead — to walk straight ahead without stopping for anything, like a farmer's plow.

[47]To buck up — to take courage.

☆ FOLLOW-UP QUESTIONS

I. At the beginning of the story, Julian and his mother are about to take the bus so that she can go to her reducing class.
   A.   Why does she have to lose weight?
   B.   How does she feel about taking the buses now that they are integrated?
   C.   Why does she worry so much about the hat she has recently bought?
   D.   What does her concern about the cost of the hat and her pleasure at the free reducing classes tell us about her financial situation?
   E.   How does Julian feel about taking her to the night classes?

II. Julian's mother says, "If you know who you are, you can go anywhere."
   A.   What does she consider herself to be?
   B.   What is implied in the author's choice of name for the grandparents? (the Godhighs)
   C.   When Julian's mother smiles at the Negro woman and her child on the bus, how would you describe her attitude toward them?
   D.   How does she treat the white woman (with protruding teeth) on the bus? Aside from color, do they seem like social equals? How can you tell?
   E.   What does Julian's mother mean when she says about Negroes, "They should rise, yes, but on their own side of the fence"?
   F.   When she says, "The world's in a mess," do you feel she has thought deeply about the world, or is she using a phrase she has heard somewhere? Does she often speak in clichés? If so, identify some of them. What do clichés reveal about the person who uses them?

III. Julian's mother's eyes "were as innocent and untouched by experience as they must have been when she was ten."
   A.   Julian constantly sees his mother as if she were a child. Can this be simply Julian's distorted view of his mother, or is there other evidence that she is childlike?
   B.   When she talks about Julian's grandparents, how does she see herself? As a young woman or as a child?
   C.   By comparison, how does Julian imagine himself when he thinks of the grandparents' house?
   D.   At the end of the story, when Julian's mother probably has a stroke from the shock of being hit by the Negro woman, who does she turn to? Who does she want to come get her?

IV. Julian says to his mother, "If you'll never learn where you are, you can at least learn where I am."
   A.   Does Julian have a clear view of "where he is"?
   B.   What does he mean by the phrase?
   C.   His mother clearly does *not* understand why she was knocked down by the Negro woman. Does Julian understand?
   D.   Where in the story is it clear that he is aware of the difference between the world as it used to be (his mother's past) and as it is now? What does he think of his own chances for the future as compared with his mother's view of them?
   E.   How does he see their present circumstances? Is their neighborhood, as he sees it, "fashionable"?

V. Julian never spoke of the Godhighs' mansion "without contempt or thought of it without longing."
    A. Although Julian knows where he is, where does he wish he were?
    B. Do you remember anything indicating that Julian feels separate and above the "general idiocy" he sees around him?
    C. One way of separating himself from those he considers his inferiors is to retreat to "the inner compartment of his mind . . . a kind of mental bubble." At one point in the story, the author writes: "he retired again into the high-ceilinged room sparsely settled with large pieces of antique furniture." What is that "room"? Why does the author connect Julian's *mind* and the Godhigh mansion?
    D. While in his "mental bubble," Julian assesses himself as well as the world. In spite of his mother, he realizes, "he had turned out so well . . . in spite of all her foolish views, he was free of prejudice and unafraid to face facts." Is Julian really as free of prejudice as he says?
VI. In one of his fantasies he imagines ways of teaching his mother a lesson, for example, by making friends with "some distinguished Negro professor or lawyer . . ."
    A. Why is it important for Julian that the Negro be "distinguished"?
    B. Why is the woman he imagines bringing home only "suspiciously Negroid"?
    C. Why doesn't he "linger" with the idea of participating in a sit-in demonstration?
    D. Do you think he is committed to Negro equality? Why?
VII. Julian prides himself on his intelligence, and especially on the fact that "instead of being blinded by love for his mother as she was for him, he had cut himself emotionally free of her and could see her with complete objectivity."
    A. What does "complete objectivity" mean?
    B. Do you think that Julian is in fact "objective" about his mother?
    C. Do you think one person can ever be completely objective about another?
    D. What small gestures does Julian make to "teach his mother a lesson"—and why is it so important to him to do so?
    E. Is there any moment in the story that you can remember where Julian is *not* feeling something toward his mother?
VIII. "True culture lies in the mind, the *mind* . . . ," Julian claims. She replies that "It's in the heart . . ."
    A. Where in the story is it clear that Julian puts intelligence, "principle," and "justice" above "the heart"? For example, when he sees his mother's dismay that the Negro woman is wearing her hat, what is Julian's reaction? At the end of the story, when his mother has been knocked down by the woman, what is Julian's immediate response?

☆ *THEME TOPICS*

1. Describe an incident that changed your feelings about a person. How did the incident affect you, and in what way did your feelings change?
2. Describe how an old person (or old people) you have known reacted to social change, i.e., different marriage patterns; changing sexual morality; new attitudes toward religion; new economic policies, etc. Did this social change bring about any conflict between generations? Why or why not?

3.   In "Everything That Rises Must Converge," Julian's mother offers a little black
     boy a penny, but the boy's mother refuses it angrily, saying, "He don't take
     nobody's pennies!" Discuss an incident in which you or someone you know tried
     to help someone or to give them something and this help was refused. Tell why you
     think the person refused the help. What does this incident suggest about people (or
     nations) helping others and how help should be offered?

The Invisible Land*
Michael Harrington

INTRODUCTION

I.   In "The Invisible Land," Michael Harrington refers to an anecdote about two famous American writers, Ernest Hemingway and F. Scott Fitzgerald. The latter remarked, "The rich are different." And Hemingway replied, "Yes, they have money."

   A. In what other ways do you feel the rich are different from other people?

   B. In your country, does the general appearance of a person necessarily indicate his economic status? Does a poor person always look poor? Does a rich person always look rich? What might be the difference between clothes worn by the middle class and clothes worn by the lower class?

   C. Are you aware of particular attitudes directed toward the very poor? Toward the very rich? What are they?

II.   In discussing the general character of poverty, Harrington refers to the labor movement in the United States. Labor unions have become a powerful economic force. They are organizations set up to represent workers in matters of wages and working conditions. The Congress of Industrial Organizations (CIO), for example, is a labor union that started to organize workers in the 1930s and today continues to represent millions of workers.

   A. Do labor unions exist in your country?

   B. If so, why have they been set up?

   C. Who joins them?

III. Social Security is a governmental program designed to cover the working people. Established in 1935, it includes old age and survivors' insurance. The individual and the employer pay for it by paying a percentage of his or her salary during the course of his or her working life. When a worker reaches a specific age (60 to 65) and retires, he or she automatically receives a sum of money each month.

   A. Does a form of social security exist in your native country?

   B. If so, what are its benefits?

   C. Has there been any criticism of that system? If so, who has the criticism come from? What arguments have been advanced against the system?

IV.   Harrington maintains that in the United States the poor are not represented by a lobby. A lobby is an organized group of people who are paid to represent a specific interest; they work to influence public officials on legislation and other policy decisions. Industries, labor unions, and professional groups hire lobbyists to help produce conditions favorable to them.

A. In the United States, lobbying is a legal means of influencing elected officials. What might be some of its advantages? Some of its drawbacks?

B. Is there a comparable system of lobbying in your native country? If so, how does it work?

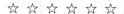

There is a familiar America. It is celebrated in speeches and advertised on television and in the magazines. It has the highest mass standard of living the world has ever known.

In the 1950s this America worried about itself, yet even its anxieties were products of abundance. The title of a brilliant book was widely misinterpreted, and the familiar America began to call itself *the affluent society.*[1] There was introspection about Madison Avenue and tailfins;[2] there was discussion of the emotional suffering taking place in the suburbs. In all this, there was an implicit assumption that the basic, grinding economic problems had been solved in the United States. In this theory the nation's problems were no longer a matter of basic human needs—of food, shelter, and clothing. Now they were seen as qualitative, a question of learning to live decently amid luxury.

While this discussion was carried on, there existed another America. In it dwelt somewhere between 40 million and 50 million citizens of this land. They were poor. They still are.

To be sure, the other America is not impoverished in the same sense as those poor nations where millions cling to hunger as a defense against starvation. This country has escaped such extremes. That does not change the fact that tens of millions of Americans are, at this very moment, maimed in body and spirit, existing at levels beneath those necessary for human decency. If these people are not starving, they are hungry, and sometimes fat with hunger, for that is what cheap foods do. They are without adequate housing and education and medical care.

The government has documented what this means to the bodies of the

---

*Reprinted with permission of Macmillan Publishing Company, Inc., from The Other America, by Michael Harrington, 1962.

---

[1] The affluent society — reference to the book, *The Affluent Society,* by the American economist, John Kenneth Galbraith. The book, published in the 1950s, was critical of many aspects of the American economy but was popularly considered (usually by people who hadn't read it) as having said that all Americans were living an affluent life.

[2] Tailfins — finlike decorations near the tail lights of an automobile. A popular design style in American cars of the 1950s. Some people considered tailfins elegant; others thought they were symbols of useless and expensive ornamentation.

poor. . . . But even more basic, this poverty twists and deforms the spirit. The American poor are pessimistic and defeated, and they are victimized by mental suffering to a degree unknown in Suburbia.[3]

This book is a description of the world in which these people live; it is about the other America. Here are the unskilled workers, the migrant farm workers,[4] the aged, the minorities, and all the others who live in the economic underworld[5] of American life. In all this, there will be statistics, and that offers the opportunity for disagreement among honest and sincere men. I would ask the reader to respond critically to every assertion, but not to allow statistical quibbling[6] to obscure the huge, enormous, and intolerable fact of poverty in America. For, when all is said and done, that fact is unmistakable, whatever its exact dimensions, and the truly human reaction can only be outrage. As W. H. Auden[7] wrote:

> *Hunger allows no choice*
> *To the citizen or the police;*
> *We must love one another or die.*

I

The millions who are poor in the United States tend to become increasingly invisible. Here is a great mass of people, yet it takes an effort of the intellect and will even to see them.

I discovered this personally in a curious way. After I wrote my first article on poverty in America, I had all the statistics down on paper. I had proved to my satisfaction that there were around 50 million poor in this country. Yet, I realized I did not believe my own figures. The poor existed in the government reports; they were percentages and numbers in long, close columns, but they were not part of my experience. I could prove that the other America existed, but I had never been there.

My response was not accidental. It was typical of what is happening to an entire society, and it reflects profound social changes in this nation. The other America, the America of poverty, is hidden today in a way that it never was before. Its millions are socially invisible to the rest of us. No wonder that so many misinterpreted Galbraith's title and assumed that *the affluent society* meant that everyone had a decent standard of life. The misinterpretation was

---

[3]Suburbia — the suburbs. Generally affluent areas or groups of people outside the big cities. The term implies uniform cultural attitudes.

[4]Migrant farm workers — people who travel from farm job to farm job according to which crops are in season.

[5]Economic underworld — workers who receive very low wages and live at or near the poverty level.

[6]Quibbling — arguing over insignificant matters.

[7]W. H. Auden — English poet and literary critic (1907–1974) who lived most of his adult life in the United States.

true as far as the actual day-to-day lives of two thirds of the nation were concerned. Thus, one must begin a description of the other America by understanding why we do not see it.

There are perennial reasons that make the other America an invisible land.

Poverty is often off the beaten track. It always has been. The ordinary tourist never left the main highway, and today he rides interstate turnpikes. He does not go into the valleys of Pennsylvania where the towns look like movie sets of Wales in the 1930s. He does not see the company houses[8] in rows, the rutted roads (the poor always have bad roads whether they live in the city, in towns, or on farms), and everything is black and dirty. And even if he were to pass through such a place by accident, the tourist would not meet the unemployed men in the bar or the women coming home from a runaway sweatshop.[9]

Then, too, beauty and myths are perennial masks of poverty. The traveler comes to the Appalachians in the lovely season. He sees the hills, the streams, the foliage—but not the poor. Or perhaps he looks at a rundown mountain house and—remembering Rousseau[10] rather than seeing with his eyes—decides that "those people" are truly fortunate to be living the way they are and that they are lucky to be exempt from the strains and tensions of the middle class. The only problem is that "those people," the quaint inhabitants of those hills, are undereducated, underprivileged, lack medical care, and are in the process of being forced from the land into a life in the cities, where they are misfits.

These are normal and obvious causes of the invisibility of the poor. They operated a generation ago; they will be functioning a generation hence. It is more important to understand that the very development of American society is creating a new kind of blindness about poverty. The poor are increasingly slipping out of the very experience and consciousness of the nation.

If the middle class never did like ugliness and poverty, it was at least aware of them. "Across the tracks"[11] was not a very long way to go. There were forays into the slums at Christmas time; there were charitable organizations that brought contact with the poor. Occasionally, almost everyone passed through the Negro ghetto[12] or the blocks of tenements,[13] if only to get downtown to work or to entertainment.

Now the American city has been transformed. The poor still inhabit the miserable housing in the central area, but they are increasingly isolated from

---

[8]Company houses — houses which companies provided for workers as part of their pay.

[9]Runaway sweatshop — factories where the employees were required to work long hours for low pay and under bad working conditions.

[10]Rousseau — Jean Jacques Rousseau (1712–1778). French philosopher who exalted the "noble savage" living in primitive nature.

[11]"Across the tracks" — the poorer section of a village or town, often located on the opposite side of the railroad tracks from the more affluent section.

[12]Negro ghetto — area of a town or city where Negroes, or blacks, live.

[13]Tenements — city apartment houses in poor condition.

contact with, or sight of, anybody else. Middle-class women coming in from Suburbia on a rare trip may catch the merest glimpse of the other America on the way to an evening at the theater, but their children are segregated in suburban schools. The business or professional man may drive along the fringes of slums in a car or bus, but it is not an important experience to him. The failures, the unskilled, the disabled, the aged, and the minorities are right there, across the tracks, where they have always been. But hardly anyone else is.

In short, the very development of the American city has removed poverty from the living, emotional experience of millions upon millions of middle-class Americans. Living out in the suburbs, . . . [we find it] easy to assume that ours is, indeed, an affluent society.

This new segregation of poverty is compounded by a well-meaning ignorance. A good many concerned and sympathetic Americans are aware that there is much discussion of urban renewal.[14] Suddenly, driving through the city, they notice that a familiar slum has been torn down and that there are towering, modern buildings where once there had been tenements or hovels. There is a warm feeling of satisfaction, of pride in the way things are working out: the poor, it is obvious, are being taken care of.

The irony in this . . . is that the truth is nearly the exact opposite to the impression. The total impact of the various housing programs in postwar America has been to squeeze more and more people into existing slums. . . . During the past decade and a half, there has been more subsidization[15] of middle- and upper income housing than there has been of housing for the poor.

Clothes make the poor invisible too: America has the best-dressed poverty the world has ever known. For a variety of reasons, the benefits of mass production have been spread much more evenly in this area than in many others. It is much easier in the United States to be decently dressed than it is to be decently housed, fed, or doctored. Even people with terribly depressed incomes can look prosperous.

This is an extremely important factor in defining our emotional and existential ignorance of poverty. In Detroit the existence of social classes became much more difficult to discern the day the companies put lockers in the plants. From that moment on, one did not see men in work clothes on the way to the factory, but citizens in slacks and white shirts. This process has been magnified . . . throughout the country. There are tens of thousands of Americans in the big cities who are wearing shoes, perhaps even a stylishly cut suit or dress, and yet are hungry. It is not a matter of planning, though it almost seems as if the affluent society had given out costumes to the poor so that they would not offend the rest of society with the sight of rags.

Then, many of the poor are the wrong age to be seen. A good number of them (over 8 million) are sixty-five years of age or better; an even larger number

[14]Urban renewal — improvement of housing and living conditions in the city.

[15]Subsidization — financial aid from the government for an individual or group.

are under eighteen. The aged members of the other America are often sick, and they cannot move. Another group of them live out their lives in loneliness and frustration: they sit in rented rooms, or else they stay close to a house in a neighborhood that has completely changed from the old days. Indeed, one of the worst aspects of poverty among the aged is that these people are out of sight and out of mind,[16] and alone.

The young are somewhat more visible, yet they too stay close to their neighborhoods. Sometimes they advertise their poverty through a lurid tabloid story[17] about a gang killing. But generally they do not disturb the quiet streets of the middle class.

And finally, the poor are politically invisible. It is one of the cruelest ironies of social life in advanced countries that the dispossessed[18] at the bottom of society are unable to speak for themselves. The people of the other America do not, by far and large, belong to unions, to fraternal organizations, or to political parties. They are without lobbies[19] of their own; they put forward no legislative program. As a group, they are atomized.[20] They have no face; they have no voice.

Thus, there is not even a cynical political motive for caring about the poor, as in the old days. Because the slums are no longer centers of powerful political organizations, the politicians need not really care about their inhabitants. The slums are no longer visible to the middle class, so much of the idealistic urge to fight for those who need help is gone. Only the social agencies have a really direct involvement with the other America, and they are without any great political power.

To the extent that the poor have a spokesman in American life, that role is played by the labor movement. The unions[21] have their own particular idealism: an ideology of concern. More than that, they realize that the existence of a reservoir of cheap, unorganized labor is a menace to wages and working conditions throughout the entire economy. Thus, many union legislative proposals— to extend the coverage of minimum-wage [laws] and Social Security,[22] to organize migrant farm laborers—articulate the needs of the poor.

---

[16] Out of sight and out of mind — neither seen nor thought about.

[17] Lurid tabloid story — a sensational story published in a newspaper that specialized in such news.

[18] The dispossessed — people who have been deprived of basic needs.

[19] Lobbies — organized groups which hire representatives to influence legislation benefiting the particular group.

[20] Atomized — separated; isolated from other groups.

[21] Unions — labor unions. Organizations which represent and bargain for the interests of groups of workers.

[22] Social Security — system administered by the United States government by which the employer and employee are required to contribute to a Social Security fund. When an employee retires, he or she is then guaranteed a certain monthly income for the rest of his or her life.

That the poor are invisible is one of the most important things about them. They are not simply neglected and forgotten as in the old rhetoric[23] of reform; what is much worse, they are not seen.

Forty to 50 million people are becoming increasingly invisible. That is a shocking fact. But there is a second basic irony of poverty that is equally important: if one is to make the mistake of being born poor, he should choose a time when the majority of the people are miserable too.

J.K. Galbraith develops this idea in *The Affluent Society* and, in doing so, defines the "newness" of the kind of poverty in contemporary America. The old poverty, Galbraith notes, was general. It was the condition of life of an entire society, or at least of that huge majority who were without special skills or the luck of birth. When the entire economy advanced, a good many of these people gained higher standards of living. Unlike the poor today, the majority poor of a generation ago were an immediate (if cynical) concern of political leaders. The old slums of the immigrants had the votes; they provided the basis for labor organizations; their very numbers would be a powerful force in political conflict. At the same time the new technology required higher skills, more education, and stimulated an upward movement for millions.

Perhaps the most dramatic case of the power of the majority poor took place in the 1930s. The Congress of Industrial Organizations [CIO] literally organized millions in a matter of years. A labor movement that had been declining and confined to a thin stratum of the highly skilled suddenly embraced masses of men and women in basic industry. At the same time this acted as a pressure upon the government, and the New Deal codified some of the social gains in laws like the Wagner Act. The result was not a basic transformation of the American system, but it did transform the lives of an entire section of the population.

In the 1930s one of the reasons for these advances was that misery was general. There was no need then to write books about unemployment and poverty. That was the decisive social experience of the entire society, and the apple-sellers even invaded Wall Street. There was political sympathy from middle-class reformers; there was an acute *élan*[24] and spirit that grew out of a deep crisis.

Some of those who advanced in the 1930s did so because they had unique and individual personal talents. But for the great mass, it was a question of being at the right point in the economy at the right time in history, and utilizing that position for [a] common struggle. Some of those who failed did so because they did not have the will to take advantage of new opportunities. But for the most part the poor who were left behind had been at the wrong place in the economy at the wrong moment in history.

---

[23]Rhetoric — the style and form of literature or public speaking. As used here, it implies empty talk about a problem, while nothing is done to solve it.

[24]*Élan* — enthusiasm; style (French word).

These were the people in the unorganizable jobs, in the South, in the minority groups, in the fly-by-night[25] factories that were low on capital and high on labor. When some of them did break into the economic mainstream—when, for instance, the CIO opened up the way for some Negroes to find good industrial jobs—they proved to be as resourceful as anyone else. . . . [The] Americans who stayed behind were not . . . primarily . . . individual failures; rather, they were victims of an impersonal process that selected some for progress and discriminated against others.

Out of the 1930s came the welfare state.[26] Its creation had been stimulated by mass impoverishment and misery, yet it helped the poor least of all. Laws like unemployment compensation, the Wagner Act, the various farm programs—all these were designed for the middle third in the cities, for the organized workers, and for the upper third in the country, for the big market farmers. If a man works in an extremely low-paying job, he may not even be covered by Social Security or other welfare programs. If he receives unemployment compensation, the payment is scaled down according to his low earnings.

One of the major laws that was designed to cover everyone, rich and poor, was Social Security. But even here the other Americans suffered discrimination. Over the years Social Security payments have not even provided a subsistence level of life. The middle third have been able to supplement the federal pension through private plans negotiated by unions, through joining [such] medical-insurance schemes . . . [as] Blue Cross,[27] and so on. The poor have not been able to do so. They lead a bitter life, and then have to pay for that fact in old age.

Indeed, the paradox that the welfare state benefits those least who need help most is but a single instance of a persistent irony in the other America. Even when the money finally trickles down—even when a school is built in a poor neighborhood, for instance—the poor are still deprived. Their entire environment, their life, their values, do not prepare them to take advantage of the new opportunity. The parents are anxious for the children to go to work; the pupils are pent up,[28] waiting for the moment when their education has complied with the law.

Today's poor, in short, missed the political and social gains of the 1930s. They are, as Galbraith rightly points out, the first minority poor in history, the first poor not to be seen, the first poor whom the politicians could leave alone.

The first step toward the new poverty was taken when millions of people proved immune to progress. When that happened, the failure was not individual and personal, but a social product. But once the historic accident takes place, it begins to become a personal fate.

---

[25] Fly-by-night — short-lasting; unreliable.

[26] Welfare state — a social system in which the state, or government, takes primary responsibility for the welfare of its citizens.

[27] Blue Cross — a medical insurance system.

[28] Pent up — restricted, with energy waiting to break loose.

The new poor of the other America saw the rest of society move ahead. They went on living in depressed areas, and often they tended to become depressed human beings. In some of the West Virginia towns, for instance, an entire community will become shabby and defeated. The young and the adventurous go to the city, leaving behind those who cannot move and those who lack the will to do so. The entire area becomes permeated with failure, and that is one more reason the big corporations shy away.[29]

Indeed, one of the most important things about the new poverty is that it cannot be defined in simple, statistical terms. . . . If a group has internal vitality, a will—if it has aspiration—it may live in dilapidated housing, it may . . . [have] an inadequate diet, and it may suffer poverty, but it is not impoverished. So it was in those ethnic slums[30] of the immigrants that played such a dramatic role in the unfolding of the American dream. The people found themselves in slums, but they were not slum-dwellers.

But the new poverty is constructed so as to destroy aspiration; it is a system designed to be impervious to hope. The other America does not contain the adventurous seeking a new life and land. It is populated by the failures, by those driven from the land and bewildered by the city, by old people suddenly confronted with the torments of loneliness and poverty, and by minorities facing a wall of prejudice.

In the past, when poverty was general in the unskilled and semiskilled work force, the poor were all mixed together. The bright and the dull, those who were going to escape into the great society and those who were to stay behind, all of them lived on the same street. When the middle third rose, this community was destroyed. And the entire invisible land of the other Americans became a ghetto, a modern poor farm for the rejects of society and of the 'economy.

It is a blow to reform and the political hopes of the poor that the middle class no longer understands that poverty exists. But, perhaps more important, the poor are losing their links with the great world. If statistics and sociology can measure a feeling as delicate as loneliness . . . , the other America is becoming increasingly populated by those who do not belong to anybody or anything. They are no longer participants in an ethnic culture from the old country; they are less and less religious; they do not belong to unions or clubs. They are not seen, and because of that they themselves cannot see. Their horizon has become more and more restricted; they see one another, and that means they see little reason to hope.

Galbraith was one of the first writers to begin to describe the newness of contemporary poverty, and that is to his credit. Yet because even he underestimates the problem, it is important to put his definition into perspective.

For Galbraith, there are two main components of the new poverty: case poverty and insular poverty. Case poverty is the plight of those who suffer from some physical or mental disability that is personal and individual and excludes

---

[29] Shy away — to avoid.

[30] Ethnic slums — poor areas of cities where people of the same nationality live crowded together.

them from the general advance. Insular poverty exists in areas like the Appalachians or the West Virginia coal fields, where an entire section of the country becomes economically obsolete.

Physical and mental disabilities are, to be sure, an important part of poverty in America. The poor are sick in body and in spirit. But this is not an isolated fact about them, an individual "case," a stroke of bad luck.[31] Disease, alcoholism, low IQ's[32]—these express a whole way of life. They are, in the main, the effects of an environment, not the biographies of unlucky individuals. Because of this, the new poverty is something that cannot be dealt with by first aid. If there is to be a lasting assault on the shame of the other America, it must seek to root out of this society an entire environment, and not just the relief of individuals.

But perhaps the idea of insular poverty is even more dangerous. To speak of "islands" of the poor (or, in the more popular term, of "pockets of poverty") is to imply that one is confronted by a serious, but relatively minor, problem. This is hardly a description of a misery that extends to 40 million or 50 million people in the United States. They have remained impoverished in spite of increasing productivity and the creation of a welfare state. That fact alone should suggest the dimensions of a serious and basic situation.

And yet, even given these disagreements with Galbraith, his achievement is considerable. He was one of the first to understand that there are enough poor people in the United States to constitute a subculture[33] of misery, but not enough of them to challenge the conscience and the imagination of the nation.

Finally, one might summarize the newness of contemporary poverty by saying: these are the people who are immune to[34] progress. But then the facts are even more cruel. The other Americans are the victims of the very inventions and machines that have provided a higher living standard for the rest of the society. They are upside-down in the economy, and for them greater productivity often means worse jobs; agricultural advance becomes hunger.

In the optimistic theory, technology is an undisguised blessing. A general increase in productivity, the argument goes, generates a higher standard of living for the whole people. And indeed, this has been true for the middle and upper thirds of American society, the people who made such striking gains in the last two decades. It tends to overstate the automatic character of the process, to omit the role of human struggle. (The CIO was organized by men in conflict, not by economic trends.) Yet it states a certain truth—for those who are lucky enough to participate in it.

But the poor, if they were given to theory, might argue the exact opposite. They might say: progress is misery.

---

[31] A stroke of bad luck — an accident; a blow of fate.

[32] Low IQ's — low intelligence quotients. The IQ test is a standardized test designed to measure a person's intelligence.

[33] Subculture — a smaller culture, or cultural group, existing within a larger one.

[34] Immune to — unaffected by.

As the society . . . [becomes] more technological, more skilled, those who learn to work the machines, who get expanding education, move up. Those who miss out at the very start find themselves at a new disadvantage. A generation ago in American life, the majority of the working people did not have high school educations. But at that time industry was organized on a lower level of skill and competence. And there was a sort of continuum in the shop: the youth who left school at sixteen could begin as a laborer, and gradually pick up skill as he went along.

Today the situation is quite different. The good jobs require much more academic preparation, much more skill from the very outset. Those who lack a high school education tend to be condemned to the economic underworld—to low-paying service industries, to backward factories, to sweeping and janitorial duties. If the fathers and mothers of the contemporary poor were penalized a generation ago for their lack of schooling, their children will suffer all the more. The very rise in productivity that created more money and better working conditions for the rest of the society can be a menace to the poor.

But then this technological revolution might have an even more disastrous consequence: it could increase the ranks of the poor as well as intensify the disabilities of poverty. At this point it is too early to make any final judgment, yet there are obvious danger signals. There are millions of Americans who live just the other side of poverty. When a recession[35] comes, they are pushed onto the relief rolls.[36] (Welfare payments in New York respond almost immediately to any economic decline.) If automation continues to inflict more and more penalties on the unskilled and the semiskilled, it could have the impact of permanently increasing the population of the other America.

Even more explosive is the possibility that people who participated in the gains of the 1930s and the 1940s will be pulled back down into poverty. Today the mass-production industries where unionization made such a difference are contracting. Jobs are being destroyed. In the process, workers who had achieved a certain level of wages, who had won [good] working conditions in the shop, are suddenly confronted with impoverishment. This is particularly true for anyone over forty years of age and for members of minority groups. Once their job[s are] . . . abolished, their chances of ever getting similar work are very slim.

It is too early to say whether or not this phenomenon is temporary, or whether it represents a massive retrogression that will swell the numbers of the poor. To a large extent, the answer to this question will be determined by the political response of the United States. . . . If serious and massive action is not undertaken, it may be necessary for statisticians to add some old-fashioned, prewelfare-state poverty to the misery of the other America.

Poverty . . . is invisible and it is new, and both these factors make it more tenacious. It is more isolated and politically powerless than ever before. It is

---

[35]Recession — period of mild economic decline, less severe than a depression.

[36]Relief rolls — lists of those people who are on relief, receiving unemployment or welfare payments from state or city governments.

laced with[37] ironies, not the least of which is that many of the poor view progress upside-down—as a menace and a threat to their lives. And if the nation does not measure up to the challenge of automation, poverty might be on the increase.

II

There are mighty historical and economic forces that keep the poor down; and there are human beings who help out in this grim business, many of them unwittingly. There are sociological and political reasons why poverty is not seen; and there are misconceptions and prejudices that literally blind the eyes. The latter must be understood if anyone is to make the necessary act of intellect and will so that the poor can be noticed.

Here is the most familiar version of social blindness: "The poor are that way because they are afraid of work. And anyway they all have big cars. If they were like me (or my father or my grandfather), they could pay their own way. But they prefer to live on the dole[38] and cheat the taxpayers."

This theory, usually thought of as a virtuous and moral statement, is one of the means of making it impossible for the poor ever to pay their way. There are, one must assume, citizens of the other America who choose impoverishment out of fear of work (though, writing it down, I really do not believe it). But the real explanation of why the poor are where they are is that they made the mistake of being born to the wrong parents, in the wrong section of the country, in the wrong industry, or in the wrong racial or ethnic group. Once that mistake has been made, they could have been paragons of will and morality, but most of them would never even have had a chance to get out of the other America.

There are two important ways of saying this: the poor are caught in a vicious circle; or: the poor live in a culture of poverty.

In a sense, one might define the contemporary poor in the United States as those who, for reasons beyond their control, cannot help themselves. All the most decisive factors making for opportunity and advance are against them. They are born going downward, and most of them stay down. They are victims whose lives are endlessly blown round and round the other America.

Here is one of the most familiar forms of the vicious circle of poverty. The poor get sick more than anyone else in the society. That is because they live in slums, jammed together under unhygienic conditions; they have inadequate diets, and cannot get decent medical care. When they become sick, they are sick longer than any other group in the society. Because they are sick more often and longer than anyone else, they lose wages and work, and find it difficult to hold a steady job. And because of this, they cannot pay for good housing, for a nutritious diet, for doctors. At any given point in the [cycle], particularly when there is a major illness, their prospect is to move to an even lower level and to begin the cycle, round and round, toward even more suffering.

---

[37]Laced with — interwoven with. Here, meaning that irony is closely tied in with the situation of poverty.

[38]On the dole — receiving welfare payments instead of working.

This is only one example of the vicious circle. Each group in the other America has its own particular version of the exeprience, . . . but the pattern, whatever its variations, is basic to the other America.

The individual cannot usually break out of this vicious circle. Neither can the group, for it lacks the social energy and political strength to turn its misery into a cause. Only the larger society, with its help and resources, can really make it possible for these people to help themselves. Yet those who could make the difference too often refuse to act because of their ignorant, smug moralisms. They view the effects of poverty—above all, the warping of the will and spirit that is a consequence of being poor—as choices. Understanding the vicious circle is an important step in breaking down this prejudice.

There is an even richer way of describing this same, general idea: poverty in the United States is a culture, an institution, a way of life.

There is a famous anecdote about Ernest Hemingway and F. Scott Fitzgerald. Fitzgerald is reported to have remarked to Hemingway: "The rich are different." And Hemingway replied: "Yes, they have money." Fitzgerald had much the better of the exchange. He understood that being rich was not a simple fact, like a large bank account, but a way of looking at reality—a series of attitudes, a special type of life. If this is true of the rich, it is ten times truer of the poor. Everything about them—from the condition of their teeth to the way in which they love—is suffused and permeated by the fact of their poverty. And this is sometimes a hard idea for a Hemingway-like middle-class America to comprehend.

The family structure of the poor, for instance, is different from that of the rest of the society. There are more homes without a father, there is less marriage, more early pregnancy, and—if Kinsey's[39] statistical findings can be used— markedly different attitudes toward sex. As a result of this, to take but one consequence of the fact, hundreds of thousands—and perhaps millions—of children in the other America never know stability and "normal" affection.

Or perhaps the policeman is an even better example. For the middle class, the police protect property, give directions, and help old ladies. For the urban poor, the police are those who arrest you. In almost any slum there is a vast conspiracy against the forces of law and order. If someone approaches asking for a person, no one there will have heard of him, even if he lives next door. The outsider is "cop," bill collector, investigator (and, in the Negro ghetto, most dramatically, he is "the Man").

While writing this book, I was arrested for participation in a civil-rights demonstration. A brief experience of a night in a cell made an abstraction personal and immediate: the city jail is one of the basic institutions of the other America. Almost everyone whom I encountered in the "tank" was poor: skid-row whites, Negroes, Puerto Ricans. Their poverty was an incitement to arrest in the first place. (A policeman will be much more careful with a well-dressed, obviously educated man who might have political connections than he will with

---

[39]Kinsey — Alfred Kinsey, who did research into sexual behavior.

someone who is poor.) They did not have money for bail[40] or for lawyers. And, perhaps most important, they [a]waited their arraignment[41] with stolidity, in a mood of passive acceptance. They expected the worst, and they probably got it.

There is, in short, a language of the poor, a psychology of the poor, a world view of the poor. To be impoverished is to be an internal alien, to grow up in a culture that is radically different from the one that dominates the society. The poor can be described statistically; they can be analyzed as a group. But they need a novelist as well as a sociologist if we are to see them. They need an American Dickens to record the smell and texture and quality of their lives. The cycles and trends, the massive forces, must be seen as affecting persons who talk and think differently.

. . . I work on an assumption that cannot be proved by government figures or even documented by impressions of the other America. It is an ethical proposition, and it can be simply stated: in a nation with a technology that could provide every citizen with a decent life, it is an outrage and a scandal that there should be such social misery. Only if one begins with this assumption is it possible to pierce through the invisibility of 40 million to 50 million human beings and to see the other America. We must perceive passionately, if this blindness is to be lifted from us. A fact can be rationalized and explained away; an indignity cannot.

What shall we tell the American poor, once we have seen them? Shall we say to them that they are better off than the Indian poor, the Italian poor, the Russian poor? That is one answer, but it is heartless. I should put it another way. I want to tell every well-fed and optimistic American that it is intolerable that so many millions should be maimed[42] in body and in spirit when it is not necessary that they should be. My standard of comparison is not how much worse things used to be. It is how much better they could be if only we were stirred.

☆ FOLLOW-UP QUESTIONS

I.   Harrington states that after having proved to his satisfaction that there were about fifty million poor in the United States, he nevertheless did not believe his own figures.

    A.   Why does he say his response was typical of what is happening in American society?

    B.   What does he mean by "the other America"?

    C.   How does the "ordinary tourist" avoid seeing poverty?

---

[40]Bail — security, usually an amount of money, given for the release from prison of a person who has been arrested and is awaiting trial. The money is offered as a guarantee that the arrested man will appear for trial.

[41]Arraignment — the act of being arraigned, or being brought before a court to answer the formal charge of a crime.

[42]Maimed — severely crippled.

D.   How do myths and natural beauty obscure poverty?

E.   In what ways has the development of the American city isolated the poor from everyone else? Is this situation true in other countries? Can you give any examples?

F.   Why do clothes make the poor "invisible"? Is this kind of "invisibility" of the poor widespread in your country?

G.   Harrington states that "many of the poor are the wrong age to be seen." Why?

H.   What does he mean by the statement, "As a group, the poor are atomized"?

I.   According to the writer, why has the labor movement been the only "spokesman" for the poor?

II. Harrington makes a comparison between the poor of the 1950s and the poor of a generation before.

A.   How does the poverty of contemporary America differ from "the old poverty"?

B.   Why were political leaders concerned with the "majority poor" of a generation ago?

C.   How did the Congress of Industrial Organizations (CIO) increase the power of the "majority poor" in the 1930s? What are some other reasons why the poor were able to advance during that time?

D.   According to Harrington, why did some people remain poor while others were progressing?

III. The writer claims that the creation of the welfare state in the 1930s "had been stimulated by mass impoverishment and misery, yet it helped the poor least of all."

A.   What are the general goals of a "welfare state"? What governments today could be considered "welfare states"?

B.   In the United States during the 1930s, who benefited from unemployment compensation and farm progress?

C.   Why have "the other Americans" suffered discrimination from the way Social Security operates?

IV. "The new poor of the other America saw the rest of society move ahead." But these "people have proved immune to progress."

A.   According to Harrington, in what ways is "the new poverty" constructed so as to "destroy aspiration"?

B.   What does he mean by the statement, "the other America is becoming increasingly populated by those who do not belong to anybody or anything"?

C.   Why are "the other Americans" victims of technology while the rest of society benefits from a general increase of productivity? In what way is there a threat that could increase the number of people belonging to "the other America"?

V.   Harrington states, "there are sociological and political reasons why poverty is not seen; and there are misconceptions and prejudices that literally blind the eyes."

A.   Describe one common theory about the poor. How does Harrington dispute the theory that "the poor are that way because they are afraid of work."

B.   What does the writer mean by "the vicious circle of poverty"?

C.   What examples does Harrington give to support his contention that poverty is "a way of looking at reality—a series of attitudes, a special type of life."

VI.   In this essay, Harrington refers to the work of another writer, J. K. Galbraith, and particularly to his widely read book, *The Affluent Society.*

    A.   Why does Harrington feel it necessary to credit Galbraith with specific ideas he discusses in "The Invisible Land"?

    B.   In what way does he disagree with Galbraith's treatment of the subject of poverty?

    C.   How are Galbraith's terms "case poverty" and "insular poverty" defined? What reasons does Harrington give for objecting to these terms?

    D.   Although he differs with him on some points, why does Harrington believe Galbraith's achievement is considerable?

    E.   Do you feel Harrington's references to a widely read book strengthen his argument? Why?

VII.   On the last page of this essay, Harrington writes, "it is an outrage and a scandal that there should be such social misery."

    A.   What other examples can you find of emotional writing in this essay?

    B.   What is Harrington's purpose in writing this essay? Do you feel his approach is strong enough to help open people's eyes? Why?

    C.   The writer states that the poor need a novelist as well as a sociologist "if we are to see them." What can a novelist achieve that a sociologist generally cannot? Can you think of any novelists who have written about the poor? About the rich? Who were they, what did they write about, and what did they achieve?

☆ THEME TOPICS

1.   Describe a work of fiction that focuses on a particular class of people. Does that writer record the smell and texture and quality of their lives? Can you give an example?

2.   Discuss an attitude (not necessarily your own) toward a particular group of people. Include your own feelings about this attitude.

3.   Discuss a social problem about which you have specific ideas. Include references to a book (or books) dealing with this problem. Support or illustrate it from your own reading.

First Views of the Enemy*
Joyce Carol Oates

INTRODUCTION

Almost everyone has experienced fear of an immediate danger. Some people, however, continuously feel anxious and uneasy. They anticipate danger which is not necessarily immediate, and may even be remote.

A. How would you calm the fears of someone who was continuously anxious about something? Do you think the statement, "It's all in your mind," would be helpful?

B. Anxiety about a speeding car can easily be justified: the car can kill you . . . However, is anxiety always restricted to fear of physical harm? What are some anxieties or fears that lead people to seek psychiatric help? Why are some people afraid of what other people think of them? Is it possible to be afraid of oneself? Why?

C. What are some ways in which people learn to be afraid of certain things? Certain groups of people? How can ignorance of other people and their different ways of life cause anxiety? Do you think the statement "fear is contagious" has any validity? Why?

D. Can you think of a situation in which you were initially afraid, but then overcame your fear? How did you accomplish this?

Just around the turn the road was alive. First to assault the eye was a profusion of heads, black-haired, bobbing, and a number of straw hats that looked oddly professional—like straw hats in a documentary film;[1] and shirts and overalls and dresses, red, yellow, beflowered, dotted, striped, some bleached by the sun, some stiff and brilliant, just bought and worn proudly out of the store. The bus in which they were traveling—a dead dark blue, colored yet without any color— was parked half on the clay road and half in the prickly high grass by the ditch. Its old-fashioned hood[2] was open, yanked[3] cruelly up and doubled on itself, and staring into its greasy, dust-flecked tangle of parts was the driver, the only fair, brown-haired one of the bunch. Annette remembered, later, that as her station

---

[1] Documentary film — a film presentation of factual, political, social, or historical events. "Documentaries" usually consist of actual news films and/or interviews, accompanied by narrative.

[2] Hood — the metal lid that covers an automobile engine and may be raised or lowered. (In British usage, "bonnet.")

[3] To yank — to pull sharply and strongly.

wagon[4] moved in astonishment toward them the driver looked up and straight at her: a big indifferent face, curious without interest, smeared with grease as if deliberately, to disguise himself. No kin of yours, lady, no kin! he warned contemptuously.

Breaking from a group of children, running with arms out for a mock embrace,[5] a boy of about seven darted right toward Annette's car. The boy's thick black hair, curled with sweat, plastered onto his forehead, framed a delicate, cruelly tanned face, a face obviously dead white beneath its tan: great dark eyes, expanded out of proportion, neat little brows like angels' brows—that unbelievable and indecent beauty of children exploited for art—a pouting mouth, still purple at the corners from the raspberries picked and hidden for the long bus ride, these lips now turning as Annette stared into a hilarious grin and crying out at her and the stricken child who cringed beside her, legs already drawn up fatly at the knees———

In agony the brakes cried, held: the scene, dizzy with color, rocked with the car, down a little, back up, giddily, helplessly, while dust exploded up on all sides. "Mommy!" Timmy screamed, fascinated by the violence, yet his wail was oddly still and drawn out, and his eyes never once turned to his mother. The little Mexican boy had disappeared in front of the car. Still the red dust arose, the faces at the bus jerked around together, white eyes, white teeth, faces were propelled toward the windows of the bus, empty a second before. "God, God," Annette murmured; she had not yet released the steering wheel, and on it her fingers began to tighten as if they might tear the wheel off, hold it up to defend her and her child, perhaps even to attack.

A woman in a colorless dress pushed out of the crowd, barefooted in the red clay, pointed her finger at Annette and shouted something—gleefully. She shook her fist, grinning, others grinned behind her; the bus driver turned back to his bus. Annette saw now the little boy on the other side of the road, popping up safe in the ditch, and jumping frantically—though the sharp weeds must have hurt his feet—and laughing, yelling, shouting as if he were insane. The air rang with shouts, with laughter. A good joke. What was the joke? Annette's brain reeled with shock, sucked for air as if drowning. Beside her Timmy wailed softly, but his eyes were fastened on the boy in the ditch. "He's safe, he's safe," Annette whispered. But others ran toward her now—big boys, tall but skinny, without shirts. How their ribs seemed to run with them, sliding up and down inside the dark tanned flesh with the effort of their legs! Even a few girls approached, hard dark faces, already aged, black hair matted and torn about their thin shoulders. They waved and cried, "Missus! Missus!" Someone even shouted, "Cadillac!"[6] though her station wagon, already a year old, was far from being a Cadillac. As if to regain attention the little boy in the ditch picked up something, a handful of pebbles, and threw it at the car, right beneath

---

[4]Station wagon — an automobile, usually rather long, with extra seats or a storage space in the rear. All storage space is visible through the car window.

[5]Mock embrace — false embrace. A gesture that appears to be an embrace but is not.

[6]Cadillac — fine, expensive American car. A symbol of luxury.

Timmy's pale gaping face. A babble of Spanish followed, more laughter, the barefoot woman who must have been the boy's mother strode mightily across the road, grabbed the boy, shook him in an extravagant mockery of punishment? sucked her lips at him, made spitting motions, rubbed his head hard with the palm of her hand — this hurt, Annette saw with satisfaction, for the child winced in spite of his bravado. At the bus the American man's back swelled damply and without concern beneath his shirt; he did not even glance around.

Annette leaned to the window, managed a smile. "Please let me through," she called. Her voice surprised her; it sounded like a voice without body or identity, channeled in over a radio.

The boys made odd gestures with their hands, not clenching them into fists, but instead striking with the edges of their hands, knife-like, into the air. Their teeth grinned and now, with them so close (the bravest were at her fender),[7] Annette could see how discolored their teeth were, though they had seemed white before. They must have been eating dirt! she thought vaguely. "Please let me through," she said. Beside her Timmy sat in terror. She wanted to reach over and put her hand over his eyes, hide this sight from him — this mob of dirty people, so hungry their tongues seemed to writhe in their mouths, their exhaustion turned to frenzy. "Missus! Missus! Si, si,[8] Cadillac!" the boys yelled, pounding on the front of the car. The women, men, even very old people — with frail white hair — watched, surprised and pleased at being entertained.

"Please. Please." Suddenly Annette pressed on the horn: what confidence that sound inspired! The boys hesitated, moved back. She toyed with[9] the accelerator, wanting to slam down on it, to escape. But suppose one of them were in the way. . . . The horor of that falling thud, the vision of blood sucked into red clay, stilled her nervousness, made her inch the big car forward slowly, slowly. And in the back those unmistakable bags of groceries, what would be showing at the tops? Maybe tomatoes, pears, strawberries — perhaps picked by these people a few days ago — maybe bread, maybe meat — Annette's face burned with something more than shame. But when she spoke her voice showed nothing. "Let me through, please. Let me through." She sounded cool and still.

Then she was past. The station wagon picked up speed. Behind her were yells, cries no longer gleeful, now insulting, vicious: in the mirror fists, shouting faces, the little boy running madly into the cloud of dust behind the car. He jerked something back behind his head, his skinny elbow swung, and with his entire body he sent a mudrock after the car which hit the back window square,[10] hard, and exploded. With her fingers still frozen to the steering wheel Annette sped home.

Beside her the child, fascinated, watched the familiar road as if seeing it for the first time. That tender smile was something strange; Annette did not like it.

---

[7]Fender — metal part covering the wheels of an automobile.

[8]Si, si. — yes, yes. (Spanish)

[9]To toy with — to play with.

[10]Square — direct.

Annette herself, twitching with fear, always a nervous woman, electric[11] as the harassed or the insanely ill are, saw with shock that her face in the mirror was warm and possessed. That was she, then, and not this wild, heart-thumping woman, afraid of those poor children in the road. . . . Her eyes leaped home; her mind anticipated its haven. Already, straightening out of a turn, she could see it: the long, low, orange-brick home, trees behind the house not yet big enough for shade, young trees, a young house, a young family. Cleared out of the acres of wheat and wood and grass fields on either side, a surprise to someone driving by, looking for all the world as if it and its fine light-green grass, so thin as to look unreal, and its Hercules fence[12] had been picked up somewhere far away and dropped down here. Two miles away, on the highway which paralleled this road, there were homes something like this, but on this road there were only, a half-mile ahead, a few farmhouses, typical, some shacks deserted and not deserted, and even a gas station and store; otherwise nothing. Annette felt for the first time the insane danger of this location, and heard with magical accuracy her first question when her husband had suggested it: "But so far out. . . . Why do you want it so far out?" City children, both of them, the hot rich smell of sunlight and these soundless distances had never been forbidding, isolating. Instead each random glance at the land strengthened in them a sense of their own cleverness. Children of fortune, to withdraw from their comfortable pasts, to raise a child in such safety!—It was fifteen miles to the nearest town, where Annette did her shopping and Timmy went to school, and forty miles to the city where her husband worked.

Annette turned into the driveway, drove slowly into the garage. Still in a trance, angry at herself, she got out of the car but stood with her hand still lingering on the steering wheel. A thin, fashionably thin young woman, for years more woman than girl, in a white dress she stood with a remote, vague smile, hand lightly on the wheel, mind enticed by something she could not name. Perplexed, incredulous: in spite of the enormity of what threatened (the migrant workers[13] were hardly a mile away) she felt slowed and meaningless. Her inertia touched even Timmy, who usually jumped out of the car and slammed the door. If only he would do this, and she could cry, "Timmy! *Please!*" calm might be restored. But no, he climbed down on his side like a little old man; he pushed the door back indifferently so that it gave a feeble click and did not even close all the way. For a while mother and son stood on opposite sides of the car; Annette could tell that Timmy did not move and was not even looking at her. Then his footsteps began. He ran out of the garage.

Annette was angry. Only six, he understood her, he knew what was to come next: he was to help her with the packages, with the doors, open the cupboards in the kitchen, he would be in charge of putting things into the

---

[11]Electric — tense; with energy.

[12]Hercules fence — a strong metal fence.

[13]Migrant workers — farm workers who travel from one section of the country to another, harvesting crops as they ripen. Migrant workers in the southwestern United States are generally of Mexican origin. For the most part, they receive low wages and live in substandard housing.

refrigerator. As if stricken by a sudden bad memory Annette stood in the garage, waiting for her mind to clear. What was there in Timmy's running out? For an instant she felt betrayed—as if he cherished the memory of that strange little boy, and ran out to keep it from her. She remembered the early days of her motherhood, how contemptuous she had been of herself, of what she had accomplished—a baby she refused to look at, a husband neurotic with worry, a waiting life of motherhood so oppressive that she felt nausea contemplating it: Is this what I have become? What is this baby to me? Where am I? Where as *I*? Impassioned, a month out of college and fearful, in spite of her attractiveness, that she would never be married, Annette had taken the dangerous gamble of tearing aside her former life, rejecting the familiar possessions and patterns that had defined her, and had plunged, with that intense confident sharp-voiced young man, into a new life she was never quite sure had not betrayed the old, stricken the old: her parents, her lovely mother, now people to write to, send greeting cards to, hint vaguely at visiting. . . .

Sighing, she began to move. She took the packages out of the car, went outside (the heat was now brilliant), put them down and, with deft angry motions in case Timmy was secretly watching, pulled down the garage door and locked it. "There!" But when she turned, her confidence was distracted. She stared at the house. Shrubbery hiding the concrete slab—basements were not necessary this far south—rosebushes bobbing roses, vulnerable, insanely gaudy, the great picture window[14] that made her think, always, someone was slyly watching her, even the faint professional sweep of grass[15] out to the road—all these in their elaborate planned splendor shouted mockery at her, mockery at themselves, as if they were safe from destruction! Annette fought off the inertia again; it passed close by her, a whiff of something like death, the same darkness that had bothered her in the hospital, delivered of her child. She left the packages against the garage (though the ice cream in its special package might be melting) and, awkward in her high heels, hurried out the drive. She shielded her eyes: nothing in sight down the road. It was a red clay road, a country road that would never be paved, and she and her husband had at first taken perverse pride in[16] it. But it turned so, she had never noticed that before, and great bankings of foliage hid it, disguised its twistings, so that she could see not more than a quarter mile away. Never before had the land seemed so *flat*.

She hurried. At the gate the sun caught up with her, without ceremony. She struggled to swing the gate around (a few rusty, loosened prongs had caught in the grass); she felt perspiration breaking out on her body, itching and prickling her, under her arms, on her back. The white dress must have hung damp and wrinkled about her legs. Panting with the exertion, she managed to get the gate loose and drag it around; it tilted down at a jocose[17] angle, scraping the gravel; then she saw that there was no lock, she would need a padlock, there was one in

---

[14]Picture window — large window not divided into individual panes; offers a good view.

[15]Professional sweep of grass — the carefully planned curve of the grass, looking as if it were designed by a landscape architect.

[16]To take perverse pride in — to be proud of something most people would be ashamed of.

the garage somewhere, and in the same instant, marvelling at her stamina, she turned back.

Hurrying up the drive, she thought again of the little Mexican boy. She saw his luxurious face, that strange unhealthy grin inside his embracing arms—it sped toward her. Cheeks drawn in as if by age, eyes protruding with—it must have been hunger—dirty hands like claws reaching out, grabbing, demanding what? What would they demand of her? If they were to come and shout for her out in the road, if she were to offer them—something—milk, maybe, the chocolate cookies Timmy loved so, maybe even money? would they go away, then, would they thank her and run back to their people? Would they continue their trip north, headed for Oregon and Washington? What would happen? Violence worried the look of the house, dizzied Annette: there were the yellow roses she tended so fondly, rich and sprawling against the orange brick. In the sunlight their petals, locked intricately inside one another, were vivid, glaringly detailed, as if their secret life were swelling up in rage at her for having so endangered their beauty.

There the packages lay against the garage, and seeing them Annette forgot about the padlock. She stooped and picked them up. When she turned again she saw Timmy standing just inside the screen door. "Timmy, open the—" she said, vexed, but he had already disappeared. Inside the kitchen she slammed the bags down, fought back the impulse to cry, stamped one heel on the linoleum so hard that her foot buzzed with pain. "Timmy," she said, her eyes shut tight, "come out in this kitchen."

He appeared, carrying a comic book.[18] That was for the look of it, of course; he had not been reading. His face was wary. Fair like his mother, blond-toned, smart for his age, he had still about his quiet plump face something that belonged to field animals, wood animals, shrewd, secret creatures that have little to say for themselves. He read the newspaper, like his father, cultivated the same thoughtful expression; encouraged, he talked critically about his school-teacher with a precocity that delighted his father, frightened Annette (to her, even now, teachers were somehow *different* from other people); he had known the days of the week, months of the year, continents of the world, planets of the solar system, major star groupings of the universe, at an astonishing age—as a child he approached professional perfection. But Annette, staring at him, was not sure, now, that she could trust him. What if, when the shouting began outside, when "Missus! Missus!" demanded her, Timmy ran out to them, joined them, stared back at her in the midst of their white eyes and dirty arms? They stared at each other as if this question had been voiced.

"You almost killed him," Timmy said.

His voice was soft. Its innocence showed that he knew how daring he was; his eyes as well, neatly fringed by pale lashes, trembled slightly in their gaze. "What?" said Annette. "What?"

---

[17]Jocose — cheerful; humorous.

[18]Comic book — a booklet of cartoons telling a continuous story. These stories may be comic, or violent and sensational.

The electric clock, built into the big white range,[19] whirred in the silence. Timmy swallowed, rustled his comic book, pretended to wipe his nose—a throwback to a habit long outgrown, hoping to mislead her—and looked importantly at the clock. "*He* hit the car. Two times," he said.

This was spoken differently. The ugly spell was over. "Yes, he certainly did," Annette said. She was suddenly busy. "He certainly did." After a moment Timmy put down the comic book to help her. They worked easily, in silence. Eyes avoided one another. But Annette felt feverishly excited; something had been decided, strengthened. Timmy, stooping to put vegetables in the bottom of the refrigerator, felt her staring at him and peered up, his little eyebrows raised in a classic look of wonder. "You going to call Daddy?" he said. Annette had been thinking of this but when Timmy suggested it, it was exposed for what it was—a child's idea. "That won't be necessary," she said. She folded bags noisily and righteously.

When they finished mother and son wandered without enthusiasm into the dining room, into the living room, as if they did not really want to leave the kitchen. Annette's eyes flinched at what she saw: crystal, polished wood, white walls, aqua lampshades, white curtains, sand-toned rug, detailed, newly cleaned, spreading regally across the room—surely no one ever walked on that rug! That was what they would say if they saw it. And the glassware off in the corner, spear-like, transparent green, a great window behind it, linking it with the green grass outside, denying a barrier, inviting in sunlight, wind, anyone's eyes approaching—Annette went to the window and pulled the draw drapes shut; that was better; she breathed gently, coaxed by the beauty of those drapes into a smile: they were white, perfectly hung, sculptured superbly in generous swelling curves. And fireproof, if it came to that. . . . Annette turned. Timmy stood before the big red swivel chair as if he were going to sit in it—he did not—and looked at her with such a queer, pinched expression, in spite of his round face, that Annette felt a sudden rush of shame. She was too easily satisfied, too easily deluded. In all directions her possessions stretched out about her, defining her, identifying her, and they were vulnerable and waiting, the dirt road led right to them; and she could be lured into smiling! That must be why Timmy looked at her so strangely. "I have something to do," she murmured, and went back to the dining room. The window there was open; she pulled it down and locked it. She went to the wall control and turned on the air conditioning. "Run, honey, and close the windows," she said. "In your room."

She went into the bedroom, closed the windows there and locked them. Outside there was nothing—smooth lawn, lawn furniture (fire-engine red) grouped casually together, as if the chairs made of tubing and spirals were having a conversation. Annette went into the bathroom, locked that window, avoided her gaze in the mirror, went, at last, into the "sewing room," which faced the road, and stood for a while staring out the window. She had never liked the color of that clay, really—it stretched up from Louisiana to Kentucky,

---

[19]Range — gas or electric stove.

sometimes an astonishing blood-red, pulsating with heat. Now it ran watery in the sunlight at the bend. Nothing there. Annette waited craftily. But still nothing. She felt that, as soon as she turned away, the first black spots would appear—coarse black hair—and the first splashes of color; but she could not wait. There was too much yet to do.

She found Timmy in the living room again, still not sitting in the chair. "I'll be right back, darling," she said. "Stay here. It's too hot outside for you. Put on the television—Mommy will be right back."

She got the clipping shears out of the closet and went outside, still teetering[20] in her high heels. There was no time to waste, no time. The yellow rosebush was farthest away, but most important. She clipped roses off, a generous amount of stem. Though hurried—every few seconds she had to stare down the road—she took time to clip off some leaves as well. Then she went to the red bushes, which now exclaimed at her ignorance: she could see they were more beautiful, really, than the yellow roses. Red more beautiful than yellow; yellow looked common, not stunning enough against the house. It took her perhaps ten minutes, and even then she had to tear her eyes away from the lesser flowers, over there in the circular bed; she did not have time for them—unaccountably she was angry at them, as if they had betrayed her already, grateful to the migrant workers who were coming to tear them to pieces! Their small stupid faces nodded in the hot wind.

Timmy awaited her in the kitchen. He looked surprised at all the roses. "The big vase," she commanded. In a flurry of activity, so pleased by what she was doing that she did not notice the dozens of bleeding scratches on her hands, she laid the roses on the cupboard, clipped at leaves, arranged them, took down a slender copper vase and filled it with water, forced some roses in, abandoned it when Timmy came in with the milk-glass vase (wedding present from a remote aunt of hers). The smell of roses filled the kitchen, sweetly drugged Annette's anxiety. Beauty, beauty—it was necessary to have beauty, to possess it, to keep it around oneself! How well she understood that now.

Finished abruptly, she left the refuse on the cupboard and brought the vases into the living room. She stood back from them, peered critically . . . saw a stain on the wood of the table already; she must have spilled some water. And the roses were not arranged well, too heavy, too many flowers, an insane jumble of flowered faces, some facing each other nose to nose, some staring down toward the water in the vase in an indecent way, some at the ceiling, some at Annette herself. But there was no time to worry over them, already new chores called to her, demanded her services. What should she do next?—The answer hit her like a blow, how could she be so stupid? The doors were not even locked! Staggered by this, she ran to the front door, with trembling fingers locked it. How could she have overlooked this? Was something in her, some secret corner, conspiring with the Mexicans down the road? She ran stumbling to the back door—that had even been left open, it could have been seen from the road! A few flies buzzed idly, she had no time for them. When she appeared, panting, in the

---

[20]Teetering — moving uncertainly, finding it difficult to get balance.

doorway she saw Timmy by the big white vase trying to straighten the flowers. . . . "Timmy," she said sharply. "You'll scratch yourself. Go away, go into the other room, watch television."

He turned at once but did not look at her. She watched him and felt, then, that it was a mistake to speak that way to him—in fact, a deliberate error, like forgetting about the doors; might not her child be separated from her if they came, trapped in the other room? "No, no, Timmy," she said, reaching out for him—he looked around, frightened—"no, come here. Come here." He came slowly. His eyes showed trust; his mouth, pursed and tightened, showed wariness, fear of that trust. Annette saw all this—had she not felt the same way about him, wishing him dead as soon as he was born?—and flicked it aside, bent to embrace him. "Darling, I'll take care of you. Here. Sit here. I'll bring you something to eat."

He allowed her to help him sit at the dining-room table. He was strangely quiet, his head bowed. There was a surface mystery about that quietness! Annette thought, in the kitchen, I'll get through that, I'll prove myself to him. At first cunningly, then anxiously, she looked through the refrigerator, touching things, rearranging things, even upsetting things—a jar of pickles—and then came back carrying some strawberry tarts, made just the day before, and the basket of new strawberries, and some apples. "Here, darling," she said. But Timmy hesitated; while Annette's own mouth watered painfully he could only blink in surprise. Impatiently she said, "Here, eat it, eat them. You love them. *Here*." "No napkins," Timmy said fearfully. "Never mind napkins, or a table cloth, or plates," Annette said angrily—how slow her child seemed to her, like one of those empty-faced children she often saw along the road, country children, staring at her red car. "Here. Eat it. Eat it." When she turned to go back to the kitchen she saw him lifting one of the tarts slowly to his mouth.

She came back almost immediately—bringing the package of ice cream, two spoons, a basket of raspberries, a plate of sliced chicken, wrapped loosely in wax paper—She was overcome by hunger. She pulled a chair beside Timmy, who had not yet eaten—he stared gravely at her—and began to eat one of the tarts. It convulsed her mouth, so delicious was it, so sweet yet at the same time sour, tantalizing; she felt something like love for it, jealousy for it, and was already reaching for another when she caught sight of Timmy's stare. "Won't Daddy be home? Won't we have dinner?" he pleaded.

But he paused. His lips parted moistly and he stared at his mother, who smiled back at him, reassuring him, comforting him, pushing one of the tarts toward him with her polished nails. Then something clicked[21] in his eyes. His lips damp with new saliva, he smiled at her, relieved, pleased. As if a secret ripened to bursting between them, swollen with passion, they smiled at each other. Timmy said, before biting into the tart, "*He* can't hit the car again, it's all locked up." Annette said, gesturing at him with sticky fingers, "Here, darling. Eat this. Eat. *Eat*."

---

[21] To click — as used here, to reveal sudden comprehension of a situation.

☆ *FOLLOW-UP QUESTIONS*

I.   "First Views of the Enemy" begins with a closely detailed description of a near accident.
  A.   How are the migrant workers dressed?
  B.   Their straw hats are described as looking "oddly professional—like straw hats in a documentary film." How does this comparison heighten our sense of what these people look like? What does it tell us about Annette herself?
  C.   We are told that Annette later remembered the driver's look. "No kin of yours, lady, no kin," he seemed to say. How is he described? From whose point of view?
  D.   How does the near accident come about?
  E.   What is Annette's state of mind when she leans out the window and says, "Please let me through"?
  F.   Annette notices how "discolored their teeth were" and vaguely thinks "they must have been eating dirt." What does this explanation reveal about Annette? About the nature of her fear?
  G.   How had "the enemy" perhaps helped make the groceries available to Annette? Is this ironic in any way?

II. When she arrives home, Annette still feels threatened by the migrant workers.
  A.   Why does the location of the house disturb her?
  B.   Once home, Annette is described as "angry at herself." Why does she feel this way?
  C.   Why is Annette disappointed when Timmy doesn't jump out of the car and slam the door?
  D.   Standing in the garage, Annette tries to analyze Timmy's running out and remembers her early days of motherhood. What makes these unhappy memories come back? What are we told about Annette's fears before she was married? What information are we given about her husband?
  E.   When Annette thinks of the little Mexican boy, she envisions "dirty hands like claws reaching out, grabbing . . ." In the same paragraph, the petals of her yellow roses are described as "locked intricately inside one another . . . glaringly detailed, as if their secret life were swelling up in rage at her for having so endangered their beauty." What do these images reveal about her state of mind?
  F.   Why does her son's "precocity" frighten Annette? In what way does she imagine he could betray her? Does she have any evidence to support her distrust of the child? When does she decide not to call her husband?

III. Annette is strongly aware of the possessions that surround her existence.
  A.   What precautions does she take to safeguard her home?
  B.   Why does she clip off the roses? Is this action in any way symbolic? If so, what does it symbolize?
  C.   What sensible precaution does she remember last? Why is this particularly ironic?
  D.   Imagining "the enemy" about to invade her home, Annette envisions their appearance as "black spots." What are these black spots? Why is it significant that these people are thought of as inanimate matter?

IV. Joyce Carol Oates focuses intently on her protagonist's state of mind. Annette is revealed through the ways she reacts to what she imagines is the immediate threat of the migrant workers.

    A.   Do you, however, sense that she also has some underlying fears? If so, what else is she afraid of?

    B.   How does her sense of being betrayed relate to her fears? In what ways does Annette feel she has been betrayed? What betrayals, if any, has she been guilty of?

V.   The story ends with Annette's insistence that Timmy eat. "Here, darling. Eat this. Eat. Eat."

    A.   How does the child react at first?

    B.   Who is the first one to begin eating?

    C.   Why is their eating together before dinner somehow conspiratorial?

    D.   Before Timmy bites into the tart, what does he say?

    E.   What does this conclusion show us about the way Annette deals with her fear and guilt?

    F.   From Annette's point of view, "the enemy" are the Mexican migrant workers. Do you feel they are her real "enemy"?

    G.   Does the ending provide the reader with a definite resolution? Is there a change in the relationship between Annette and her son?

VI.   "First Views of the Enemy" is written in the third person. Annette does not tell us the story directly. For example, on the first page we read, "First to assault the eye was a profusion of heads, black-haired, bobbing . . ."

    A.   If Annette were telling the story directly in the first person (I . . .), how would the quotation read?

    B.   Though this is a third-person narrative, the story seems to be told through Annette's point of view, emerging through her feelings, observations, and memories. Which word in the quotation above most clearly indicates that it is Annette's view of the migrant workers?

    C.   What are some other examples in which Annette's point of view seems to dominate the story?

    D.   We find out almost everything about Annette: her thoughts, feelings, words, and actions. Do you feel the story would have been less effective if the writer had chosen to let us know less about the protagonist's emotions?

    E.   Does Joyce Carol Oates judge Annette? For example, does she state specifically whether Annette's treatment of her son is wrong?

☆ THEME TOPICS

1.   Describe a situation in which you (or a person you know or have read about) had to deal with people whose way of life was totally different from yours (or from that person's).

2.   Describe a moment of intense fear you have experienced. Include the circumstances that led up to the moment, and the way you coped (or didn't cope) with your fear.

3.   If you were her friend, how would you go about helping the protagonist of "First Views of the Enemy"? What questions would you ask her? What advice would you give?

The Role of the Undesirables*
Eric Hoffer

INTRODUCTION

I. Someone who rejects or is rejected by the society in which he lives may be called an undesirable. The same term is sometimes applied to groups of people.

    A. Can you think of any groups of people who are or have been treated as undesirables?

    B. What characteristics do the people in these groups have in common?

    C. Who determines whether an individual or group is undesirable?

    D. Could every criminal be called an undesirable? Why or why not?

    E. Why is a person without a home and job often considered an undesirable? Why might someone find it difficult to hold a steady job?

    F. Do some people prefer to be without permanent homes and steady jobs? If so, what reasons might they give to justify their choice? What arguments might one present in favor of the person who rejects society's values?

II. During the 1930s, the United States suffered a severe economic depression in which there was widespread unemployment and poverty. Many of the people who were out of work wandered from place to place looking for jobs. Sometimes people could find jobs as "migrant workers," picking the fruits and vegetables of different areas as they became ready for harvest.

    A. What attitudes do you think migrant workers would hold toward the more settled or established people in society?

    B. Do you think anyone might ever choose to be a migrant worker if he wasn't forced into it by economic need? Why or why not?

III. The pioneers of any new country were the first people who settled in a territory. They left their homes to go into the wilderness, often enduring great hardship. Large numbers of pioneers settled the United States, Brazil, and Australia, for example.

    A. What characteristics are generally attributed to pioneers?

    B. What are some of the reasons people became pioneers?

C. Are all pioneers motivated by a desire for land and possible wealth?

D. Do you think it likely that people who were successful and secure would deliberately leave their homes and go into the wilderness? Why or why not?

In the winter of 1934, I spent several weeks in a federal transient camp[1] in California. These camps were originally established by Governor Rolph in the early days of the Depression[2] to care for single homeless unemployed of the state. In 1934 the federal government took charge of the camps for a time, and it was then that I first heard of them.

How I happened to get into one of the camps is soon told. Like thousands of migrant agricultural workers[3] in California I then followed the crops from one part of the state to the other. Early in 1934 I arrived in the town of El Centro, in the Imperial Valley. I had been given a free ride on a truck from San Diego, and it was midnight when the truck driver dropped me on the outskirts of El Centro. I spread my bedroll by the side of the road and went to sleep. I had hardly dozed off when the rattle of a motorcycle drilled itself into my head and a policeman was bending over me saying, "Roll up,[4] mister." It looked as though I was in for something[5]; it happened now and then that the police got overzealous and rounded up the freight trains. But this time the cop[6] had no such thought. He said, "Better go over to the federal shelter and get yourself a bed and maybe some breakfast." He directed me to the place.

I found a large hall, obviously a former garage, dimly lit, and packed with cots.[7] A concert of heavy breathing shook the thick air. In a small office near the door, I was registered by a middle-aged clerk. He informed me that this was the "receiving shelter" where I would get one night's lodging and breakfast. The meal was served in the camp nearby. Those who wished to stay on, he said, had to enroll in the camp. He then gave me three blankets and excused himself for not having a vacant cot. I spread the blankets on the cement floor and went to sleep.

---

[1]Federal transient camp — a camp, or shelter, for single, homeless, and unemployed men.

[2]The Depression — the economic Depression of the 1930s, in which there was a great deal of unemployment.

[3]Migrant agricultural workers — workers who travel from place to place, planting or harvesting crops according to the season.

[4]"Roll up" — Here the policeman is asking Hoffer to roll up his bedroll, or sleeping bag.

[5]To be in for something — to be about to have an unpleasant experience.

[6]Cop — slang term meaning "policeman."

[7]Cot — folding bed.

I awoke with dawn amid a chorus of coughing, throat clearing, the sound of running water, and the intermittent flushing of toilets in the back of the hall. There were about fifty of us, of all colors and ages, all of us more or less ragged and soiled. The clerk handed out tickets for breakfast, and we filed out to the camp located several blocks away, near the railroad tracks.

From the outside the camp looked like a cross between a factory and a prison. A high fence of wire enclosed it, and inside were three large sheds and a huge boiler topped by a pillar of black smoke. Men in blue shirts and dungarees were strolling across the sandy yard. A ship's bell in front of one of the buildings announced breakfast. The regular camp members—there was a long line of them—ate first. Then we filed in through the gate, handing our tickets to the guard.

It was a good, plentiful meal. After breakfast our crowd dispersed. I heard some say that the camps in the northern part of the state were better, that they were going to catch a northbound freight. I decided to try this camp in El Centro.

My motives in enrolling were not crystal clear. I wanted to clean up. There were shower baths in the camp and wash tubs and plenty of soap. Of course I could have bathed and washed my clothes in one of the irrigation ditches, but here in the camp I had a chance to rest, get the wrinkles out of my belly,[8] and clean up at leisure. In short, it was the easiest way out.

A brief interview at the camp office and a physical examination were all the formalities for enrollment. There were some two hundred men in the camp. They were the kind I had worked and traveled with for years. I even saw familiar faces—men I had worked with in orchards and fields. Yet my predominant feeling was one of strangeness. It was my first experience of life in intimate contact with a crowd. For it is one thing to work and travel with a gang, and quite another thing to eat, sleep, and spend the greater part of the day cheek by jowl[9] with two hundred men.

I found myself speculating on a variety of subjects: the reason for their chronic belly-aching and beefing[10]—it was more a ritual than the expression of a grievance; the amazing orderliness of the men; the comic seriousness with which they took their games of cards, checkers, and dominoes; the weird manner of reasoning one overheard now and then. Why, I kept wondering, were these men within the enclosure of a federal transient camp? Were they people temporarily hard up?[11] Would jobs solve all their difficulties? Were we indeed like the people outside?

Up to then I was not aware of being one of a specific species of humanity. I had considered myself simply a human being—not particularly good or bad, and on the whole harmless. The people I worked and traveled with I knew as Americans and Mexicans, Whites and Negroes, Northerners and Southerners,

---

[8]To "get the wrinkles out of my belly" — to relax, to rest.

[9]Cheek by jowl — in crowded conditions, with little or no privacy.

[10]Belly-aching and beefing — slang terms meaning "complaining."

[11]Hard up — poor, deprived.

etc. It did not occur to me that we were a group possessed of peculiar traits, and that there was something—innate or acquired—in our make-up[12] which made us adopt a particular mode of existence.

It was a slight thing that started me on a new track.

I got to talking to a mild-looking, elderly fellow. I liked his soft speech and pleasant manner. We swapped trivial experiences. Then he suggested a game of checkers. As we started to arrange the pieces on the board I was startled by the sight of his crippled right hand. I had not noticed it before. Half of it was chopped off lengthwise, so that the horny stump with its three fingers looked like a hen's leg. I was mortified that I had not noticed the hand until he dangled it, so to speak, before my eyes. It was, perhaps, to bolster my shaken confidence in my powers of observation that I now began paying close attention to the hands of the people around me. The result was astounding. It seemed that every other man had been mangled in some way. There was a man with one arm. Some men limped. One young, good-looking fellow had a wooden leg. It was as though the majority of the men had escaped the snapping teeth of a machine and left part of themselves behind.

It was, I knew, an exaggerated impression. But I began counting the cripples as the men lined up in the yard at mealtime. I found thirty (out of two hundred) crippled either in arms or legs. I immediately sensed where the counting would land me.[13] The simile preceded the statistical deduction: we in the camp were a human junk pile.

I began evaluating my fellow tramps as human material, and for the first time in my life I became face-conscious. There were some good faces, particularly among the young. Several of the middle-aged and the old looked healthy and well-preserved. But the damaged and decayed faces were in the majority. I saw faces that were wrinkled, or bloated, or raw as the surface of a peeled plum. Some of the noses were purple and swollen, some broken, some pitted with enlarged pores. There were many toothless mouths (I counted seventy-eight). I noticed eyes that were blurred, faded, opaque, or bloodshot. I was struck by the fact that the old men, even the very old, showed their age mainly in the face. Their bodies were still slender and erect. One little man over sixty years of age looked a mere boy when seen from behind. The shriveled face joined to a boyish body made a startling sight.

My diffidence had now vanished. I was getting to know everybody in the camp. They were a friendly and talkative lot. Before many weeks I knew some essential fact about practically everyone.

And I was continually counting. Of the two hundred men in the camp there were approximately as follows:

Cripples. 30
Confirmed drunkards 60

---

[12]Make-up — as used here: character, temperament.

[13]"Where the counting would land me" — what conclusions the counting would lead me to.

Old men (55 and over)....................................... 50
Youths under twenty... 10
Men with chronic diseases, heart, asthma, TB[14] 12
Mildly insane.. 4
Constitutionally lazy[15] 6
Fugitives from justice....................................... 4
Apparently normal 70

(The numbers do not tally up to two hundred since some of the men were counted twice or even thrice—as cripples and old, or as old and confirmed drunks, etc.)

In other words: less than half the camp inmates (seventy normal, plus ten youths) were unemployed workers whose difficulties would be at an end once jobs were available. The rest (60 percent) had handicaps in addition to unemployment.

I also counted fifty war veterans, and eighty skilled workers representing sixteen trades. All the men (including those with chronic diseases) were able to work. The one-armed man was a wizard[16] with the shovel.

I did not attempt any definite measurement of character and intelligence. But it seemed to me that the intelligence of the men in the camp was certainly not below the average. And as for character, I found much forbearance and genuine good humor. I never came across one instance of real viciousness. Yet, on the whole, one would hardly say that these men were possessed of strong characters. Resistance, whether to one's appetites or to the ways of the world, is a chief factor in the shaping of character; and the average tramp is, more or less, a slave of his few appetites. He generally takes the easiest way out.

The connection between our make-up and our mode of existence as migrant workers presented itself now with some clarity.

The majority of us were incapable of holding onto a steady job. We lacked self-discipline and the ability to endure monotonous, leaden hours. We were probably misfits from the very beginning. Our contact with a steady job was not unlike a collision. Some of us were maimed, some got frightened and ran away, and some took to drink.[17] We inevitably drifted in the direction of least resistance—the open road. The life of a migrant worker is varied and demands only a minimum of self-discipline. We were now in one of the drainage ditches of ordered society. We could not keep a footing in the ranks of respectability and were washed into the slough[18] of our present existence.

Yet, I mused, there must be in this world a task with an appeal so strong

---

[14]TB — tuberculosis.

[15]Constitutionally lazy — lazy by nature.

[16]Wizard — as used here: very skillful.

[17]To take to drink — to begin taking alcoholic drinks immoderately; to become a drunkard.

[18]Slough — swamp.

that were we to have a taste of it we would hold on and be rid for good of our restlessness.

My stay in the camp lasted about four weeks. Then I found a haying job not far from town, and finally, in April, when the hot winds began blowing, I shouldered my bedroll and took the highway to San Bernardino.

It was the next morning, after I got a lift to Indio by truck, that a new idea began to take hold of me. The highway out of Indio leads through waving date groves, fragrant grapefruit orchards, and lush alfalfa fields; then, abruptly, passes into a desert of white sand. The sharp line between garden and desert is very striking. The turning of white sand into garden seemed to me an act of magic. This, I thought, was a job one would jump at—even the men in the transient camps. They had the skill and the ability of the average American. But their energies, I felt, could be quickened only by a task that was spectacular, that had in it something of the miraculous. The pioneer task of making the desert flower would certainly fill the bill.[19]

Tramps as pioneers? It seemed absurd. Every man and child in California knows that the pioneers had been giants, men of boundless courage and indomitable spirit. However, as I strode on across the white sand, I kept mulling over the idea.

Who were the pioneers? Who were the men who left their homes and went into the wilderness? A man rarely leaves a soft spot and goes deliberately in search of hardship and privation. People become attached to the places they live in; they drive roots. A change of habitat is a painful act of uprooting. A man who has made good and has a standing in his community stays put.[20] The successful businessmen, farmers, and workers usually stayed where they were. Who then left for the wilderness and the unknown? Obviously those who had not made good: men who went broke[21] or never amounted to much; men who though possessed of abilities were too impulsive to stand the daily grind;[22] men who were slaves of their appetites—drunkards, gamblers, and women chasers; outcasts—fugitives from justice and ex-jailbirds.[23] There were no doubt some who went in search of health—men suffering with TB, asthma, heart trouble. Finally there was a sprinkling of young and middle-aged in search of adventure.

All these people craved change, some probably actuated by the naïve belief that a change in place brings with it a change in luck. Many wanted to go to a place where they were not known and there make a new beginning. Certainly they did not go out deliberately in search of hard work and suffering. If in the end they shouldered enormous tasks,[24] endured unspeakable hardships, and ac-

---

[19]To fill the bill — to meet all the requirements.

[20]To stay put — to stay in one place.

[21]To go broke — to lose all one's money.

[22]Daily grind — the routine of the daily job.

[23]Jailbirds — slang term for prisoner or ex-prisoner.

[24]To shoulder a task — to take on a difficult task.

complished the impossible, it was because they had to. They became men of action on the run. They acquired strength and skill in the inescapable struggle for existence. It was a question of do or die.[25] And once they tasted the joy of achievement, they craved for more.

Clearly the same types of people which now swelled the ranks of migratory workers and tramps had probably in former times made up the bulk of pioneers. As a group the pioneers were probably as unlike the present-day "native sons"—their descendants—as one could well imagine. Indeed, were there to be today a new influx of typical pioneers, twin brothers of the forty-niners,[26] only in modern garb, the citizens of California would consider it a menace to health, wealth, and morals.

With few exceptions, this seems to be the case in the settlement of all new countries. Ex-convicts were the vanguard in the settling of Australia. Exiles and convicts settled Siberia. In this country, a large portion of our earlier and later settlers were failures, fugitives, and felons. The exceptions seemed to be those who were motivated by religious fervor, such as the Pilgrim Fathers and the Mormons.

Although quite logical, the train of thought seemed to me then a wonderful joke. In my exhilaration I was eating up the road[27] in long strides, and I reached the oasis of Elim in what seemed almost no time. A passing empty truck picked me up just then and we thundered through Banning and Beaumont, all the way to Riverside. From there I walked the seven miles to San Bernardino.

Somehow, this discovery of a family likeness between tramps and pioneers took a firm hold on my mind. For years afterward it kept intertwining itself with a mass of observations which on the face of them had no relation to either tramps or pioneers. And it moved me to speculate on subjects in which, up to then, I had had no real interest, and of which I knew very little.

I talked with several old-timers—one of them over eighty and a native son—in Sacramento, Placerville, Auburn, and Fresno. It was not easy, at first, to obtain the information I was after. I could not make my questions specific enough. "What kind of people were the early settlers and miners?" I asked. They were a hard-working, tough lot, I was told. They drank, fought, gambled, and wenched.[28] They wallowed in luxury, or lived on next to nothing with equal ease. They were the salt of the earth.[29]

Still it was not clear what manner of people they were.

If I asked what they looked like, I was told of whiskers, broad-brimmed hats, high boots, shirts of many colors, sun-tanned faces, horny hands. Finally I asked: "What group of people in present-day California most closely resembles

---

[25] A question of do or die — the need to do a job in order to survive.

[26] Forty-niners — people who went to California in 1849 in search of gold.

[27] To eat up the road — to walk quickly along the road, covering a long distance.

[28] To wench — to have sexual intercourse with prostitutes or loose women.

[29] Salt of the earth — the most admirable people on the earth; people with basic goodness.

the pioneers?" The answer, usually after some hesitation, was invariably the same: "The Okies[30] and the fruit tramps."[31]

I tried also to evaluate the tramps as potential pioneers by watching them in action. I saw them fell timber, clear firebreaks,[32] build rock walls, put up barracks, build dams and roads, handle steam shovels, bulldozers, tractors, and concrete mixers. I saw them put in a hard day's work after a night of steady drinking. They sweated and growled, but they did the work. I saw tramps elevated to positions of authority as foremen and superintendents. Then I could notice a remarkable physical transformation: a seamed face gradually smoothed out and the skin showed a healthy hue; an indifferent mouth became firm and expressive; dull eyes cleared and brightened; voices actually changed; there was even an apparent increase in stature. In almost no time these promoted tramps looked as if they had been on top all their lives. Yet sooner or later I would meet up with them again in a railroad yard, on some skid row,[33] or in the fields— tramps again. It was usually the same story: they got drunk or lost their temper and were fired, or they got fed up with the steady job and quit. Usually, when a tramp becomes a foreman he is careful in his treatment of the tramps under him; he knows the day of reckoning[34] is never far off.

In short it was not difficult to visualize the tramps as pioneers. I reflected that if they were to find themselves in a singlehanded life-and-death struggle with nature, they would undoubtedly display persistence. For the pressure of responsibility and the heat of battle steel a character. The inadaptable would perish, and those who survived would be the equal of the successful pioneers.

I also considered the few instances of pioneering engineered from above— that is to say, by settlers possessed of lavish means, who were classed with the best where they came from. In these instances, it seemed to me, the resulting social structure was inevitably precarious. For pioneering de luxe usually results in a plantation society, made up of large landowners and peon labor, either native or imported. Very often there is a racial cleavage between the two. The colonizing activities of the Teutonic barons in the Baltic, the Hungarian nobles in Transylvania, the English in Ireland, the planters in our South, and the present-day plantation societies in Kenya and other British and Dutch colonies are cases in point. Whatever their merits, they are characterized by poor adaptability. They are likely eventually to be broken up either by a peon[35] revolution or by an influx of typical pioneers—who are usually of the same race

---

[30] Okies — farmers who went from Oklahoma to settle in California.

[31] Fruit tramps — migrant workers who pick fruit in season.

[32] Firebreak — a strip of land that has been cleared to prevent a forest fire from spreading.

[33] Skid row — slang term for a district inhabited by drunkards, vagrants, or other "failures."

[34] Day of reckoning — Judgment Day. The time when one will be punished for one's bad actions in the past.

[35] Peon — Spanish word for peasant, a poor farmer, or unskilled farm laborer. This term is often used in the Southwestern United States, where there has been a strong Spanish-language influence.

or nation as the landowners. The adjustment is not necessarily implemented by war. Even our old South, had it not been for the complication of secession, might eventually have attained stability without war: namely, by the activity of its own poor whites or by an influx of the indigent[36] from other states.

There is in us a tendency to judge a race, a nation, or an organization by its least worthy members. The tendency is manifestly perverse and unfair; yet it has some justification. For the quality and destiny of a nation are determined to a considerable extent by the nature and potentialities of its inferior elements. The inert mass of a nation is in its middle section. The industrious, decent, well-to-do, and satisfied middle classes—whether in cities or on the land—are worked upon and shaped by minorities at both extremes: the best and the worst.

The superior individual, whether in politics, business, industry, science, literature, or religion, undoubtedly plays a major role in the shaping of a nation. But so do the individuals at the other extreme: the poor, the outcasts, the misfits, and those who are in the grip of some overpowering passion. The importance of these inferior elements as formative factors lies in the readiness with which they are swayed in any direction. This peculiarity is due to their inclination to take risks ("not giving a damn") and their propensity for united action. They crave to merge their drab, wasted lives into something grand and complete. Thus they are the first and most fervent adherents of new religions, political upheavals, patriotic hysteria, gangs, and mass rushes to new lands.

And the quality of a nation—its innermost worth—is made manifest by its dregs as they rise to the top: by how brave they are, how humane, how orderly, how skilled, how generous, how independent or servile; by the bounds they will not transgress in their dealings with a man's soul, with truth, and with honor.

The average American of today bristles[37] with indignation when he is told that this country was built, largely, by hordes of undesirables from Europe. Yet, far from being derogatory, this statement, if true, should be a cause for rejoicing, should fortify our pride in the stock from which we have sprung.

This vast continent with its towns, farms, factories, dams, aqueducts, docks, railroads, highways, powerhouses, schools, and parks is the handiwork of common folk from the Old World, where for centuries men of their kind had been beasts of burden, the property of their masters—kings, nobles, and priests—and with no will and no aspirations of their own. When on rare occasions one of the lowly had reached the top in Europe he had kept the pattern intact and, if anything, tightened the screws.[38] The stuffy little corporal from Corsica[39] harnessed the lusty forces released by the French Revolution to a

---

[36]Indigent — very poor; lacking basic necessities.

[37]To bristle — to become angry or indignant.

[38]To tighten the screws — to allow less freedom than before.

[39]The stuffy little corporal from Corsica — Napoleon Bonaparte (1769–1821), Emperor of the French (1804–1815).

gilded state coach, and could think of nothing grander than mixing his blood with that of the Hapsburg masters and establishing a new dynasty. In our day a bricklayer in Italy,[40] a house painter in Germany,[41] and a shoemaker's son in Russia[42] have made themselves masters of their nations; and what they did was to re-establish and reinforce the old pattern.

Only here, in America, were the common folk of the Old World given a chance to show what they could do on their own, without a master to push and order them about. History contrived an earth-shaking joke when it lifted by the nape of the neck lowly peasants, shopkeepers, laborers, paupers, jailbirds, and drunks from the midst of Europe, dumped them on a vast, virgin continent and said: "Go to it; it is yours!"

And the lowly were not awed by the magnitude of the task. A hunger for action, pent up for centuries, found an outlet. They went to it with ax, pick, shovel, plow, and rifle; on foot, on horse, in wagons, and on flatboats. They went to it praying, howling, singing, brawling, drinking, and fighting. Make way for the people! This is how I read the statement that this country was built by hordes of undesirables from the Old World.

Small wonder that we in this country have a deeply ingrained faith in human regeneration. We believe that, given a chance, even the degraded and the apparently worthless are capable of constructive work and great deeds. It is a faith founded on experience, not on some idealistic theory. And no matter what some anthropologists, sociologists, and geneticists may tell us, we shall go on believing that man, unlike other forms of life, is not a captive of his past—of his heredity and habits—but is possessed of infinite plasticity, and his potentialities for good and for evil are never wholly exhausted.

☆ FOLLOW-UP QUESTIONS

I.   The writer of this essay looks back upon several weeks he spent in a camp for homeless, unemployed men during the Depression. He analyzes these men as a group with particular characteristics that have led to their becoming "undesirables."

   A.   How did Hoffer happen to get into the federal transient camp?
   B.   What did the camp look like from the outside?
   C.   What were the writer's reasons for enrolling in this camp?
   D.   How did he go about collecting information about "practically everyone in the camp"?

[40] A bricklayer in Italy — Benito Mussolini (1883–1945), Fascist Premier of Italy from 1922 to 1943.

[41] A housepainter in Germany — Adolf Hitler (1889–1945), Austrian-born fascist Chancellor of Germany from 1934–1945.

[42] A shoemaker's son in Russia — Josef Stalin (1879–1953), General Secretary of the Communist Party of the Soviet Union (1922–1953); Premier (1941–1953).

    E.   What categories did he divide the men into? Why did he call the remaining category normal?

    F.   What did he conclude about intelligence and character?

    G.   What reasons does he give for claiming that the men did not have strong characters?

    H.   How does he link the character make-up and the "mode of existence" of the men?

    I.   Hoffer states, "We were probably misfits from the very beginning." What were some of the ways these men seemed poorly adjusted to their environment?

II.   The American pioneers, "those men who left their homes and went into the wilderness," are generally regarded with respect and admiration. Therefore, it seems ironic that Hoffer finds a great many similarities between the "undesirables," the migratory workers and tramps, and the pioneers.

    A.   How does he justify the statement that those who left for the wilderness "had not made good"?

    B.   What negative characteristics does he attribute to those men who became pioneers?

    C.   According to Hoffer, what particular wish did they all have in common?

    D.   Hoffer describes the pioneers as unlikely types of people to work hard and endure hardships. Nevertheless, they did. How does he explain this?

    E.   How did Hoffer get information about the early California settlers and miners?

    F.   How were they described to him?

    G.   Trying to "evaluate the tramps as potential pioneers," the writer makes specific observations about the manner in which they worked.

        1. What became apparent when the tramps were given positions of authority?

        2. What ultimately happened to them?

III. Hoffer states that "there is in us a tendency to judge a race, a nation or an organization by its least worthy members." He admits this tendency is unfair, but to some extent, he justifies it.

    A.   What is the writer's theory about the roles of the middle class and "the minorities at both extremes"?

    B.   According to Hoffer, what characteristics of "the poor, the outcast and the misfits" have led them to play an important part in the shaping of a nation?

    C.   Why does he believe Americans should be proud of the fact that the United States was built "largely by hordes of undesirables from Europe"?

IV. Hoffer's way of gathering the information that supports his impressions is direct; he talks to people and notes his own observations.

    A.   Which sections of the essay emphasize Hoffer's powers of observation?

    B.   Are these methods valid kinds of research? Why or why not?

    C.   Do you think the writer's theory about "tramps as pioneers" is convincing? Why or why not?

V.   Hoffer has written this essay from his own experiences and observations.

    A.   Do you consider this essentially a personal essay? Why or why not?

    B.   What does the writer reveal about himself?

    C.   What do Hoffer's theories tell us about the man himself?

☆ *THEME TOPICS*

1. Write an essay about a group of people who are (or were) considered undesirables. Discuss the characteristics these people have (had) in common. Include reasons why they are (were) rejected by society.
2. Discuss a particular theory you hold about a group of people. Use your own observations and information or impressions you have gotten from others to support your theory.

A Clear and Simple Style*
Donald Hall

INTRODUCTION

I. Style is an important consideration in writing and in other fields, especially in the arts.

    A. Two pianists playing the same piece of music will invariably play it differently. What determines the difference? What do we mean when we say, "I like her style of playing that piece"?

    B. Similarly, there are always differences among any of the thousands of paintings done of a common subject, for example, the Madonna and Child. What elements make one painter's style different from another's?

II. This essay is concerned with style as it applies to language.

    A. Imagine a simple situation: A boy is asked to do an errand for his mother. He says "All right," stops what he is doing, and goes out the door. From this description, do you have any idea of how the boy feels about doing the errand? In what ways other than the words he uses and the fact that he goes out might he show his feelings? If he doesn't want to do the errand, what facial expression might he have? What tone of voice might he use? How might he leave the room? How could you rewrite the "story" to indicate that the boy does the errand *unwillingly*? For instance, " 'All right,' John groaned. . . ."

    B. Have you ever paused in conversation to "choose the right word," or noticed another person's choice of words? How often have you said to another person: "Why did you use *that* word?" or "Don't put it *that* way!" How can the choice of one word rather than another affect the meaning of a sentence?

    C. When do we use words other than in written and spoken language? When you are thinking, do you use words? Do words occur in your dreams?

Ezra Pound,[1] George Orwell,[2] James Thurber,[3] and Ernest Hemingway[4] don't have much in common: a great poet who became a fascist,[5] a disillusioned left-wing satirist,[6] a comic essayist and cartoonist,[7] and a great novelist. If anything, they could represent the diversity of modern literature. Yet one thing unites them. They share a common idea of good prose[8] style, an idea of the virtues of clarity and simplicity. This attitude toward style was not unknown to earlier writers, but never before has it been so pervasive and so exclusive.

Style is the manner of a sentence, not its matter. Yet the distinction between manner and matter is a slippery one; manner affects matter. When Time[9] used to tell us that President Truman[10] slouched into one room, while General Eisenhower[11] strode into another, their manner was attempting to prejudice our feelings. The hotel which invites me to enjoy my favorite beverage at the Crown Room[12] is trying not to sound crass ("Have a drink at the bar"). One linguist in discussing this problem took Caesar's[13] "I came — I saw — I conquered," and revised it into "I arrived on the scene of the battle, I observed the situation, I won the victory." Here the matter is the same, but the tone of arrogant dignity in Caesar disappears into the pallid pedantry of the longer version. It is impossible to say that the matter is unaffected. Still, let us say that this kind of difference, in the two versions of Caesar, is what we mean by style. One of the things we *don't* mean by style is grammar.

In the phrase "good writing" or "good style," the word "good" has usually meant "beautiful" or "proficient" — like a good Rembrandt[14] or a good kind of

[1] Ezra Pound — American poet and literary critic (1885–1972).

[2] George Orwell — English novelist and essayist (1903–1950). Author of the political satires *Animal Farm* and *1984*.

[3] James Thurber — American cartoonist and writer of humorous stories and essays (1894–1961).

[4] Ernest Hemingway — American novelist and short story writer (1899–1961). Author of *For Whom the Bell Tolls, The Sun Also Rises, A Farewell to Arms,* and numerous other works.

[5] Fascist — one who advocates or practices fascism, a dictatorship of the extreme right wing. Originally, a supporter of the government of Benito Mussolini in Italy (1922–1943).

[6] Satirist — a writer of satire, a form of literature which uses irony or humor to ridicule and expose human foolishness or wickedness.

[7] Cartoonist — one who makes humorous drawings for newspapers or magazines. Cartoons, often with written captions, are frequently used to ridicule their subjects.

[8] Prose — any speech or writing that is not in poetic form.

[9] *Time* — a popular weekly news magazine published in the United States. This magazine is famous for its own special writing style, which is often designed to influence people's opinions.

[10] President Truman — thirty-third president of the United States (1945–1953).

[11] General Eisenhower — American general in World War II. Thirty-fourth president of the United States (1953–1961).

[12] Crown Room — typical name of a bar serving alcoholic drinks in a better hotel.

[13] Caesar — Roman general who was Emperor of Rome from 49 to 44 B.C.

[14] Rembrandt — Dutch painter and graphic artist (1606–1669).

soap. Now it means honest, as opposed to fake. Bad writing happens when the writer lies to himself, or to others, or to both. Probably it is usually necessary to lie to yourself in order to lie to others; advertising men[15] use the products they praise. Bad writing may be proficient: It may persuade us to buy a poor car or to vote for an imbecile, but it is bad because it is tricky, false in its enthusiasm, and falsely motivated. It appeals to a part of us that wants to deceive itself. I am encouraged to tell myself that I am enjoying my favorite beverage when I am really only getting sloshed.[16]

"If a man writes clearly enough any one can see if he fakes," says Hemingway. Orwell reverses the terms: "The great enemy of clear language is insincerity. . . . When there is a gap between one's real and one's declared aims, one turns as it were instinctively to long words and exhausted idioms, like a cuttlefish squirting out ink." Pound talks about the "gap between one's real and one's declared aims" as the distance between expression and meaning. In "The New Vocabularianism," Thurber speaks of the political use of clichés to hide a "menacing Alice in Wonderland[17] meaninglessness."

As Robert Graves[18] says, "The writing of good English is thus a moral matter." And the morality is a morality of truth-telling. Herbert Read[19] declares that "the only thing that is indispensable for the possession of a good style is personal sincerity." We can agree, but must add that personal sincerity is not always an easy matter, nor always available to the will. "Real aims," we must understand, are not necessarily conscious ones. The worst liars in the world may consider themselves sincere. Analysis of one's own style, in fact, can act as a test of one's own feelings. And certainly, many habits of bad style are bad habits of thinking as well as of feeling.

There are examples of the modern attitude toward style in older writers. Jonathan Swift,[20] maybe the best prose writer of the language, sounds like George Orwell when he writes: ". . . our English tongue is too little cultivated in this kingdom, yet the faults are nine in ten owing to affectation, not to want of understanding. When a man's thoughts are clear, the properest words will generally offer themselves first, and his own judgment will direct him in what order to place them, so as they may be best understood." Here Swift appears

---

[15]Advertising men — people who are in the business of preparing advertisements or notices designed to call public attention to a commercial product.

[16]Getting sloshed — slang term for getting drunk.

[17]*Alice in Wonderland* — title of a children's book by the English author Lewis Carroll (1832–1898). In this book there are many humorous speeches and incidents that are apparently absurd and meaningless.

[18]Robert Graves — an English poet, novelist, and literary critic (born 1895).

[19]Herbert Read — English art critic, poet, and editor (1893–1968).

[20]Jonathan Swift — English poet and novelist, famous for his satires. Author of *Gulliver's Travels* (1667–1745).

tautological.[21] Clear thoughts only *exist* when they are embodied in clear words. But he goes on: "When men err against this method, it is usually on purpose." Purposes, we may add, which we often disguise from ourselves.

Aristotle[22] in his "Rhetoric" makes a case for plainness and truth-telling. "The right thing in speaking really is that we should be satisfied not to annoy our hearers, without trying to delight them: we ought in fairness to fight our case with no help beyond the bare facts." And he anticipates the modern stylist's avoidance of unusual words: "Clearness is secured by using the words . . . that are current and ordinary." Cicero[23] attacks the Sophists[24] because they are "on the lookout for ideas that are neatly put rather than reasonable . . ."

Yet when we quote Cicero, the master rhetorician,[25] on behalf of honest clarity, we must remember that the ancients did not really think of style as we do. Style until recent times has been a division of rhetoric. To learn style, one learned the types of figures of speech, and the appropriateness of each to different levels of discourse—high, middle, and low. The study of style was complex, but technical rather than moral. For some writers, Latin was high and the vernacular[26] low, but in the Renaissance[27] the vernacular took in[28] all levels. It is only with modern times that style divorces itself[29] from rhetoric—rhetoric belongs to the enemy, to the advertisers and the propagandists—and becomes a matter of ethics and introspection.

Ezra Pound, like some French writers before him, makes the writer's function social. "Good writers are those who keep the language efficient. That is to say, keep it accurate, keep it clear." We must ask why this idea of the function of good style is so predominantly a modern phenomenon. Pound elsewhere speaks of the "assault," by which he means the attack upon our ears and eyes of words used dishonestly to persuade us, to convince us to buy or to believe. Never before have men been exposed to so many words—written words, from newspapers and billboards[30] and paperbacks[31] and flashing signs and the sides

---

[21]Tautological — needless repetition, giving the same meaning in different words. In logic, a tautology is a statement that is true because it includes all the logical possibilities. For example: "A person is either here or not here."

[22]Aristotle — Greek philosopher, author of works on literature and style (384–322 B.C.).

[23]Cicero — Roman statesman and orator (106–43 B.C.).

[24]Sophists — members of a pre-Socratic school of philosophy in ancient Greece. They were known for their devious and complex reasoning, which was often used to advance their own purposes.

[25]Rhetorician — an expert in rhetoric, the study of styles and forms used in literature and public speaking.

[26]Vernacular — the everyday, common speech of a country or district.

[27]Renaissance — the period of revival, or "rebirth" of the arts and learning that began in 14th century Italy and later spread throughout Europe.

[28]Took in — included.

[29]Divorces itself — separates itself from.

[30]Billboards — outdoor advertising signs.

[31]Paperbacks — books with paper covers, generally less expensive than those published with hard, or "cloth" covers.

of buses; spoken words, from radio and television and loudspeakers. Everyone who wishes to keep his mind clear and his feelings his own must make an effort to brush away these words like cobwebs from the face.

The assault of the phony[32] is a result of technology combined with a morality that wishes to use this technique for persuasion. The persuasion is for purposes of making money, as in advertising, or winning power, as in war propaganda and the slogans of politicians. Politicians have always had slogans, but they never before had the means to spread their words so widely. The cold war[33] of rhetoric between communism and capitalism has killed no soldiers, but the air is full of the small corpses[34] of words that were once alive; democracy, freedom, liberation.

It is because of the assault, primarily, that writers have become increasingly concerned with the honesty of their style to the exclusion of other qualities. Concentration upon honesty is the only way to exclude the sounds of the bad style that assault us all. These writers are concerned finally *to be honest about what they see, feel and know.* For some of them, like William Carlos Williams,[35] we can only trust the evidence of our eyes and ears, our real knowledge of our immediate environment.

Our reading of good writers, and our attempt to write like them, can help to guard us against the dulling onslaught. But we can only do this if we are able to look into ourselves with some honesty: an ethic of clarity demands intelligence and self-knowledge. Really the ethic is not only a defense against the assault (nothing good is ever merely defensive) but is a development of the same inwardness which is reflected in psychoanalysis.[36] One cannot, after all, examine one's motives and feelings carefully if one takes a naive view that the appearance of a feeling is the reality of that feeling.

Sometimes the assault is merely pompous. Some people say "wealthy" instead of "rich" in order to seem proper, or "home" instead of "house" in order to seem genteel. Years ago, James Russell Lowell ridiculed the newspapers which translated "A great crowd came to see" into "A vast concourse was assembled to witness . . ." None of these examples is so funny as a Colonel's[37] statement on television that one of our astronauts[38] "has established visual contact" with a piece of equipment. He meant that the astronaut had *seen* it.

---

[32]Phony — slang term meaning false, dishonest.

[33]Cold war — intense conflict or hostility between countries or ideologies which stops short of actual war. The term was first used to describe the rivalry between the United States and the Soviet Union that developed immediately after the Second World War.

[34]Corpses — dead bodies. Used here to mean words that are no longer alive or useful.

[35]William Carlos Williams — American poet and medical doctor (1883–1963).

[36]Psychoanalysis — literally, "examination of the soul." The method developed by Sigmund Freud that uses dream interpretation and analysis of a person's thoughts to study mental processes and, in some cases, to attempt to relieve mental distress.

[37]Colonel — an Army officer of high rank, standing just above major and just below general.

[38]Astronauts — people trained to operate spacecraft or to fly in them.

Comic as these pomposities are, they are signs that something has gone wrong somewhere. (My father normally spoke a perfectly good plain English, but occasionally when he was unhappy with himself he would fall off[39] dreadfully; I remember him admonishing me at dinner. "It is necessary to masticate[40] thoroughly.") The Colonel must be worried about the intellectual respectability of the space program, if he resorts to phrases like "visual contact." The lady who speaks of "luncheon" instead of "lunch" is worried about her social status. She gives herself away.[41] Something has gone wrong, and it has gone wrong inside her mind and her emotions.

The style is the man. Again and again, the modern stylists repeat this idea. By a man's metaphors[42] you shall know him. When a commencement orator advises students to "enrich themselves culturally," chances are that he is more interested in money than in poetry. When a university president says that his institution turned out 1,432 B.A.'s last year, he tells us that he thinks he is running General Motors. The style is the man. Rémy de Gourmont used the analogy that the bird's song was conditioned by the shape of the beak. And Paul Valéry said, ". . . what makes the style is not merely the mind applied to a particular action; it is the whole of a living system extended, imprinted and recognizable in expression."

These statements are fine, but they sound too deterministic,[43] as if one expresses an unalterable self, and can no more change the style of that self than a bird can change the shape of its beak. Man is a kind of bird that can change his beak.

A writer of bad prose, in order to become a writer of good prose, must alter his character. He does not have to become good in terms of conventional morality, but he must become honest in the expression of himself, which means that he must know himself. There must be no gap between expression and meaning, between real and declared aims. For some people, some of the time, this simply means *not* telling deliberate lies. For most people, it means learning when they are lying and when they are not. It means learning the real names of their feelings. It means not saying or thinking, "I didn't *mean* to hurt your feelings," when there really existed a desire to hurt. It means not saying "luncheon" or "home" for the purpose of appearing upper-class or well-educated. It means not using the passive mood to attribute to no one in particular opinions that one is unwilling to call one's own. It means not disguising banal thinking by polysyllabic writing, or the lack of feeling by clichés[44] which purport to[45] display feeling.

---

[39]Fall off — as used here: to decline in quality or standards.

[40]Masticate — chew.

[41]Gives herself away — betrays or reveals herself. Shows her true nature.

[42]Metaphors — figures of speech which describe one feeling or thing by comparing it with another. For example: "My love is a rose." "All the world's a stage."

[43]Deterministic — following the belief that everything is predetermined, or fated to happen.

[44]Clichés — expressions that were perhaps fresh at one time but which have become stale through being used too often. "Face the music." "Sell like hot cakes." "Take by storm." Etc.

[45]Purport to — pretend to.

The style is the man, and the man can change himself by changing his style. Prose style is the way you think and the way you understand what you feel. Frequently we feel for each other a mixture of strong love and strong hate; if we call it love, and disguise the hate to ourselves by sentimentalizing over love, we are thinking and feeling badly. Style is ethics and psychology; clarity is a psychological sort of ethic, since it involves not general moral laws but truth to the individual self. The scrutiny of style is a moral and psychological study. By trying to scrutinize our own style we try to understand ourselves. Editing our own writing, or going over in memory our own spoken words, or even inwardly examining our thought, we can ask *why* we resorted to the passive in this case, or to clichés in that.

When the smoke of bad prose fills the air, something is always on fire somewhere. If the style is really the man, the style becomes an instrument for discovering and changing the man. Language is expression of self, but language is also the instrument by which to know that self.

☆ FOLLOW-UP QUESTIONS

I.   "Style is the manner of a sentence, not its matter."
   A.   By "manner" does Hall mean grammar? If not, what does he mean?
   B.   In the example given from *Time* magazine, how do the two expressions "slouched into" and "strode into" differ? (Both are ways of saying "came in.")
   C.   What is the difference between Caesar's description of what he did and the linguist's version? How does the linguist's version—which describes the same action in a different manner—change the meaning of the sentence?
   D.   When Hall distinguishes "manner" from "matter," does he mean that style is entirely separate from the meaning of a sentence? Or that style affects the meaning?

II.   Good prose style, according to many modern writers, has "the virtues of clarity and simplicity." This attitude, Hall writes, has "never before . . . been so pervasive and so exclusive."
   A.   What earlier writers does Hall quote who also believed in clear and simple expression?
   B.   Until recently, however, how did writers generally think of style?
   C.   What is "rhetoric"? Why might the study of various techniques of expression have nothing to do with "clarity" or "simplicity"?

III.   "It is only with modern times that style divorces itself from rhetoric—rhetoric belongs to the enemy, to the advertisers and the propagandists."
   A.   How has technology contributed to the proliferation of spoken and written words?
   B.   Does Hall regret the fact that we have never before "been exposed to so many words"? Or does he disapprove of *the purposes* which these "many words" are used for?
   C.   What do advertisers and propagandists try to persuade people to do?

D.   Explain what Hall means when he says: "the cold war of rhetoric . . . has killed no soldiers, but the air is full of the small corpses of words that were once alive: democracy, freedom, liberation." How can a word be "alive" or "dead"? How have these words been "killed"?

E.   "Good style" has usually meant "beautiful" or "proficient," Hall writes. Can advertising or political propaganda be both "beautiful" and "proficient" and yet be *bad style* according to the definition established by modern writers? Why? What is "the assault of the phony"?

IV.   "The great enemy of clear language is insincerity."

A.   In what sense is the writing of good English "a moral matter"?

B.   What does Hall mean when he talks of the "gap between one's real and one's declared aims"?

C.   Sometimes this "gap" may be comic. What is the significance of the Colonel's description of what the astronaut did? Does Hall think the space program is immoral? Does he think the Colonel is immoral? In what sense?

D.   What other examples of "bad," i.e., "immoral" or insincere style does Hall give? Explain the difference between the word "luncheon" and "lunch." What significance does Hall find in the expression "enrich" used by a commencement orator? or "turned out" used by a university president?

V.   "An ethic of clarity demands intelligence and self-knowledge."

A.   Does Hall feel that it is easy to be a good—i.e., an honest—writer?

B.   Why does he say that good style demands introspection?

C.   Good style is partly a "defense against the phony," but also a "development of the same inwardness which is reflected in psychoanalysis." In what way is the process of psychoanalysis similar to the process of becoming a good writer, according to Hall?

D.   Good writers are concerned "to be honest about what they see, feel and know." What is a patient in analysis concerned about?

VI.   "The style is the man." What does Hall mean by this phrase?

A.   Does Hall agree with the analogy that the connection between one's way of expressing oneself and what one really feels is analogous to a bird's song and the shape of its beak?

B.   Does Hall believe that a person's style is a reflection of his or her character?

C.   On the other hand, Hall writes that this analogy is "too deterministic." What does he mean? Does he think it is possible to change one's character, and therefore one's style?

D.   "Man is a kind of bird that can change his beak." Explain.

VII.   "Language is expression of self, but language is also the instrument by which to know that self."

A.   How can one become a good writer, according to Hall?

B.   Is analysis of the language one uses a good way of discovering one's real feelings?

C.   Is Hall concerned only with the problems of good writing?

D.   By style, does Hall mean only written or spoken language? What about the words we use silently when we are thinking?

E.   Do you think this essay is concerned exclusively with "how to become a good writer" or "how to judge good writing"? Why or why not? Does it have relevance to people who are not writers?

☆ *THEME TOPICS*

1. Discuss the importance of language in politics. Consider such things as the influence of political slogans. Why are politicians often considered immoral? Why is censorship of the written word often considered essential to the safety of governments in power?

2. Compare styles of writing in forms where the purposes and readers are very different, e.g., advertising, personal letters, diaries, news reports, student compositions.

3. What is the difference between ethics or morality as meant by Hall and conventional morality?

Why I Write*
George Orwell

INTRODUCTION

I. In this essay, George Orwell, a British novelist and essayist, examines the reasons why he became a writer.

    A. Are the motives that influence a person's choice of profession generally materialistic? What are some other considerations? What might be the dominant motivation to become a doctor? A teacher? A politician? A pilot? A businessman? A policeman? A farmer?

    B. Children sometimes declare their ambitions very early in life. Would the child who wants to be an opera singer be more serious about his goal than the child who wants to become a fireman? Why or why not? Do gifted children always become exceptional in their chosen field when they mature?

    C. Many individuals aren't able to develop and use their talents. What effect might this failure have on them?

    D. What are some of the pressures that might lead one to choose the wrong profession? Can you think of any examples of people who realize they are in the wrong profession but often stay in it even though they are unhappy?

From a very early age, perhaps the age of five or six, I knew that when I grew up I should be a writer. Between the ages of about seventeen and twenty-four I tried to abandon this idea, but I did so with the consciousness[1] that I was outraging[2] my true nature and that sooner or later I should have to settle down and write books.

I was the middle child of three, but there was a gap of five years on either side, and I barely saw my father before I was eight. For this and other reasons I was somewhat lonely, and I soon developed disagreeable mannerisms[3] which made me unpopular throughout my schooldays. I had the lonely child's habit of

---

---

[1]Consciousness — knowledge; awareness.

[2]To outrage — as used here: to violate or betray.

[3]Mannerism — a distinctive habit; a characteristic gesture, speech trait, or way of dressing. *Mannerism* implies behavior that is "put on" or affected; unnatural.

making up stories and holding conversations with imaginary persons, and I think from the very start my literary ambitions were mixed up with the feeling of being isolated and undervalued. I knew that I had a facility with words and a power of facing unpleasant facts, and I felt that this created a sort of private world in which I could get my own back[4] for my failure in everyday life. Nevertheless the volume of serious—i.e., seriously intended—writing which I produced all through my childhood and boyhood would not amount to half a dozen pages. I wrote my first poem at the age of four or five, my mother taking it down to dictation. I cannot remember anything about it except that it was about a tiger and the tiger had "chair-like teeth"—a good enough phrase, but I fancy the poem was a plagiarism[5] of Blake's "Tiger, Tiger." At eleven, when the war of 1914–18 broke out, I wrote a patriotic poem which was printed in the local newspaper, as was another, two years later, on the death of Kitchener. From time to time, when I was a bit older, I wrote bad and usually unfinished "nature poems" in the Georgian style.[6] I also, about twice, attempted a short story which was a ghastly failure. That was the total of the would-be serious work that I actually set down on paper during all those years.

However, throughout this time I did in a sense engage in literary activities. To begin with there was the made-to-order stuff which I produced quickly, easily and without much pleasure to myself. Apart from school work, I wrote *vers d'occasion,*[7] semi-comic poems which I could turn out at what now seems to me astonishing speed—at fourteen I wrote a whole rhyming play, in imitation of Aristophanes,[8] in about a week—and helped to edit school magazines, both printed and in manuscript. These magazines were the most pitiful burlesque[9] stuff that you could imagine, and I took far less trouble with them than I now would with the cheapest journalism.[10] But side by side with all this, for fifteen years or more, I was carrying out a literary exercise of a quite different kind: this was the making up of a continuous "story" about myself, a sort of diary existing only in the mind. I believe this is a common habit of children and adolescents. As a very small child I used to imagine that I was, say, Robin Hood, and picture myself as the hero of thrilling adventures, but quite soon my "story" ceased to be narcissistic[11] in a crude way and became more and more a mere description of

---

[4]To get one's own back — to get revenge.

[5]Plagiarism — presenting someone else's ideas or writings as if they were your own.

[6]Georgian style — in English literature, the style of writing (often dealing with nature) typical of the period 1714–1830 when George I, George II, George III, and George IV ruled Great Britain.

[7]*vers d'occasion* — poetry written to celebrate a particular event or occasion. (French expression)

[8]Aristophanes — Greek playwright (448?–380? B.C.), author of many satirical comedies.

[9]Burlesque — a literary work that makes a subject appear ridiculous by approaching it in an inappropriate style; a mocking imitation of something.

[10]Cheapest journalism — the worst kind of sensational or trivial writing for newspapers or magazines.

[11]Narcissistic — self-loving. From the Greek myth of Narcissus, who fell in love with his own image in a pool and was changed into a flower.

what I was doing and the things I saw. For minutes at a time this kind of thing would be running through my head: "He pushed the door open and entered the room. A yellow beam of sunlight, filtering through the muslin curtains, slanted on to the table, where a matchbox, half open, lay beside the inkpot. With his right hand in his pocket he moved across to the window. Down in the street a tortoiseshell cat was chasing a dead leaf," etc., etc. This habit continued till I was about twenty-five, right through my non-literary years. Although I had to search, and did search, for the right words, I seemed to be making this descriptive effort almost against my will, under a kind of compulsion from outside. The "story" must, I suppose, have reflected the styles of the various writers I admired at different ages, but so far as I remember it always had the same meticulous descriptive quality.

When I was about sixteen I suddenly discovered the joy of mere words, *i.e.,* the sounds and associations of words. The lines from *Paradise Lost*—

So hee[12] with difficulty and labour hard
Moved on: with difficulty and labour hee,

which do not now seem to me so very wonderful, sent shivers down my backbone; and the spelling "hee" for "he" was an added pleasure. As for the need to describe things, I knew all about it already. So it is clear what kind of books I wanted to write, in so far as I could be said to want to write books at that time. I wanted to write enormous naturalistic novels[13] with unhappy endings, full of detailed descriptions and arresting similes,[14] and also full of purple passages[15] in which words were used partly for the sake of their sound. And in fact my first completed novel, *Burmese Days,* which I wrote when I was thirty but projected much earlier, is rather that kind of book.

I give all this background information because I do not think one can assess a writer's motives without knowing some thing of his early development. His subject matter will be determined by the age he lives in—at least this is true in tumultuous, revolutionary ages like our own—but before he even begins to write he will have acquired an emotional attitude from which he will never completely escape. It is his job, no doubt, to discipline his temperament and avoid getting stuck at some immature stage, or in some perverse mood: but if he escapes from his early influences altogether, he will have killed his impulse to write. Putting aside the need to earn a living, I think there are four great motives for writing, at any rate for writing prose. They exist in different degrees in every writer, and in any one writer the proportions will vary from time to time, according to the atmosphere in which he is living. They are:

---

[12] Hee — archaic spelling of *he.*

[13] Naturalistic novels — novels based on the literary theories of the French author Emile Zola (1840–1902). Naturalistic fiction was seen as an extreme form of realism and often dealt with unpleasant aspects of life.

[14] Arresting similes — explicit comparisons, using the words *like* or *as,* that catch (or *arrest*) the reader's attention.

[15] Purple passages — lush, often overwritten, descriptive passages in novels or stories.

(1) Sheer egoism. Desire to seem clever, to be talked about, to be remembered after death, to get your own back on grownups who snubbed you in childhood, etc., etc. It is humbug[16] to pretend that this is not a motive, and a strong one. Writers share this characteristic with scientists, artists, politicians, lawyers, soldiers, successful businessmen—in short, with the whole top crust[17] of humanity. The great mass of human beings are not acutely selfish. After the age of about thirty they abandon individual ambition—in many cases, indeed, they almost abandon the sense of being individuals at all—and live chiefly for others, or are simply smothered under drudgery. But there is also the minority of gifted, wilful people who are determined to live their own lives to the end, and writers belong in this class. Serious writers, I should say, are on the whole more vain and self-centered than journalists, though less interested in money.

(2) Esthetic[18] enthusiasm. Perception of beauty in the external world, or, on the other hand, in words and their right arrangement. Pleasure in the impact of one sound on another, in the firmness of good prose or the rhythm of a good story. Desire to share an experience which one feels is valuable and ought not to be missed. The esthetic motive is very feeble in a lot of writers, but even a pamphleteer or a writer of textbooks will have pet words and phrases which appeal to him for non-utilitarian reasons; or he may feel strongly about typography, width of margins, etc. Above the level of a railway guide, no book is quite free from esthetic considerations.

(3) Historical impulse. Desire to see things as they are, to find out true facts and store them up for the use of posterity.

(4) Political purpose—using the word "political" in the widest possible sense. Desire to push the world in a certain direction, to alter other people's idea of the kind of society that they should strive after. Once again, no book is genuinely free from political bias. The opinion that art should have nothing to do with politics is itself a political attitude.

It can be seen how these various impulses must war against one another, and how they must fluctuate from person to person and from time to time. By nature—taking your "nature" to be the state you have attained when you are first adult—I am a person in whom the first three motives would outweigh the fourth. In a peaceful age I might have written ornate or merely descriptive books, and might have remained almost unaware of my political loyalties. As it is I have been forced into becoming a sort of pamphleteer.[19] First I spent five years in an unsuitable profession (the Indian Imperial Police, in Burma), and then I underwent poverty and the sense of failure. This increased my natural hatred of authority and made me for the first time fully aware of the existence of the working classes, and the job in Burma had given me some understanding of the nature of imperialism: but these experiences were not enough to give me an accurate

---

[16]Humbug — nonsense; something intended to fool or deceive people.

[17]Top crust — upper level.

[18]Esthetic — having to do with taste, with the appreciation of beauty.

[19]Pamphleteer — writer of pamphlets, usually on political or social themes.

political orientation. Then came Hitler, the Spanish civil war, etc. By the end of 1935 I had still failed to reach a firm decision. I remember a little poem that I wrote at that date, expressing my dilemma:

A happy vicar I might have been
Two hundred years ago,
To preach upon eternal doom
And watch my walnuts grow;

But born, alas, in an evil time,
I missed that pleasant haven,
For the hair has grown on my upper lip
And the clergy are all clean-shaven.

And later still the times were good,
We were so easy to please,
We rocked our troubled thoughts to sleep
On the bosoms[20] of the trees.

All ignorant we dared to own[21]
The joys we now dissemble;[22]
The greenfinch[23] on the apple bough
Could make my enemies tremble.

But girls' bellies and apricots,
Roach[24] in a shaded stream,
Horses, ducks in flight at dawn,
All these are a dream.

It is forbidden to dream again;
We maim our joys or hide them;
Horses are made of chromium steel
And little fat men shall ride them.

I am the worm who never turned,[25]
The eunuch[26] without a harem;[28]
Between the priest and the commissar[28]
I walk like Eugene Aram;[29]

And the commissar is telling my fortune
While the radio plays,
But the priest has promised an Austin Seven,[30]
For Duggie always pays.

I dreamed I dwelt in marble halls,[31]
And woke to find it true;
I wasn't born for an age like this;
Was Smith? Was Jones? Were you?

The Spanish war and other events in 1936–7 turned the scale[32] and thereafter I knew where I stood. Every line of serious work that I have written since 1936

---

[20] Bosoms — breasts. In this case, poetically, the branches of the trees.

[21] To own — as used here: to confess, to admit.

[22] To dissemble — to pretend; to present a false appearance.

[23] Greenfinch — brightly colored bird.

[24] Roach — a freshwater fish of northern Europe.

[25] "The worm who never turned" — the expression "the worm turned" refers to a moment when a lowly creature (represented by the worm) suddenly asserted itself ("turned") and took some positive action.

[26] Eunuch — a castrated man. Eunuchs were often the attendants in harems (see footnote 27) of Oriental, Middle Eastern, or Roman rulers or nobility.

[27] Harem — the house or section of a house reserved for women members of a Moslem household; the women themselves.

[28] Commissar — a member of the Communist Party, especially in the Soviet Union, who is responsible for political indoctrination and enforcing party loyalty.

[29] Eugene Aram — an English philologist of the 18th century. He was arrested and later hanged for the murder of his friend.

[30] Austin Seven — a British-made car.

[31] "I dreamed I dwelt in marble halls" — words from an operetta, "The Bohemian Girl," by Alfred Bunn (1796–1860). The passage refers to someone dreaming of luxurious living.

[32] To turn the scale — to make a decisive difference in one's life.

has been written, directly or indirectly, *against* totalitarianism and *for* democratic socialism, as I understand it. It seems to me nonsense, in a period like our own, to think that one can avoid writing of such subjects. Everyone writes of them in one guise or another. It is simply a question of which side one takes and what approach one follows. And the more one is conscious of one's political bias, the more chance one has of acting politically without sacrificing one's esthetic and intellectual integrity.

What I have most wanted to do throughout the past ten years is to make political writing into an art. My starting point is always a feeling of partisanship, a sense of injustice. When I sit down to write a book, I do not say to myself, "I am going to produce a work of art." I write it because there is some lie that I want to expose, some fact to which I want to draw attention, and my initial concern is to get a hearing. But I could not do the work of writing a book, or even a long magazine article, if it were not also an esthetic experience. Anyone who cares to examine my work will see that even when it is downright propaganda it contains much that a full-time politician would consider irrelevant. I am not able, and I do not want, completely to abandon the world-view that I acquired in childhood. So long as I remain alive and well I shall continue to feel strongly about prose style, to love the surface of the earth, and to take a pleasure in solid objects and scraps of useless information. It is no use trying to suppress that side of myself. The job is to reconcile my ingrained likes and dislikes with the essentially public, non-individual activities that this age forces on all of us.

It is not easy. It raises problems of construction and of language, and it raises in a new way the problem of truthfulness. Let me give just one example of the cruder kind of difficulty that arises. My book about the Spanish civil war, *Homage to Catalonia,* is, of course, a frankly political book, but in the main it is written with a certain detachment and regard for form. I did try very hard in it to tell the whole truth without violating my literary instincts. But among other things it contains a long chapter, full of newspaper quotations and the like, defending the Trotskyists[33] who were accused of plotting with Franco.[34] Clearly such a chapter, which after a year or two would lose its interest for any ordinary reader, must ruin the book. A critic whom I respect read me a lecture about it. "Why did you put in all that stuff?" he said. "You've turned what might have been a good book into journalism." What he said was true, but I could not have done otherwise. I happened to know, what very few people in England had been allowed to know, that innocent men were being falsely accused. If I had not been angry about that I should never have written the book.

In one form or another this problem comes up again. The problem of language is subtler and would take too long to discuss. I will only say that of late years I have tried to write less picturesquely and more exactly. In any case I find

---

[33]Trotskyists — followers of Leon Trotsky (1877–1940), a Russian communist revolutionary who was expelled from the Soviet Union by the leaders of the Communist Party in 1929 and was assassinated in Mexico in 1940.

[34]Franco — Francisco Franco was chief of the Spanish state from 1939 through 1975. Franco was an enemy of the communists.

that by the time you have perfected any style of writing, you have always out-grown it. *Animal Farm* was the first book in which I tried, with full consciousness of what I was doing, to fuse political purpose and artistic purpose into one whole. I have not written a novel for seven years, but I hope to write another fairly soon. It is bound to be a failure, every book is a failure, but I do know with some clarity what kind of book I want to write.

Looking back through the last page or two, I see that I have made it appear as though my motives in writing were wholly public-spirited. I don't want to leave that as the final impression. All writers are vain, selfish and lazy, and at the very bottom of their motives there lies a mystery. Writing a book is a horrible, exhausting struggle, like a long bout[35] of some painful illness. One would never undertake such a thing if one were not driven on by some demon whom one can neither resist nor understand. For all one knows that demon is simply the same instinct that makes a baby squall for attention. And yet it is also true that one can write nothing readable unless one constantly struggles to efface[36] one's own personality. Good prose is like a window pane. I cannot say with certainty which of my motives are the strongest, but I know which of them deserve to be followed. And looking back through my work, I see that it is invariably where I lacked a *political* purpose that I wrote lifeless books and was betrayed into purple passages, sentences without meaning, decorative adjectives and humbug generally.

[1947]

---

[35] Bout — battle; struggle (as in a boxing bout).

[36] To efface — to wipe out.

☆ FOLLOW-UP QUESTIONS

I.   Orwell states that from an early age, perhaps five or six, he knew he would grow up to become a writer.

    A.   Why was he somewhat lonely when he was a child?

    B.   How did he compensate for his lack of popularity throughout his school days?

    C.   What abilities was he aware of?

    D.   What were his literary accomplishments at the age of fourteen? How does Orwell, looking back, regard them?

    E.   What kind of novels did he want to write when he was about sixteen?

II.   Orwell describes his literary exercise of keeping a "sort of diary existing only in the wind." He quotes an example of the content of this continuous "story" about himself:

> He pushed the door open and entered the room. A yellow beam of sunlight filtering through the muslin curtains, slanted on the table, where a matchbox, half open, lay beside the inkpot. With his right hand in his pocket he moved across to the window. Down in the street a tortoiseshell cat was chasing a dead leaf.

    A. How does the writer regard the style of this prose?

    B. What seems to be its dominant characteristic?

    C. Do you think that meticulous descriptive prose usually adds to or detracts from a piece of writing? Why? What did Orwell mean by saying that in his later years he tried to write "less picturesquely and more exactly"?

    D. What does Orwell mean when he says that as he grew old he stopped writing "purple passages"?

III. Orwell says, "Putting aside the need to earn a living, I think there are four great motives for writing, at least for writing prose."

    A. What are those motives?

    B. How does Orwell characterize the writer's "sheer egoism"? With whom does the writer share this motive? What constitutes the writer's selfishness? Do you agree with Orwell's evaluation of "the minority of gifted, wilful people who are determined to live their own lives to the end"?

    C. How does Orwell define "esthetic enthusiasm"? Why does he claim this motive is feeble in many writers? Nevertheless, he states that "above the level of a railway guide, no book is quite free from esthetic considerations." Why does he think this is so?

    D. What does the writer mean by the term *historical impulse*?

    E. Orwell states that no book is genuinely free from "political purpose," his fourth motive. Why does he use the word *political* in the widest possible sense?

    F. Can you think of any other motives for writing?

    G. If you analyzed your own professional motives, would they have any resemblance to Orwell's "four great motives for writing"? In what ways?

IV. Orwell states that "in a peaceful age I might have written ornate or merely descriptive books."

    A. According to Orwell, what mainly determines an author's subject matter?

    B. What personal experiences and political events influenced the direction of his writing?

    C. How does the last stanza of the poem written in 1935 express his "dilemma"?

    D. After the Spanish Civil War and other events of 1936–37, what became Orwell's major reasons for writing?

    E. How does he explain his desire to make political writing into an art? What does he maintain about his work even when it is "downright propaganda"?

V. Orwell says, "by the time you have perfected any style of writing, you have always outgrown it."

    A. From your own reading, do you think this is necessarily true of every serious writer? Why? Can you name any writers who at some point in their careers seemed to have perfected their styles, but nevertheless went on to write in a different style? What reasons might have led them to make the changes?

    B. When you look back on something you've thought or written years before, how do you generally react?

    C. Orwell claims that "every book is a failure." Whose point of view is he expressing? Why doesn't the inevitability of failure seem to discourage him? How does the word *demon* explain the "mystery" involved in the "horrible, exhausting struggle" to write a book?

    D. What does Orwell mean when he states that "good prose is like a window pane"?

☆ *THEME TOPICS*

1. Describe the motives that have led you to choose your line of work or field of study.
2. Discuss the work of a writer (other than Orwell) whose writing has been affected by world events, and who has taken a specific political stand.
3. Describe a political situation (national or international) from your own point of view.

The Happy Medium*
Leonard Bernstein

INTRODUCTION

In this essay, Leonard Bernstein describes the difficulties involved in talking about music.

A. Can a description of a work of art have the same effect as the work itself? Why or why not?
B. Why might it be easier to describe a story than a painting?
C. Which would you find easier to talk about, a movie or a musical composition? Why?
D. How would you describe the way you feel about your favorite painting?
E. Would you always agree with someone else's feelings about the same painting?
F. What particular musical compositions do you react to emotionally? Why? Are you able to analyze your reactions to them logically? Why do some compositions have power over your emotions while others do not?

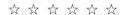

Ever since I can remember I have talked about music, with friends, colleagues, teachers, students, and just plain, simple citizens. But in the last few years I have found myself talking about it publicly, thus joining the long line of well-meaning but generally doomed folk who have tried to explain the unique phenomenon of human reaction to organized sound. It is almost like trying to explain a freak of nature[1] (whatever *that* may be). Ultimately one must simply accept the loving fact that people enjoy listening to organized sound (*certain* organized sounds, anyway); that this enjoyment can take the form of all kinds of responses from animal excitement to spiritual exaltation; and that people who can organize sounds so as to evoke the most exalted responses are commonly called geniuses. These axioms can neither be denied nor explained. But, in the great tradition of man burrowing through the darkness with his mind, hitting his head on cave walls, and sometimes perceiving a pinpoint of light, we can at least try to explain; in fact, there's no stopping us.

*Reprinted by permission of Simon & Schuster, A Division of Gulf & Western Corporation, from *The Joy of Music,* by Leonard Bernstein, Copyright © 1954, 1955, 1956, 1957, 1958, 1959. Reprinted by permission of Laurence Pollinger Ltd., from *The Joy of Music,* by Leonard Bernstein, Copyright © 1954, 1955, 1956, 1957, 1958, 1959.

[1]Freak of nature — an abnormally formed person, animal, or thing.

There have been more words written about the *Eroica* symphony than there are notes in it; in fact, I should imagine that the proportion of words to notes, if anyone could get an accurate count, would be flabbergasting.[2] And yet, has anyone ever successfully "explained" the *Eroica*?[3] Can anyone explain in mere prose the wonder of one note following or coinciding with another so that we feel that it's exactly how those notes *had* to be? Of course not. No matter what rationalists we may profess to be, we are stopped cold[4] at the border of this mystic area. It is not too much to say *mystic* or even *magic*: no art lover can be an agnostic when the chips are down.[5] If you love music, you are a believer, however dialectically you try to wriggle out of it.[6]

The most rational minds in history have always yielded to a slight mystic haze when the subject of music has been broached, recognizing the beautiful and utterly satisfying combination of mathematics and magic that music is. Plato[7] and Socrates[8] knew that the study of music is one of the finest disciplines for the adolescent mind, and insisted on it as a *sine qua non*[9] of education: and just for those reasons of its combined scientific and "spiritual" qualities. Yet when Plato speaks of music—scientific as he is about almost everything else—he wanders into vague generalizations about harmony, love, rhythm, and those deities who could presumably carry a tune. But he knew that there was nothing like piped music to carry soldiers inspired into battle—and everyone else knows it too. And that certain Greek modes[10] were better than others for love or war or wine festivals or crowning an athlete. Just as the Hindus, with their most mathematically complicated scales, rhythms and "ragas,"[11] knew that certain ones had to be for morning hours, or sunset, or Siva[12] festivals, or marching, or windy days. And no amount of mathematics could or can explain that.

We are still, in our own day, faced with this magical block.[13] We try to be scientific about it, in our bumbling[14] way—to employ principles of physics,

---

[2]Flabbergasting — amazing; astounding.

[3]*Eroica* — the Third Symphony ("The Heroic") by the German composer Ludwig van Beethoven (1770–1827).

[4]To be stopped cold — to be stopped completely, with no possibility of advancing.

[5]When the chips are down — when there is a moment of decision or crisis. The expression is taken from gambling, where chips (representing money) are placed on particular numbers, as in the game of roulette, for example.

[6]To wriggle out of it — to evade a difficult question or problem.

[7]Plato — Greek philosopher (427?–347 B.C.).

[8]Socrates — Greek philosopher and teacher (470?–399 B.C.).

[9]*Sine qua non* — an essential element or condition. (Latin, meaning literally "without which not").

[10]Greek modes — one of several formal patterns employed in the music of classical Greece.

[11]Raga — a traditional form in Hindu music.

[12]Siva — Hindu god of destruction and reproduction.

[13]Block — as used here: an obstacle.

[14]Bumbling — awkward, clumsy.

acoustics, mathematics, and formal logic. We employ philosophical devices like empiricism and teleological method. But what does it accomplish for us? The "magic" questions are still unanswered. For example, we can try to explain the "shape" of a theme from a Beethoven quartet by saying that it follows the formal principle of synthesis: that there is a short statement (thesis), followed by a "questioning answer" (antithesis), followed by a development arising out of the conflict of the two (synthesis). The Germans call this form "*Stollen.*"[15] Others say "syllogistic." Words, words, words. Why is the theme beautiful? There's the rub.[16] We can find a hundred themes shaped in this way, or based on variants of this principle; but only one or two will be *beautiful.*

When I was at Harvard,[17] Professor Birkhoff had just published a system of aesthetic[18] *measure*—actually trying to evolve a mathematical system whereby any object of art could be awarded a beauty-rating on a given continuum of aesthetic worth. It was a noble effort; but when all is said and done, it comes to a dead end. The five human senses are capable of measuring objects up to a certain point (the eye can decide that "X" is twice as long as "Y"; the ear can guess that one trombone is playing twice as loud as the other); but can the senses' own aesthetic responses be measured? How far is the smell of pork from the smell of beans? What beans? Cooked how? Raw? In what climate? If the *Eroica* earns a grade of 3.2, what mark do you give *Tristan*?[19] Or a one-page Bach[20] prelude?

We bumble. We imitate scientific method in our attempts to explain magic phenomena by fact, forces, mass, energy. But we simply can't explain human reaction to these phenomena. Science can "explain" thunderstorms, but can it "explain" the fear with which people react to them? And even if it can, in psychology's admittedly unsatisfactory terminology, how does science explain the sense of *glory* we feel in a thunderstorm, break down this sense of glory into its parts? Three parts electrical stimulation, one part aural excitement, one part visual excitement, four parts identification-feelings with the beyond,[21] two parts adoration of almighty forces—an impossible cocktail.

But some people *have* "explained" the glory of a thunderstorm—now and then, with varying degrees of success—and such people are called poets. Only artists can explain magic; only art can substitute for nature. By the same token, only art can substitute for art. And so the only way one can really say anything about music is to write music.

---

[15] *Stollen* — a German Christmas cake.

[16] "There's the rub." — "There's the difficulty." From Shakespeare's play, *Hamlet*: "Aye, there's the rub."

[17] Harvard — Harvard University, located in Cambridge, Massachusetts. Bernstein was a student at Harvard, and later he was a lecturer on music there.

[18] Aesthetic — (often spelled "esthetic.") Having to do with taste, especially a sense of the beautiful.

[19] *Tristan* — the opera, *Tristan and Isolde,* by German composer Richard Wagner (1813–1883).

[20] Bach — Johann Sebastian Bach (1685–1750), German composer.

[21] The beyond — beyond the everyday world of earth. Outside the area of ordinary experience.

Still we go on trying to shed some light on the mystery. There is a human urge to clarify, rationalize, justify, analyze, limit, describe. There is also a great urge to "sell" music, arising out of the transformation of music in the last 200 years into an industry. Suddenly there are mass markets, a tremendous recording industry, professional careerists, civic competitiveness, music chambers of commerce. And out of this has come something called "Music Appreciation"—once felicitously called by Virgil Thomson[22] the "Music Appreciation Racket."[23] It is, in the main,[24] a racket, because it is in the main specious and commercial. It uses every device to sell music—cajoling, coyness, flattery, oversimplification, irrelevant entertainment, tall tales[25]—all in order to keep the music business humming.[26] And in so doing it has itself become a business. The next step is obviously a new parasitic development—music-appreciation appreciation.

The "racket" operates in two styles, depending on the audience involved; and one is duller than the other. Type A is the bird-bees-and-rivulets variety, which invokes anything at all under the sun as long as it is extra-musical.[27] It turns every note or phrase or chord into a cloud or crag or Cossack.[28] It tells homey tales about the great composers, either spurious or irrelevant. It abounds in anecdotes, quotes from famous performers, indulges itself in bad jokes and unutterable puns, teases the hearer, and tells us nothing about music. I have used such devices myself: everyone who speaks about music at all must do it sometime or other. But I hope that I have done it always and only when the anecdote, the analogy, or the figure of speech makes the music clearer, more simply accessible, and not just to entertain or—much worse—to take the listener's mind *off* the music, as the Racket does.

Type B is concerned with analysis—a laudably serious endeavor, but it is as dull as Type A is coy. It is the now-comes-the-theme-upside-down-in-the-second-oboe variety. A guaranteed soporific. What it does, ultimately, is to supply you with a road map of themes, a kind of Baedeker[29] to the bare geography of a composition; but again it tells us nothing about music except those superficial geographical facts.

Luckily all talk about music is not restricted to the level of music appreciation. There are writers in the learned journals who make sense, but only to other

---

[22]Virgil Thomson — American composer and music critic (born 1896).

[23]Racket — an illegal or dishonest activity carried on with the aim of making money.

[24]In the main — for the most part; primarily.

[25]Tall tales — entertaining stories that are not true. Such stories either exaggerate the truth or are completely fictional.

[26]Humming — busy; successful. "Humming with activity."

[27]Extra-musical — outside the boundary or scope of music.

[28]Cossack — Russian cavalryman.

[29]Baedeker — author of a famous series of guidebooks for tourists. These books were called "Baedekers."

musicians, or to the cultivated amateur. The musical layman is harder put[30] to find intelligent talk about music. But every once in a while a non-musician has appeared who has been able to give the layman some insight into music, if only into a cadence, or a melodic contour, or a single harmonic progression. Such people are rare and invaluable. Plato had some moments, as did Shakespeare.[31] Certain critics can be perceptive and at the same time intelligible to the layman—men like Sullivan and Newman and Thomson.[32] Certain novelists, like Mann and Huxley,[33] have turned out memorable paragraphs, or even chapters, on musical matters. But most novelists, and writers in general, tend to put their feet in their mouths[34] whenever they part lips to speak of music. And they do it often. For some reason literary minds seem magnetized by musical terminology—probably because they are awe-struck by the abstractness of it all. Nothing can be more different from the representational literary mind, with its literal conceptuality, than the non-objective musical mind, with its concentration on shapes, lines, and sonorous intensities. And this fascinates the writer—makes him even a little envious, I have found—so that he longs for some participation in that strange, foreign medium. As a result, when he reaches for the elusive *mot juste* he often winds up with *glissando* or *crescendo* to express (usually wrongly) what he means—precisely *because* the musical words seem so elusive. Besides, it's so *pretty*! What chic and grace those Italian words carry with them! *Scherzo. Vivace. Andantino. Crescendo.* We are constantly running across the word *crescendo* in literature, almost always used synonymously with *climax*. "The storm rose to a great crescendo." "As they kissed, their hearts reached a crescendo of pounding passion." Nonsense. Obviously *crescendo* can mean only "growing," "increasing"—specifically, getting louder. So a crescendo can mean growing to a climax of storm or passion or anything you wish; but it can't be what you grow *to*.

This digression is only by way of pointing up the rarity of intelligent musical talk, even among first-class writers. The Huxleys and the Manns[35] of this world are few and far between.[36] Huxley's description of part of Beethoven's Op. 132 in *Point Counterpoint* is unforgettable, as is his paragraph on a Mozart quintet in *Antic Hay*. Mann has some thrilling passages on music in *The Magic Mountain* and in *Dr. Faustus*. And because of people like these—who can sometimes evoke with words the quality of a piece of music, or some

---

[30]To be hard put — to have a difficult time doing something.

[31]Shakespeare — English playwright (1564–1616).

[32]Sullivan and Newman and Thomson — music critics.

[33]Mann and Huxley — Thomas Mann, German novelist, playwright, and essayist (1875–1955). Aldous Huxley, English novelist and critic (1894–1963).

[34]To put one's foot in one's mouth — to make a tactless or awkward statement.

[35]The Huxleys and the Manns — here meant in a general sense: great authors who can write well about music.

[36]Few and far between — rare, uncommon.

sense of its essential weight or thrust—because of them we musicians are encouraged to go on trying to elucidate, in the hope that, even if only here and there, we can shed a little light on[37] that terrible bugaboo,[38] musical meaning.

"Meaning" in music has preoccupied aestheticians, musicians, and philosophers for centuries. The treatises pile up, and usually succeed only in adding more words to an already obscure business. In all this mass of material we can discern four levels of meaning in music:

1) Narrative-literary meanings (*Till Eulenspiegel,*[39] *The Sorcerer's Apprentice,*[40] etc.).
2) Atmospheric-pictorial meanings (*La Mer,*[41] *Pictures at an Exhibition,*[42] etc.).
3) Affective-reactive[43] meanings such as triumph, pain, wistfulness, regret, cheerfulness, melancholy, apprehension—most typical of nineteenth-century romanticism.
4) Purely musical meanings.

Of these, the last is the only one worthy of *musical* analysis. The first three may involve associations which are good to know (if the composer intended them); otherwise they are concerned only with arbitrary justification, or prettifying for the commercial reasons mentioned before. If we are to try to "explain" music, we must explain the *music,* not the whole array of appreciators' extra-musical notions which have grown like parasites around it.

Which makes musical analysis for the layman extremely difficult. Obviously we can't use musical terminology exclusively, or we will simply drive the victim away. We must have intermittent recourse to certain extra-musical ideas, like religion, or social factors, or historical forces, which may have influenced music. We don't ever want to talk down,[44] but how *up* can we talk without losing contact? There is a happy medium somewhere between the music-appreciation racket and purely technical discussion; it is hard to find, but it can be found.

It is with this certainty that it can be found that I have made so bold as to discuss music on television, on records, and in public lectures. Whenever I feel that I have done it successfully, it is because I may have found that happy medium. And finding it is impossible without the conviction that the public is *not* a great beast, but an intelligent organism, more often than not longing for insight

---

[37]To shed light on — to clarify; to make intelligent comments on a difficult subject.

[38]Bugaboo — a source of worry or concern.

[39]*Till Eulenspiegel* — tone poem by the German composer Richard Strauss (1864–1949).

[40]*The Sorcerer's Apprentice* — short musical composition by the French composer Paul Dukas (1865–1935).

[41]*La Mer* — "The Sea," by the French composer Claude Debussy (1862–1918).

[42]*Pictures at an Exhibition* — by the Russian composer Modest Mussorgsky (1835–1881).

[43]Affective-reactive — emotional.

[44]To talk down — to talk to someone as if he or she were inferior or stupid.

and knowledge. So that, wherever possible, I try to talk about music—the *notes* of music; and wherever extra-musical concepts are needed for referential or clarifying purposes, I try to choose concepts that are musically relevant, such as nationalistic tendencies, or spiritual development, which may even have been part of the composer's own thinking. For example, in explaining jazz, I have avoided the usual pseudo-historical discussions (up-the-river-from-New Orleans) and concentrated on those aspects of melody, harmony, rhythm, etc., which make jazz different from all other music. In talking of Bach I have had to make references to his religious and spiritual convictions, but always in terms of the notes he produced. In trying to convey the problem of selection that confronts every composer, I have had recourse to actual rejected sketches for the first movement of Beethoven's *Fifth*. In other words, music appreciation doesn't *have* to be a racket. The extra-musical kind of reference can be useful if it is put in the service of explaining the notes; and the road-map variety[45] can also be serviceable if it functions along with some central idea that can engage the intelligence of the listener.

---

[45] "The road-map variety" — the kind of explanation that traces the development of music from one geographical area to another.

☆ *FOLLOW-UP QUESTIONS*

I. The title of this essay, "The Happy Medium," is a pun because it has a double meaning which the author uses with a humorous effect.
   A. *Medium* refers to a means of artistic expression. How does this definition relate to the title?
   B. *Medium* also refers to something in the middle. What is the meaning of the title in this case?
II. Bernstein states that anyone who attempts to talk about music faces almost certain failure.
   A. Why is it extremely difficult to explain "the unique phenomenon of human reaction to organized sound"?
   B. Why does the writer use the words *mystic* and *magic* in describing one's reaction to music?
   C. According to Bernstein, how have "the most rational minds in history" dealt with the subject of music?
   D. What is ironic about the way these "rational minds" have written about music?
III. Bernstein refers to a "magical block" against which we employ "principles of physics, acoustics, mathematics and formal logic."
   A. How does the word *block* suggest the difficulty in talking about music?
   B. Why does he call this block "magical"?
   C. In what situations other than music might the word *block* be used?
IV. The writer describes a system of aesthetic measure which a professor developed to rate any work of art, using a uniform grading scale.
   A. What is Bernstein's attitude toward this system?
   B. Why does he feel it is invalid?

V.   The writer states that "we imitate scientific method in our attempts to explain magic phenomena. . . . But we simply can't explain human reaction to these phenomena."
    A.   Why does he use the thunderstorm as an example of a magic phenomenon?
    B.   What are some other examples of magic phenomena?

VI.   Bernstein speaks of the "Music Appreciation Racket."
    A.   What value judgment do you find in his use of the word *racket*?
    B.   How is the word *racket* used?
    C.   Is a racket necessarily illegal?
    D.   Describe the two styles of music rackets.
    E.   Bernstein confesses that he has been guilty of using the "Type A" racket. How does he justify this?

VII.   The author names non-musicians and musicians who have been able to give the layman some insight into music.
    A.   Why does he feel, however, that most writers "put their feet in their mouths" when they use musical terms?
    B.   Why do many writers like to use musical terms even when they are not writing about music?
    C.   What are some of the musical terms Bernstein says writers tend to use incorrectly?
    D.   What is the distinction between *crescendo* and *climax*?

VIII.   Bernstein says we can discern four levels of meaning in music.
    A.   What are the four levels that he describes?
    B.   Why does he select only "purely musical meanings" as worthy of analysis?

IX.   The author states that "we don't ever want to talk down" to the layman.
    A.   When you talk down to an audience, what attitude do you have toward it?
    B.   Can you think of any radio or television programs that talk down to their audience by condescending or oversimplifying?

X.   The writer states that there is a happy medium "somewhere between the music appreciation racket and purely technical discussion." He adds that it is hard to find but it can be found.
    A.   How does Bernstein say he has achieved the happy medium in his own discussion of music?
    B.   Ultimately, is his "happy medium" a solution or a compromise? Why?

☆ *THEME TOPICS*

1.   Bernstein believes "the public is not a great beast, but an intelligent organism, more often than not longing for insight and knowledge." Do you think that the mass media—newspapers, magazines, TV, radio—share this view? Discuss, including specific references to the media.

2.   Describe, and if possible, analyze, a work of art—a painting, musical composition, dance, poem, etc.—that you feel has made a lasting impression on you. Attempt to blend accurate description with your emotional reaction.

The Bus*
Shirley Jackson

INTRODUCTION

I.   Many works of fiction are concerned with the difficulty of distinguishing between reality and unreality. Reading a work of this kind may be disturbing in that it mirrors the confusion we sometimes feel about what is real and what is unreal.

    A. How do dreams resemble reality?

    B. How do you know that you are awake?

    C. Can a dream affect your state of mind? How might you feel upon awakening from (a) a nightmare, (b) a happy dream in which your wishes are fulfilled?

    D. Do you always dream about people and places that you know?

    E. How is it possible to dream about people you don't know and places you haven't seen?

    F. Can you think of any dreams you have had that later came true? How did you feel when this happened?

    G. Even though your memory may be mostly dependable, can you think of any events that have become so confused in your mind that you are not certain they actually happened?

        1. How would you react if you became confused about what was real and what was not? For example, you remember a significant conversation with a friend who claims it never took place.

        2. How would you react if someone else became confused about what was real and what was not? For example, a friend remembers a conversation with you that you are certain never took place.

    H. It has been said that many people live their lives as if they were dreaming.

        1. What does this statement mean to you?

        2. What do you feel is the distinction between people who seem to live in a dream and people who seem to live in the world of reality?

        3. Is this a difficult distinction to make? Why?

II.   In response to the unpleasantness she is faced with, the main character in "The Bus" thinks about a letter of complaint she would like to write.

A. What circumstances might lead one to write such a letter about a
public service or something bought in a store?
B. What would you be trying to accomplish by writing a letter of
complaint?

Miss Harper was going home, although the night was wet and nasty. Miss
Harper disliked traveling at any time, and she particularly disliked traveling on
this dirty small bus, which was her only way of getting home; she had frequently
complained to the bus company about their service, because it seemed that no
matter where she wanted to go, they had no respectable[1] bus to carry her.
Getting *away* from home was bad enough, Miss Harper was fond of pointing out
to the bus company, but getting *home* seemed very close to impossible. Tonight
Miss Harper had no choice: If she did not go home by this particular bus, she
could not go for another day. Annoyed, tired, depressed, she tapped irritably on
the counter of the little tobacco store which served also as the bus station. Sir,
she was thinking, beginning her letter of complaint, Although I am an elderly
lady of modest circumstances[2] and must curtail my fondness for travel, let me
point out that your bus service falls far below . . .

Outside, the bus stirred noisily, clearly not anxious to be moving; Miss
Harper thought she could already hear the weary sound of its springs sinking out
of shape. I just can't make this trip again, Miss Harper thought; even seeing
Stephanie isn't worth it; they really go out of their way to make you uncomfortable. "Can I get my ticket, please?" she said sharply, and the old man at the
other end of the counter put down his paper and gave her a look of hatred.

Miss Harper ordered her ticket, deploring her own cross voice, and the old
man slapped it down on the counter in front of her and said, "You got three
minutes before the bus leaves."

He'd love to tell me I missed it, Miss Harper thought, and made a point of
counting her change.

The rain was beating down, and Miss Harper hurried the few exposed
steps to the door of the bus. The driver was slow in opening the door, and as Miss
Harper climbed in she was thinking: Sir, I shall never travel with your company
again. Your ticket salesmen are ugly, your drivers are surly, your vehicles
indescribably filthy . . .

There were already several people sitting in the bus, and Miss Harper
wondered where they could possibly be going; were there really this many small
towns served only by this bus? Were there really other people who would endure
this kind of trip to get somewhere, even home? I'm very out of sorts,[3] Miss
Harper thought, very out of sorts; it's too strenuous a visit for a woman of my

---

[1] Respectable — in good condition; having a clean, acceptable appearance.

[2] Of modest circumstances — lacking the money to buy luxuries.

[3] Out of sorts — irritable; in a bad mood; a little bit sick.

age; I need to get home. She thought of a hot bath and a cup of tea and her own bed, and sighed. No one offered to help her put her suitcase on the rack, and she glanced over her shoulder at the driver sitting with his back turned and thought: He'd probably rather put me off the bus than help me; and then, perceiving her own ill nature, she smiled. The bus company might write a letter of complaint about *me,* she told herself, and felt better. She had providentially[4] taken a sleeping pill before leaving the bus station, hoping to sleep through as much of the trip as possible, and at last, sitting near the back, she promised herself that it would not be unbearably long before she had a bath and a cup of tea, and tried to compose the bus company's response to her letter of complaint. Madam, a lady of your experience and advanced age ought surely to be aware of the problems confronting a poor but honest little company which wants only . . .

She was aware that the bus had started, because she was rocked and bounced in her seat, and the feeling of rattling and throbbing beneath the soles of her shoes stayed with her even when, at last, she slept. She lay back uneasily, her head resting on the seat back, moving with the motion of the bus, and around her other people slept, or spoke softly, or stared blankly out the windows at the passing lights and the rain.

Sometime during her sleep Miss Harper was jostled by someone moving into the seat behind her; her head was pushed and her hat disarranged. For a minute, bewildered by sleep, she clutched at her hat, and then said vaguely, "Who?"

"Go back to sleep," a young voice said, and giggled. "I'm just running away from home, that's all."

Miss Harper was not awake, but she opened her eyes a little and looked up at the ceiling of the bus. "That's wrong," she said as clearly as she could. "That's wrong. Go back."

There was another giggle. "Too late," the voice said. "Go back to sleep."

Miss Harper did. She slept uncomfortably and awkwardly, her mouth a little open. Sometime, perhaps an hour later, her head was jostled again and the voice said, "I think I'm going to get off here. 'Bye, now."

"You'll be sorry," Miss Harper said, asleep. "Go back."

Then, still later, the bus driver was shaking her. "Look, lady," he was saying, "I'm not an alarm clock. Wake up and get off the bus."

"What?" Miss Harper stirred, opened her eyes, felt for her pocketbook.

"I'm not an alarm clock," the driver said. His voice was harsh and tired. "I'm not an alarm clock. Get off the bus."

"What?" said Miss Harper, again.

"This is as far as you go. You got a ticket to here. You've arrived. And I am not an alarm clock waking up people to tell them when it's time to get off; you got here, lady, and it's not part of my job to carry you off the bus. I'm not—"

"I intend to report you,"[5] Miss Harper said, awake. She felt for her

---

[4]Providentially — by good fortune.

[5]To report someone — to inform a supervisor, for example, that an employee has done something wrong.

pocketbook and found it in her lap, moved her feet, straightened her hat. She was stiff, and moving was difficult.

"Report me. But from somewhere else. I got a bus to run. Now will you please get off so I can go on my way?"

His voice was loud, and Miss Harper was sickeningly aware of faces turned toward her from along the bus—grins, amused comments. The driver turned and stamped off down the bus to his seat, saying, "She thinks I'm an alarm clock," and Miss Harper, without assistance and moving clumsily, took down her suitcase and struggled with it down the aisle. The suitcase banged against seats, and she knew that people were staring at her; she was terribly afraid that she might stumble and fall.

"I'll certainly report you," she said to the driver, who shrugged.

"Come on, lady," he said. "It's the middle of the night and I got a bus to run."

"You ought to be *ashamed* of yourself," Miss Harper said wildly, wanting to cry.

"Lady," the driver said with elaborate patience, "please get off my bus."

The door was open, and Miss Harper eased herself and her suitcase onto the steep step. "She thinks everyone's an alarm clock, got to see she gets off the bus," the driver said behind her, and Miss Harper stepped onto the ground. Suitcase, pocketbook, gloves, hat—she had them all. She had barely taken stock[6] when the bus started with a jerk, almost throwing her backward, and Miss Harper, for the first time in her life, wanted to run and shake her fist at someone. I'll report him, she thought; I'll see that he loses his job. And then she realized that she was in the wrong place.

Standing quite still in the rain and the darkness, Miss Harper became aware that she was not at the bus corner of her town, where the bus should have left her. She was on an empty crossroads in the rain. There were no stores, no lights, no taxis, no people. There was nothing, in fact, but a wet dirt road under her feet and a signpost where two roads came together. Don't panic, Miss Harper told herself, almost whispering, don't panic; it's all right, it's all right, you'll see that it's all right, don't be frightened.

She took a few steps in the direction the bus had gone, but it was out of sight, and when Miss Harper called falteringly, "Come back" and "Help," there was no answer to the shocking sound of her own voice except the steady drive of the rain. I sound old, she thought, but I will not panic. She turned in a circle, her suitcase in her hand, and told herself: Don't panic, it's all right.

There was no shelter in sight, but the signpost said Ricket's Landing.[7] So that's where I am. Miss Harper thought; I've come to Ricket's Landing and I don't like it here. She set her suitcase down next to the signpost and tried to see down the road; perhaps there might be a house, or even some kind of barn or shed, where she could get out of the rain. She was crying a little, and lost and

---

[6]To take stock — to think over or analyze one's situation. In business, to take stock means to take an inventory of the stock (or goods) one has on hand.

[7]Landing — a place for taking on or letting off passengers or cargo.

hopeless, saying, Please, won't someone come?, when she saw headlights far off down the road and realized that someone was really coming to help her. She ran to the middle of the road and stood waving, her gloves wet and her pocketbook draggled. "Here," she called, "here I am. Please come and help me."

Through the sound of the rain she could hear the motor, and then the headlights caught her and, suddenly embarrassed, she put her pocketbook in front of her face. The lights belonged to a small truck, and it came to an abrupt stop beside her and the window near her was rolled down and a man's voice said furiously, "You want to get killed? You trying to get killed or something? What you doing in the middle of the road, trying to get killed?" The young man turned and spoke to the driver. "It's some dame.[8] Running out in the road like that."

"Please," Miss Harper said, as he seemed about to close the window again, "please help me. The bus put me off here when it wasn't my stop and I'm lost."

"Lost?" The young man laughed richly. "First I ever heard anyone getting lost in Ricket's Landing. Mostly they have trouble *finding* it." He laughed again, and the driver, leaning forward over the steering wheel to look curiously at Miss Harper, laughed too. Miss Harper put on a willing smile, and said, "Can you take me somewhere? Perhaps a bus station?"

"No bus station." The young man shook his head profoundly. "Bus comes through here every night, stops if he's got any passengers."

"Well," Miss Harper said, her voice rising in spite of herself; she was suddenly afraid of antagonizing these young men; perhaps they might even leave her here, in the wet and dark. "Please," she said, "can I get in with you, out of the rain?"

The two young men looked at each other. "Take her down to the old lady's," one of them said.

"She's pretty wet to get in the truck," the other one said.

"Please," Miss Harper said. "I'll be glad to pay you what I can."

"We'll take you to the old lady,"[9] the driver said. "Come on, move over," he said to the other young man.

"Wait—my suitcase." Miss Harper ran back to the signpost, no longer caring how she must look, stumbling about in the rain, and brought her suitcase over to the truck.

"That's awful wet," the young man said. He opened the door and took the suitcase from Miss Harper. "I'll just throw it in the back," he said, and turned and tossed the suitcase into the back of the truck. Miss Harper heard the sodden thud of its landing, and wondered what things would look like when she unpacked. My bottle of cologne, she thought despairingly. "Get *in*," the young man said, and, "My God, you're wet."

Miss Harper had never climbed up into a truck before, and her skirt was tight and her gloves were slippery from the rain. Without help from the young

---

[8]Dame — as used here: a slang term, somewhat disrespectful, for a woman.

[9]"The old lady" — slang term for the woman who runs the roadhouse. Here it is a term of familiarity and does not simply imply old age.

man, she put one knee on the high step and somehow hoisted herself in. This cannot be happening to me, she thought clearly. The young man pulled away fastidiously as Miss Harper slid onto the seat next to him.

"You are pretty wet," the driver said, leaning over the wheel to look around at Miss Harper. "Why were you out in the rain like that?"

"The bus driver." Miss Harper began to peel off her gloves; somehow she had to make an attempt to dry herself. "He told me it was my stop."

"That would be Johnny Talbot," the driver said to the other young man. "He drives that bus."

"Well, I'm going to report him," Miss Harper said. There was a little silence in the truck, and then the driver said, "Johnny's a good guy. He means all right."

"He's a bad bus driver," Miss Harper said sharply.

The truck did not move. "You don't want to report old Johnny," the driver said.

"I most certainly—" Miss Harper began, and then stopped. Where am I? she thought. What is happening to me? "No," she said at last, "I won't report old Johnny."

The driver started the truck, and they moved slowly down the road, through the mud and the rain. The windshield wipers swept back and forth hypnotically, there was a narrow line of light ahead from their headlights, and Miss Harper thought, What is happening to me?

"We're going down to the old lady's," the driver said. "She'll know what to do."

"What old lady?" Miss Harper did not dare to move, even to turn her head. "Is there any kind of a bus station? Or even a taxi?"

"You could," the driver said consideringly, "you could wait and catch that same bus tomorrow night when it goes through. Johnny'll be driving her."

"I just want to get home as soon as possible," Miss Harper said. The truck seat was dreadfully uncomfortable, she felt clammy[10] and sticky and chilled through, and home seemed so far away that perhaps it did not exist at all.

"Just down the road a mile or so," the driver said reassuringly.

"I've never heard of Ricket's Landing," Miss Harper said. "I can't imagine how he came to put me off there."

"Maybe somebody else was supposed to get off there and he thought it was you by mistake." This deduction seemed to tax the young man's mind[11] to the utmost, because he said, "See, someone else might've been supposed to get off instead of you."

"Then *he's* still on the bus," said the driver, and they were both silent, appalled.

---

[10]Clammy — wet and uncomfortable.

[11]To tax the young man's mind — to place a great burden on his mind, to require a great effort from it.

Ahead of them a light flickered, showing dimly through the rain, and the driver pointed and said, "There, that's where we're going." As they came closer, Miss Harper was aware of a growing dismay. The light belonged to what seemed to be a roadhouse,[12] and Miss Harper had never been inside a roadhouse in her life. The house itself was only a dim shape looming in the darkness, and the light over the side door illuminated a sign, hanging crooked, which read

BEER

BAR & GRILL[13]

"Is there anywhere else I could go?" Miss Harper asked timidly, clutching her pocketbook. "I'm not at all sure, you know, that I ought—"

"Not many people here tonight," the driver said, turning the truck into the driveway and pulling up in the parking lot, which had once, Miss Harper was sad to see, been a garden. "The rain, probably."

Peering through the window and the rain, Miss Harper felt, suddenly, a warm stir of recognition, of welcome. It's the house, she thought; why, of *course,* the house is lovely. It had clearly been an old mansion once, solidly and handsomely built, with the balance and style that belonged to a good house of an older time. "Why?" Miss Harper asked, wanting to know why such a good house should have a light tacked on over the side door, and a sign hanging crooked but saying BEER BAR & GRILL. "Why?" asked Miss Harper, but the driver said, "This is where you wanted to go . . . Get her suitcase," he told the other young man.

"In here?" asked Miss Harper, feeling a kind of indignation on behalf of the fine old house. "Into this saloon?" Why, I used to live in a house like this, she thought; what are they doing to our old houses?

The driver laughed. "You'll be safe," he said.

Carrying her suitcase and her pocketbook, Miss Harper followed the two young men to the lighted door and passed under the crooked sign. Shameful, she thought; they haven't even bothered to take care of the place; it needs paint and tightening all around and probably a new roof. And then the driver said, "Come on, come on," and pushed open the heavy door.

"I used to live in a house like this," Miss Harper said, and the young men laughed.

"I bet you did," one of them said, and Miss Harper stopped in the doorway, staring, and realized how strange she must have sounded. Where there had certainly once been comfortable rooms, high-ceilinged and square, with tall doors and polished floors, there was now one large dirty room, with a counter running along one side and half a dozen battered tables; there was a jukebox[14] in

---

[12]Roadhouse — a somewhat disreputable restaurant, drinking place, and hotel, located by the side of a road.

[13]Bar and Grill — place where food and alcoholic drinks are served.

[14]Jukebox — a coin-operated machine which plays recordings of popular songs. The machine is usually set in a highly lighted cabinet of garish colors. As a rule, jukeboxes are found only in cheaper eating places.

a corner, and torn linoleum on the floor. "Oh, no," Miss Harper said. The room smelled unpleasant, and the rain slapped against the bare windows.

Sitting around the tables and standing around the jukebox were perhaps a dozen young people, resembling the two who had brought Miss Harper here, all looking oddly alike, all talking and laughing flatly. Miss Harper leaned back against the door; for a minute she thought they were laughing about her. She was wet and disheartened, and these noisy people did not belong at all in the old house. Then the driver turned and gestured to her. "Come and meet the old lady," he said; and then, to the room at large: "Look, we brought company."

"Please," Miss Harper said, but no one had given her more than a glance. She followed the two young men across to the counter; her suitcase bumped against her legs and she thought: I must not fall down.

"Belle, Belle," the driver said, "look at the stray cat we found."

An enormous woman swung around in her seat at the end of the counter and looked at Miss Harper. Looking up and down, looking at the suitcase and Miss Harper's wet hat and wet shoes, looking at Miss Harper's pocketbook and gloves squeezed in her hand, the woman seemed hardly to move her eyes. It was almost as though she absorbed Miss Harper without any particular effort. "Hell you say," the woman said at last. Her voice was surprisingly soft. "Hell you say."[15]

"She's wet," the second young man said. The two young men stood one on either side of Miss Harper, presenting her. "Please," Miss Harper said; here was a woman, at least—someone who might understand and sympathize, "please, they put me off my bus at the wrong stop and I can't seem to find my way home. Please."

"Hell you say," the woman said, and laughed, a gentle laugh. "She sure is wet," she said.

"Please," Miss Harper said.

"You'll take care of her?" the driver asked. He turned and smiled down at Miss Harper, obviously waiting, and, remembering, Miss Harper fumbled in her pocketbook for her wallet. How much? She was wondering, not wanting to ask; it was such a short ride, but if they hadn't come I might have gotten pneumonia, and paid all those doctor bills; I have caught cold, she thought with great clarity, and she took two five-dollar bills from her wallet. They can't argue over five dollars each, she thought, and sneezed. The two young men and the large woman were watching her with great interest, and all of them saw that after Miss Harper took out the two five-dollar bills there were a single and two tens left in the wallet. The money was not wet. I suppose I should be grateful for that, Miss Harper thought, moving slowly. She handed a five-dollar bill to each young man and felt that they glanced at each other over her head.

"Thanks," the driver said. I could have gotten away with a dollar each, Miss Harper thought. "Thanks," the driver said again, and the other man said, "Say, thanks."

---

[15]"Hell you say." — a slang expression of surprise.

"Thank *you*," Miss Harper said formally.

"I'll put you up for the night," the woman said. "You can sleep here. Go tomorrow." She looked Miss Harper up and down again. "Dry off a little," she said.

"Is there anywhere else?" Then, afraid that this might seem ungracious, Miss Harper said, "I mean, is there any way of going on tonight? I don't want to impose."

"We got rooms for rent." The woman half turned back to the counter. "Cost you ten for the night."

She's leaving me bus fare home, Miss Harper thought; I suppose I *should* be grateful. "I'd better, I guess," she said, taking out her wallet again. "I mean, thank you."

The woman accepted the bill. "Upstairs," she said. "Take your choice. No one's around." She glanced sideways at Miss Harper. "I'll see you get a cup of coffee in the morning."

"Thank you." Miss Harper knew where the staircase would be, and she turned and, carrying her suitcase and her pocketbook, went to what had once been the front hall, and there was the staircase, so lovely in its proportions that she caught her breath. She turned back and saw the large woman staring at her, and said, "I used to live in a house like this. Built about the same time, I guess. One of those good old houses that were made to stand forever, and where people—"

"Hell you say," the woman said, and turned back to the counter.

The young people scattered around the big room were talking; in one corner a group surrounded the two who had brought Miss Harper, and now and then they laughed. Miss Harper was touched with a little sadness now, looking at them, so at home in the big, ugly room which had once been so beautiful. It would be nice, she thought, to speak to these young people, perhaps even become their friend, talk and laugh with them; perhaps they might like to know that this spot where they came together had been a lady's drawing room. Hesitating a little, Miss Harper wondered if she might call "Good night" or "Thank you" again, or even "God bless you all." Then, since no one looked at her, she started up the stairs. Halfway, there was a landing with a stained-glass window, and Miss Harper stopped, holding her breath. When she had been a child the stained-glass window on the stair landing in her house had caught the sunlight and scattered it on the stairs in a hundred colors. Fairyland colors, Miss Harper thought, remembering; I wonder why we don't live in these houses now. I'm lonely, Miss Harper thought, and then she thought: But I must get out of these wet clothes; I really am catching cold.

Without thinking, she turned at the top of the stairs and went to the front room on the left; that had always been her room. The door was open and she glanced in; this was clearly a bedroom for rent, and it was ugly and drab and cheap. Miss Harper turned on the light and stood in the doorway, saddened by the peeling wallpaper and the sagging floor. What have they done to the house? she thought; how can I sleep here tonight?

At last she moved to cross the room and set her suitcase on the bed. I must get dry, she told herself; I must make the best of things. The bed was correctly placed, between the two front windows, but the mattress was stiff and lumpy, and Miss Harper was frightened at the sour smell and the creaking springs. I will not think about such things, Miss Harper thought; this might be the room where I slept as a girl. The windows were almost right—two across the front, two at the side—and the door was placed correctly. How they did build these old places to a square-cut pattern, Miss Harper thought: how they did put them together; there must be a thousand houses all over the country built exactly like this. The closet, however, was on the wrong side. Some oddness of construction had set the closet to Miss Harper's right as she sat on the bed, when it ought really to have been on her left; when she was a girl the big closet had been her playhouse and her hiding place, but it had been on the left.

The bathroom was wrong, too, but that was less important. Miss Harper had thought wistfully of a hot tub before bed, but a glance at the bathtub discouraged her; she could wait until she got home. She washed her face and hands, and the warm water comforted her. She was further comforted to find that her bottle of cologne had not broken in her suitcase and that nothing inside had got wet. At least she could sleep in a dry nightgown, although in a cold bed.

She shivered once in the cold sheets, remembering a child's bed. She lay in the darkness with her eyes open, wondering where she was and how she had got here: first the bus and then the truck; and now she lay in the darkness, and no one knew where she was or what was to become of her. She had only her suitcase, and a little money in her pocketbook. She was very tired, and she thought that perhaps the sleeping pill she had taken much earlier had still not quite worn off; perhaps the sleeping pill had been affecting all her actions, since she had been following docilely, wherever she was taken. In the morning, she told herself sleepily, I'll show them I can make decisions for myself.

The jukebox noise downstairs faded softly into a distant melody. My mother is singing in the drawing room,[16] Miss Harper thought, and the company is sitting on the stiff little chairs, listening; my father is playing the piano. She could not quite distinguish the song, but it was one she had heard her mother sing many times. I could creep out to the top of the stairs and listen, she thought, and then she became aware that there was a rustling in the closet, but the closet was on the wrong side, on the right instead of the left. It is more a rattling than a rustling, Miss Harper thought, wanting to listen to her mother singing; it is as though something wooden were being shaken around. Shall I get out of bed and quiet it so I can hear the singing? Am I too warm and comfortable; am I too sleepy—

The closet was on the wrong side, but the rattling continued, just loud enough to be irritating, and at last, knowing she would never sleep until it stopped, Miss Harper swung her legs over the side of the bed and, sleepily, padded barefoot over to the closet door.

---

[16]Drawing room — a formal reception or sitting room, found in more elegant houses.

"What are you doing in there?" she asked aloud, and opened the door. There was just enough light for her to see that it was a wooden snake, head lifted, stirring and rattling itself against the other toys. Miss Harper laughed. "It's my snake," she said aloud, "it's my old snake, and it's come alive." In the back of the closet she could see her old toy clown, bright and cheerful, and as she watched, enchanted, the toy clown flopped languidly forward and back, coming alive. Then Miss Harper saw the big beautiful doll sitting on a small chair, the doll with long golden curls and wide blue eyes and a stiff organdy party dress. As Miss Harper held out her hands in joy, the doll opened her eyes and stood up.

"Rosabelle," Miss Harper cried out, "Rosabelle, it's me."

The doll turned, looking widely at her, smile painted on. The red lips opened and the doll quacked, outrageously, a flat, slapping voice coming out of that fair mouth. "Go away, old lady," the doll said, "go away, old lady, go away."

Miss Harper backed away, staring. She slammed the closet door and leaned against it. Behind her, the doll's voice went on and on. Crying out, Miss Harper turned and fled. "Mommy," she screamed, "Mommy, Mommy."

Screaming, she fled, past the bed, out the door, to the staircase. "Mommy," she cried, and fell, going down and down into darkness, turning, trying to catch onto something solid and real, crying.

"Look, lady," the bus driver said. "I'm not an alarm clock. Wake up and get off the bus."

"You'll be sorry," Miss Harper said distinctly.

"Wake up," he said, "wake up and get off the bus."

"I intend to report you," Miss Harper said. Pocketbook, gloves, hat, suitcase.

"I'll certainly report you," she said, almost crying.

"This is as far as you go," the driver said.

The bus lurched,[17] moved, and Miss Harper almost stumbled in the driving rain, her suitcase at her feet, under the sign reading Ricket's Landing.

---

[17]To lurch — to start forward suddenly, throwing people off balance.

☆ FOLLOW-UP QUESTIONS

I.   Describing Miss Harper's state of mind and the situations she faces, the writer uses language that emphasizes unpleasantness and discomfort.
   A.   Read the first few paragraphs again. What expressions do you notice that give a sense of the negative?
   B.   What details does Shirley Jackson select to describe the bus, the bar and grill, the room in the old house?
II. Throughout the story, Miss Harper is treated with coldness and rudeness. We are told on the first page that the man who sells her the bus ticket gives her a "look of hatred."

    A.   What are some other examples of rude, unpleasant, or downright cruel treatment?

    B.   Does there seem to be a connection between Miss Harper's personality and the treatment she receives?

III.   In the first few paragraphs we are told very little about Miss Harper's background. Nevertheless, by describing the situation through Miss Harper's point of view, the writer gives us a strong sense of her character and circumstances.

    A.   About how old is she?

    B.   How much do we know about her financial status?

    C.   Does she seem to be a totally disagreeable woman? Why or why not?

    D.   Does her attempt to compose the bus company's response to her letter of complaint indicate that she has a sense of humor? How?

IV.   When Miss Harper hears the "young voice" on the bus, she is described as "not awake." A few lines down we read, " 'you'll be sorry,' Miss Harper said, asleep."

    A.   How do these statements contribute to confusion about the state Miss Harper is in?

    B.   How does she react to the young voice's intention of running away from home?

    C.   Are we ever told specifically to whom the young voice belongs?

    D.   In light of what happens during the rest of the story, do you have any theories about the source of the young voice?

V.   Put off the bus by the rude driver, Miss Harper finds herself in Ricket's Landing.

    A.   What does the place look like?

    B.   Is it Miss Harper's town?

    C.   Could there be any significance in the name, Ricket's Landing? What does "rickets" mean?

VI.   When the two young men in the truck take her to the "old lady," Miss Harper finds many of the things in the house strangely familiar.

    A.   What does the old house remind her of?

    B.   Why is it easy for her to find the staircase?

    C.   What are some other familiar characteristics of the house?

    D.   What details of the room conflict with Miss Harper's memories of her own room?

VII.   As she drifts into sleep, Miss Harper seems to hear her mother singing in the drawing room and then becomes aware of a rattling in the closet.

    A.   How does she react to the sight of the wooden snake?

    B.   How does the doll, Rosabelle, transform what seems like a recreation of happy memories into a nightmare?

    C.   When the bus driver wakes her from what seems like a nightmare, where is she let off?

    D.   Could you have predicted the ending some pages before you came to it?

VIII.   "The Bus" blends and confuses dream and reality. We cannot be sure when one begins and the other ends. Nevertheless, it is possible to develop interpretations of Miss Harper's experiences. Perhaps they are a series of dreams (or nightmares) interrupted by moments of reality.

    A.   If you find this theory believable, which parts do you feel are dreams and which are reality? Why?

B. Trace the sequence of events which lead Miss Harper back to her childhood.

C. Why is the ending particularly disturbing and confusing?

D. Why does the ending give the impression that what has happened will be repeated?

E. Can we determine from the ending whether Miss Harper will ever get home safely?

F. Is it possible that in a strange way Ricket's Landing *is* Miss Harper's home? Why?

IX. Shirley Jackson has written "The Bus" in an understated, matter-of-fact style. There is no attempt to exaggerate the events of the trip.

A. How does this approach emphasize the strangeness of the ending?

B. At what point did you feel that Miss Harper's experiences became unreal?

C. If "The Bus" is a horror story, what constitutes the horror?

D. No matter how we interpret the events of the story, what can we conclude about how Miss Harper feels about her own life?

E. If "The Bus" were made into a movie, would the ending be dramatically effective even though it is confusing?

F. Would you make any changes in the story itself if you were changing it into a movie?

G. What visual devices would you use to convey a sense of strangeness? Would extremely unusual ones be necessary?

☆ *THEME TOPICS*

1. Describe an experience that seemed unreal as it was happening or one that time or memory has distorted so that you have come to think of it as unreal or confused.

2. Describe a trip you have taken during which strange, unpredictable, or absurd events took place.

3. Describe a dream you have had and tell what effect, if any, it had upon your life or your understanding of your life.

Is War Inevitable?*
Julian Huxley

INTRODUCTION

I.   In this essay, Julian Huxley, the well-known British biologist, questions the inevitability of war. In examining this problem, he tries to determine whether it is possible to prevent something which many people consider an inevitable result of basic human desires.

    A. What things, if any, do you consider to be inevitable?

    B. Are there things besides wars which many people believe are inevitable and which you believe do not have to occur? If so, what are they? How do you think they could be avoided?

II.   Huxley's essay suggests that major social and political changes must be put into practice if war is to be prevented. Proposals of drastic social change are often called *utopian,* a word which carries positive or negative connotations according to the way we look at it.

    A. Have any plans which could be called utopian been proposed or put into practice in your country? How successful were they? What were the reasons for their success or failure?

    B. Do you think that major social change is necessary in your society? Why? If change is needed, how should it be carried out?

    C. Since problems like war, air pollution, distribution of natural resources, etc., are now becoming worldwide, do you think it would be easier to solve them if nations gave up some or all of their sovereignty? Do you think a strong world government would be desirable? Why or why not?

In order to answer the question whether the human species possesses a war instinct[1] or not we must first define the two terms "war" and "instinct." This sounds irritatingly academic[2] but is not really so: on the correct answer depends the answer to the further intensely practical question, whether or not it is worth our trying to prevent war. For if war is instinctive in man, the only way to prevent

---

* © 1946 by The New York Times Company. Reprinted by permission. Reprinted by permission of A. D. Peters & Co., Ltd.

[1]Instinct — an inborn part of behavior that does not have to be learned; a natural and inevitable part of human nature.

[2]Academic — as used in this context: of only theoretical interest; of no practical value.

it would be generations of selective breeding[3] devoted to reducing or abolishing or altering his war instinct, just as man by selection has altered the instinctive savagery of the wolf to the friendly loyalty of the dog, or modified the dog's hunting instinct toward pointing in pointers,[4] retrieving in retrievers,[5] coursing by sight[6] in greyhounds, or hunting by scent in foxhounds.

Even if we could start at once on such large-scale eugenics,[7] there would be ample chance for war to destroy civilization before the lengthy process of selection had had an effect on our war instinct. If we are endowed with the instinct to make war, then the best anti-war social or economic or political machinery could only somewhat reduce the frequency of war or perhaps alter its manifestations—never prevent it. But if there is no such thing as a war instinct, then there is hope that something effective could be done and that war might really be abolished, or at any rate that it might be reduced to the status of a rare curiosity or a local and essentially unimportant phenomenon.

First, then, war. We may begin by making clear what war is not. Fighting between individuals is not war, even if it involves bloodshed or death. This applies to man—a duel is not war, nor is a murder—and also to animals—half a dozen lions fighting over a carcass are not engaged in war, nor are two stags[8] fighting for a harem of hinds.[9] Competition between two different species is not war.

The introduced American gray squirrel has ousted[10] the indigenous[11] red squirrel over much of Britain: but that has not involved war. We speak of the war against disease germs or against pests: but that is only war in a metaphorical[12] sense. Still less is it war when one kind of animal preys upon another. We speak of the lion as the natural enemy of the zebra, or owls as the enemies of mice; but

---

[3]Selective breeding — the breeding of animals (or in this case, of human beings) to emphasize certain characteristics that are considered desirable and to reduce or eliminate undesirable characteristics.

[4]Pointer — a type of hunting dog that stands in a fixed position and "points" out the game bird or animal the hunter is trying to shoot.

[5]Retriever — a type of hunting dog that is trained to bring game birds or animals back to the hunter who has shot them.

[6]Coursing by sight — hunting with dogs that are trained to chase game by sight instead of by scent.

[7]Eugenics — the study or practice of ways to improve human beings through genetic control. *Eugenics* is always used with a singular verb.

[8]Stag — an adult male deer.

[9]Hind — an adult female deer.

[10]To oust — to drive out.

[11]Indigenous — native; living naturally in an area.

[12]Metaphorical — figurative. A metaphor is an implied comparison, in which our knowledge and feelings about one thing are applied to another. For example: "The autumn of life" to refer to old age.

that again is metaphorical: the word enemy is used in a different sense from that of the enemy in a human war.

War means only one thing—organized conflict between groups of the same (or closely related) species, aimed at the imposing of the will of one group on the other. Strictly speaking, it means organized physical conflict, and it is in this sense that I shall use the term, though it might be extended to cover other types of group conflict, such as economic war, trade war, or class war.

Under this definition there are only three kinds of animals that practice war. One is a mammal—man; the other two are certain kinds of social insects— some bees and some ants.

There are other animal activities that represent stages on the way toward war, namely, fighting over breeding or feeding territory. Such fighting occurs regularly among the males of most songbirds, among various lizards and a few fish, and a number of mammals. But it is not true war, for it does not involve fighting between groups organized for the purpose.

Where, however, as in some ants, there are battles between ants' nests which are too close to each other, so that they compete for the same food territory, then we may speak of war. Thus Forel writes: "Among ants . . . collective ownership is represented by a portion of meadow, a tree or several trees, a wood or even a stretch of sand. A strong colony tries to enlarge its domain at its neighbor's expense. . . . This is the source of war." He adds that "if the two formicaries[13] are approximately equal in strength, they exterminate each other without any definite result"—a moral lesson for man!

Fighting of this sort is still a primitive sort of warfare. It is essentially unorganized as compared with the more specialized kinds of animal warfare found in other ants. Organized slave-raiding wars have been waged by the "bloody ant," Formica sanguinea, against Formica glebaria, in which the sanguinea transported all the glebaria pupae[14] to their own nest, where they were destined to grow up as unconscious slaves.

But the most remarkable ant wars occur between neighboring nests of Harvester ants. Harvesters collect seeds from various wild grasses and store them in underground granaries in their nests. Sometimes a colony will sally forth[15] to try to seize the grain belonging to another nest.

Battles between hive-bee colonies have also been recorded, the prize here being the stored honey.

Thus the most developed types of warfare among social insects concern property—slaves and food-stores.

For our purpose, however, the most important fact concerning the wars of social insects is that they have a truly instinctive basis. In wars between nests of the same species, the tactics will be identical on both sides, so that the issue is

---

[13]Formicary — a nest of ants.

[14]Pupae — the inactive stage of development in many insects, between the larval and the adult stages.

[15]To sally forth — to rush out from a defensive position to make a sudden attack.

usually decided by mere weight of numbers. In wars between different species, however, the fighting methods and tactics will be instinctively different, and may give a real advantage to one type. Their natural selection can here step in to improve the instincts involved in war.

As regards the more important question of a specific war-making instinct (as opposed to those concerned in the waging of wars once begun) there are all gradations. At the bottom we have the "territorial instinct" to defend the nest of the food-domain. We then have the instinct to enlarge the food territory at the expense of neighboring colonies of the same species, which is the beginning of truly aggressive warfare. And as a specialized brand, not found anywhere else in the animal world, we have the highly organized warfare of slave-making ants against other species.

The "territorial instinct" grows directly out of the instinct of pugnacious[16] self-defense. This is widespread, but by no means universal. There are many animals like hares and rabbits, deer and antelopes which run away rather than fight, and either do not actively defend themselves, or do so only when actually cornered. And there are others which seek to escape detection by remaining immobile, or even "sham dead"[17] in various ways, never resorting to violence.

However, though human beings will, of course, in certain circumstances seek safety by flight or by concealment, they certainly have a good dose of self-preservative pugnacity. Furthermore, this pugnacity can also readily be called into play[18] on what in animals we generally call "territorial" grounds—defense of home, mate, family or property. In human evolution, moreover, this territorial pugnacity seems to have played an important role for a long period. It must have been operative during the pre-human, semi-human and early human periods. It was doubtless operative whenever the social units came into competition for food or other territorial needs.

In the more developed societies of the hunting phase this territorial pugnacity often became the basis of true warfare. The classical example is that of many American Indians.

What can be studied among the Indians holds good for[19] all the more complex manifestations of war in the evolution from settled barbarism to industrial civilization. The only element which can possibly be called instinctive in war is man's propensity to fight, his innate pugnacity. But this is not an instinct in the strict or biological sense of the word. For one thing, it is not always elicited, and when elicited is not always a reaction to the same stimulus or set of circumstances; nor does it manifest itself in the same stereotyped way or within the same innately determined limits. Thus it is best called an impulse, urge or drive rather than an instinct. But we will not be pedantic,[20] and will say that there

---

[16]Pugnacious — eager to fight or quarrel.

[17]To "sham dead" — to pretend to be dead.

[18]To call into play — to use a quality or an ability which the person has.

[19]To hold good for — to be true for.

[20]Pedantic — insisting too strongly on distinctions that may not be meaningful.

does exist an instinctive basis on which war depends, in the shape of man's pugnacity.

However, whereas a true war instinct would make war inevitable, man's pugnacious impulses merely make it possible. In order that the possibility shall become realized in actual war, our pugnacious impulses must be disciplined, developed, rationalized, organized. Above all, they must be combined with all sorts of other impulses, motives and complex emotions and dispositions, to form what McDougall calls a *sentiment*—an organized system or piece of mental structure—in this case focused upon war.

Among the psychological elements which may thus be combined with the impulse of pugnacity to produce the complex war sentiment we may catalogue patriotism, love of power, love of glory, self-interest, fear, dislike of what is alien, the feeling of superiority, the sense of shame, belief in one's ideals and those of one's group, and many more. Such a sentiment or disposition cannot be inherited as such, but must be built up anew in every individual.

Furthermore, it will not be the same in every individual of a given society, nor will its different elements occur in the same proportions, or even always recur, in different societies or in the same society, at different times. The arrogant belief in Germanic superiority, which was combined with their leader's lust for power to bring the German people into the last war,[21] were ingredients almost wholly lacking from the war sentiment of the British, in which self-preservation and the upholding of a particular way of life were prominent, or from that of the Americans, to which an idealization of the democratic free enterprise principle contributed, and also a certain missionary spirit.

The war sentiment may be deliberately cultivated as part of the very existence of the tribe or nation, as among the American Indians in old days or in Nazi Germany in its brief appalling career. Or it may be provoked by attack, as happened to Britain when Germany invaded Poland, or to America when the Japanese attacked Pearl Harbor, or to Russia in June, 1941.

Even after provocation, however, it requires cultivating and intensifying: we all know the orgy of propaganda and patriotic campaigns, both general and special, which were found necessary for the British and American and Russian war effort. Propaganda is indeed specially necessary in anti-militarist countries like the United States, which has always mistrusted the mere suspicion of a standing army;[22] or Britain, where the soldier in peace time has almost invariably been looked at askance.[23]

But though the war sentiment always needs to be cultivated or stimulated in some way, if it is to develop to a stage which makes war possible, its development also demands a certain kind of environment. The conditions which

---

[21] The last war — the Second World War (1939–1945), the last major war before this article was written.

[22] Standing army — a permanent army.

[23] To look at (something) askance — to view something with disapproval or skepticism.

permit the development of war sentiment and of actual warfare seem various enough, but in reality they all fall under one of two main heads.

The first main condition is that the human beings concerned shall be organized in separate compact societies, be they[24] tribes or kingdoms, empires or modern nation-states. And the second is that there should be serious competition of some sort between those groups, whether for hunting-grounds or sources of oil, for living space or world markets.

Even if war is not the automatic product of a war instinct in man, but only an expression of a war sentiment which needs particular conditions for its development, yet, as Norman Cousins[25] well puts it, "the expression of man's nature will continue to be warlike if the same conditions are continued that have provoked warlike expression in him in the past."

These conditions, we have seen, boil down to[26] two essentials—organization in separate groups, and serious competition. So we should be able to reduce the incidence and possibility of war either by reducing the separateness of human organized groups (in other words, by promoting unitary world organization) or by reducing the intensity of competition between groups (in other words, by promoting all-round productivity) or preferably, of course, by doing both at once.

One of the factors which make war more possible is unrestricted national sovereignty. If we want to reduce war from the status of a likely to an unlikely phenomenon, we must not abolish nationhood by any means, but subordinate it to world sovereignty. National Governments must somehow become agencies within a single world government, just as local and regional authorities are agencies of government within nations.

But even with a single World Government, there would still be the possibility (though assuredly by a reduced possibility) of war—in this case civil war or rebellion.

To minimize this risk, we must reduce to a minimum the competition between different groups or regions for the good things of the world. And this means, as indicated above, planning for a world of abundance. Furthermore, the abundance must not be too unevenly spread; or else, even if the thin-spread regions really have enough for health and comfort, the contrast with the heavy spreading of other regions may still promote jealousy and unrest and war. In particular, the United States must beware of concentrating solely or mainly on developing her own productivity and prosperity to unexampled heights. Apart from the envies and jealousies to which this will undoubtedly give rise, it is likely to lead to an imbalance in the world's economic structure, which will one day crash, bringing down rich and poor countries alike in its fall.

---

[24]"Be they" — "regardless of whether they are" (archaic).

[25]Norman Cousins — formerly, Editor of *The Saturday Review,* a general magazine designed for people interested in literature, politics, and the arts.

[26]To boil down to — to be condensed into.

There is finally the task of finding and providing what William James[27] called "a moral equivalent of war"—some outlet for frustration and repressed hate and aggressivity, some canalization[28] of man's basic urges to pugnacity and self-assertion. Though the causes of the former may be removed by a proper economic and social system, the latter will always be with us, and need to be got rid of in some form of activity, preferably a sublimated[29] one. This task cannot be adequately or fully tackled[30] until the more urgent problems of providing the world with a unitary government and a high all-round standard of life have been coped with.[31]

When the time comes, however, I do not see why it should not be successfully tackled. It will need a good deal of psychology to find out what kind of activities are most suitable and satisfying for what people; a good deal of organization, to see that the requisite jobs and leisure activities can actually be provided in the right proportions; and a good deal of education and of propaganda in the right sense of the word, to make people realize that the jobs and activities are not only worth while, but will provide deep and full satisfactions.

To sum up very briefly, the biologist denies emphatically that there are human war instincts, either for the waging of war in a particular way, or to make war in general. But there does exist a human drive or impulse of pugnacity, which can be used as the foundation of a war sentiment; and this will continue to express itself in war as long as external conditions encourage or permit this expression of human nature. It is up to us to alter the conditions so as to prevent human pugnacity from expressing itself in war, and to encourage its use in other sentiments leading to activities and outlets of use or value. And to do this we need a unitary World Government, a general high level of productivity, and outlets and activities which will provide a moral equivalent of war.

---

[27] William James — 19th century American philosopher.

[28] Canalization — channeling; direction into a particular outlet.

[29] To sublimate — a psychological term meaning to change the natural expression of an instinctive impulse into some socially acceptable kind of behavior. For example, people may sublimate aggression by participating in sports instead of fighting.

[30] To tackle — to deal with a difficult problem.

[31] To cope with — again, to deal with something difficult.

☆ *FOLLOW-UP QUESTIONS*

I.   In the first paragraph of "Is War Inevitable?" Huxley states that "in order to answer the question of whether the human species possesses a war instinct or not we must first define the two terms *war* and *instinct*."

A.   Why doesn't he immediately define the two terms in the first paragraph?

B.   Why does Huxley believe it is essential to consider the meaning of these terms?

      C.   What non-human examples of "selective breeding" does he give?

      D.   Why does he claim that "selective breeding" for the purpose of "reducing or abolishing" man's war instinct might be impractical?

II.   Huxley chooses to clarify *war* by examining what it is not.

      A.   Do you feel this is a good way of leading up to a definition? Why?

      B.   What examples does he give of violence and death that do not constitute war?

      C.   What is the writer's definition of war? Do you agree with it?

      D.   What two kinds of animals practice war?

      E.   Reacting to the information that "if the two formicaries are approximately equal in strength, they exterminate each other without any definite result," Huxley exclaims, "a moral lesson for man." What analogy is he drawing?

      F.   What instinct does he attribute to "social insects"?

      G.   How does "territorial instinct" operate in some animals? Though it seems widespread, some animals seem to be without it. Give some examples.

III.   Huxley recognizes the importance of man's "territorial pugnacity." He states, however, that this element does not constitute a true war instinct.

      A.   Why isn't it considered an instinct in the "biological sense"?

      B.   According to the writer, why are the terms *impulse, urge* or *drive* more correct than *instinct* in this case?

      C.   What are some of the psychological elements that may help to produce the "complex war sentiment"?

IV.   Huxley divides the conditions which permit the development of "war sentiment" and of actual warfare into "organization in separate groups and serious competition."

      A.   Why does he claim that unrestricted national sovereignty makes war more possible?

      B.   How does he suggest National Governments should function to decrease the chances of war?

      C.   Is he in favor of abolishing "nationhood"?

      D.   Why would there still be the possibility of war even with a single world government? How would he minimize this risk?

      E.   Huxley suggests we reduce to a minimum the competition "for the good things of the world." What does he mean by the "good things"? Does he supply a specific, detailed plan to minimize competition? Do you agree with his theory? Why?

V.   In two paragraphs, Huxley deals briefly with the psychological elements relating to war.

      A.   What problems does the writer say have to be dealt with before certain undesirable urges of man can be tackled?

      B.   How do you interpret Williams James' phrase, "a moral equivalent of war"?

      C.   What are some of the activities the writer suggests will help eliminate war by providing an alternate outlet for man's "pugnacity and self-assertion"?

      D.   Do you agree that certain job and leisure activities . . . education . . . and propaganda in the right sense of the word" would help eliminate man's dissatisfactions and frustrations? Why?

      E.   In today's world, do Huxley's suggested solutions seem practical or do they seem utopian? Why?

       F.   Can you think of alternative solutions? How would you go about applying them?

VI.   Huxley sums up his ideas in one paragraph.

       A.   What purpose does this summary serve? Does it clarify his basic ideas?

       B.   Why aren't there specific references in the summary to insects that practice war?

       C.   Read the summary again, and then attempt to rephrase it in your own words.

☆ THEME TOPICS

1.   Subject Huxley's concept of "a united world government" to a critical examination. Include specific references to international problems that exist today.

2.   Discuss your own conception of a better world. Include ways in which you would go about achieving your plan.

3.   Discuss the inevitability of a major human concern, for example, loneliness, frustration, hate. Introduce specific examples in your discussion.